Canadian Cataloguing in Publication Data

Main entry under title:
A guidebook: the waterfront trail, explore yesterday, today and tomorrow along the shores of Lake Ontario

Includes bibliographical references.
ISBN 0-7778-4082-0

1. Ontario, Lake, Region (N.Y. and Ont.) – Guides books. 2. Waterfronts – Ontario, Lake, Region (N.Y. and Ont.) – Guidebooks. 3. Ontario, Lake, Region (N.Y. and Ont.) – I. Ontario. Waterfront Regeneration Trust.

GV182.G84   917.13'5044   C95-964047-9

Cover Photograph Credits:
Dingle Park, Oakville: Town of Oakville
Pickering, 1898: Ontario Archives 13098-53.
Heron Sketch: Aleta Karstad
Fisherboy: © 1995 Dean Berry/Liason/Creative Stock

Proceeds from the sale of this book will be used for Waterfront Trail projects.

The Environment and Waterfront Regeneration Trust

The Waterfront Regeneration Trust is concerned about the environment. Accordingly this guidebook has been manufactured under these guidelines:

The text paper meets the Canadian Environmental Choice Program (E.C.P.) guidelines; its manufacturing process is in full compliance with environmental regulations. The paper contains 50% post commercial waste with a minimum 10% post consumer waste. Kinder to the environment, the paper is acid free and can be expected to last longer without becoming brittle or changing colour.

All printing inks are manufactured from renewable vegetable base resources that replace traditional petroleum base inks. The text pages were printed on non-polluting coldset printing presses that do not emit hydrocarbons into the atmosphere.

Cover and text pages are recyclable.

Publisher's Note
Otabind (Ota-bind). This book has been bound using the patented Otabind process. You can open this book at any page, gently run your finger down the spine, and the pages will lie flat.

Printed in Canada

Printed by Webcom Limited

THE WATERFRONT TRAIL

Waterfront Regeneration Trust
Toronto · May 1995

207 Queen's Quay West, Ste. 580
Toronto, Ontario
M5J 1A2
Telephone 416-314-9490
Facsimile 416-314-9497

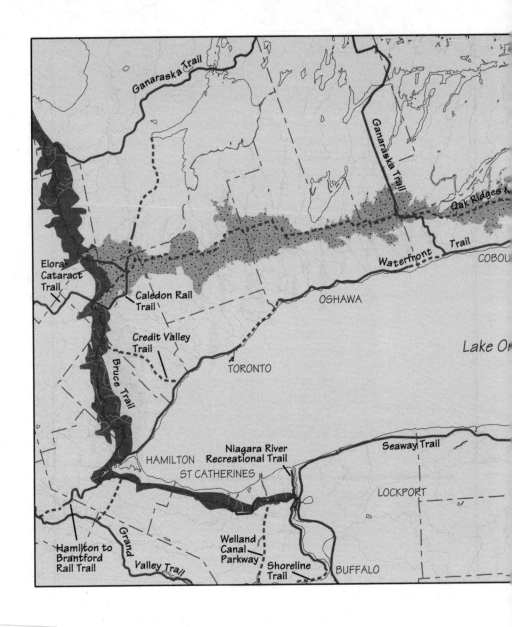

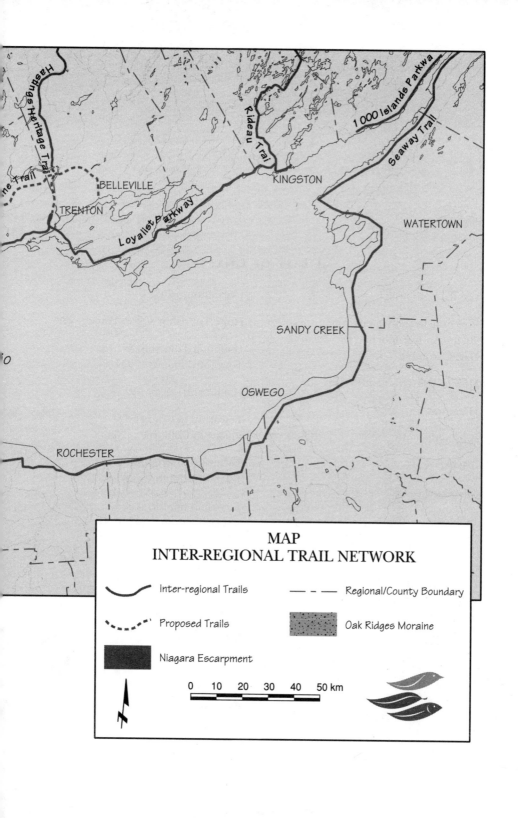

MAP
INTER-REGIONAL TRAIL NETWORK

‒‒‒‒‒ Inter-regional Trails   — — — Regional/County Boundary

▪▪▪▪▪ Proposed Trails   ▨ Oak Ridges Moraine

▬ Niagara Escarpment

0 10 20 30 40 50 km

A List of Chapters

Contents

This book represents the efforts of many people. It has been made possible by the generous support of waterfront communities. They deserve the thanks of all those who, from now on, will have the opportunity to enjoy the Waterfront Trail.

We thank those who drafted accounts of the various sections of the Waterfront Trail, not an easy task given that portions of the Trail were still under construction, unsigned, and often, under a foot of snow. They are Eileen Argyris, John Barker, Jim Bate, Don Bell, Peter Carruthers, Judy Collar, Mary Curtis, Sheila Creighton, Mike Filey, Beth Jefferson, Steve LaForest, Sher Leetooze, Tija Luste, Don McClement, Brian McHattie, Liz Mueller, Bernadette Murray, Jocelyn Neysmith, Monica Rayson, Ron Reid, Irene Rota, John Sabean, Honor Sylvester, John Thompson, Don Tyreman, and Rob Washburn.

We also wish to acknowledge the local archivists and historians, people who are passionately devoted to their communities, and who shared generously and patiently the very great deal they know.

The illustrated maps were created by Aleta Karstad who, already busy with the production of her own book, *A Place to Walk: A Naturalist's Guide to the Lake Ontario Waterfront,* found time to meet our deadlines. Helping her were Molly Brass, Tim Smith, Jiin Kim, Kim Fijan, and Fred Schueler. Brian Byrnes of Envirosense provided the sketches on the trail notes pages.

The following people generously contributed their time: Barry Linetsky compiled the photographic essay, and Deborah Ross and Heather Houghton assisted with chapter reviews.

Credits

Editor Sheila Kieran took the disparate voices and perspectives of the many contributors and shaped a cohesive story that is a pleasure to read. She brought to each chapter her wealth of knowledge, appreciation for history, commitment to accuracy, and a determination to make this first guidebook something people will use and enjoy.

Production Co-ordinator Don Bell and other production team members, Heather Iounno (researcher), Susan Lawrence and David Kilgour (copy editors), Michael Edwards of Ryan MacDonald Edwards (design), Oksana Ruczenczyn of Leslie Smart and Associates (desk-top publishing), Patricia McQuaig (production consultant), and Sarah Campbell (student assistant), all worked long and hard, and their dedication and talent are evident in this book.

Bibliography and index were provided by Janet Hollingsworth, manager of the Canadian Waterfront Resource Centre.

Finally, the staff of the Waterfront Regeneration Trust demonstrated their readiness to meet this publishing challenge with enthusiasm and professionalism. It would not have been possible to deliver this book without their support and dedication. In particular, we thank the following chapter co-ordinators: Martha Blandon, Elaine Collicott, Darcy Baker, Suesan Danesh, Anne Dixon, Charity Landon, Alice LeBlanc, Lisa Ohata, Irene Rota, Kim Sahadth, Denine Snowden, and Colleen Zanello. We also thank David Carter and Suzanne Barrett for their leadership, guidance, and advice.

Marlaine Koehler,
Project Direction

As *you come to better
understand the waterfront,
you will also come to
a deeper commitment to the
potential of its regeneration*

WELCOME TO THE
Waterfront
Trail

A SYMBOL OF HISTORY IN THE MAKING...

Step onto the Waterfront Trail, and you help make history!

Now, if you have just arrived for a Sunday afternoon stroll, or to try out your new in-line skates, that statement must seem more than a little overblown. So perhaps a little explanation is in order.

The Waterfront Trail is a symbol of a historic change in attitude towards the Lake Ontario waterfront. And when you use the Trail, you are a testament to that changing view.

For most of this century, many people in Ontario thought of the waterfront, if they thought of it at all, as a place of commerce and industry – a place with wharfs and factories and warehouses and rail lines. The water itself was a convenient and cheap place to dump our wastes – sewage and industrial effluents, even the rubble and soil from nearby construction sites.

And gradually, inevitably, the reputation of the lake became more and more tarnished. The lake was polluted, everybody knew that. To walk along the shoreline, if you could even get to the shoreline, was to be assaulted by the smell of rotting fish and windrows of algae. Often, in summer, you couldn't swim, for fear of bacterial pollution; you couldn't eat the fish at any time of the year, for fear of toxic contamination. Along many parts of the Lake Ontario shore, communities turned their back on the waterfront – for who would want to go there anyway?

But a few determined individuals were convinced that this tarnished jewel was not beyond redemption, and with the

increasing awareness of environmental concerns from the 1970s
onward, those few became many. People began to dare to hope that
the decline of Lake Ontario was not inevitable, that the downward
spiral of neglect could be reversed. Stung by the harsh indictments
of a concerned public, who believed that Lake Erie was dead and
Lake Ontario not far behind, governments at all levels began to
respond. That historic change was beginning.

Like most changes, this one took time to gather
speed. Many of the most basic actions needed were not the kind to
garner headlines. Municipalities and the province invested tens of
millions of dollars to upgrade sewage treatment plants and new
sewer pipes. New regulations, often mind-numbingly complex, were
applied to chemicals with unpronounceable names. A long slow
process of acquiring bits and pieces of waterfront land was carried
out by conservation authorities and municipalities.

These were important moves, absolutely essential to
the recovery of the lake, but largely invisible to the citizen on the
street. Over time, communities began to see their waterfronts in a
new light: Ajax reserved a wide swath of parkland along almost its
entire waterfront, which soon became a favourite destination for
nearby residents. Oshawa reversed a death sentence for Second
Marsh, which had been slated for industrial dredging, and created a
nature sanctuary instead. The city of Burlington worked in partnership with other groups to consolidate a major regional park at
Burlington Beach. Along the Toronto waterfront, the federal
government created Harbourfront, the Province of Ontario created
Ontario Place, and the City of Toronto and the Toronto Star
established the Martin Goodman Trail. In Port Credit, Bronte
Harbour and Cobourg – as in many other waterfront communities –
marinas sprang up in response to renewed interest in boating on
Lake Ontario.

In 1988, the federal government established the Royal
Commission on the Future of the Toronto Waterfront, which I was
asked to chair. Fifteen months later, the Province of Ontario took
on co-responsibility for the Commission, making it only the second
time in Canadian history a royal commission represented both federal and provincial concerns simultaneously. As a result, the focus

expanded from concern about Toronto to concern about the Lake Ontario shore from Hamilton to Trenton and to the entire bioregion (the basin formed by the Niagara Escarpment on the west, the Oak Ridges Moraine to the north and east, and Lake Ontario shoreline to the south).

The Royal Commission served to both promote and record the emerging change in attitude in many communities about their waterfront – a re-discovery of the value and attractiveness of the water's edge, a determination to conquer past neglect, an awakening of the potential of the waterfront to lead economic as well as environmental renewal. We even tagged a word to crystallize that process – regeneration.

From the many people and groups who contributed their thoughts to the work of the Commission, we were able to develop a list of nine principles to capture their expectations. People told us that they want the Lake Ontario waterfront to be clean, green, accessible, diverse, attractive, connected, open, useable and affordable.

The Commission discovered what would be needed to achieve these expectations and made a series of recommendations in its final report, *Regeneration,* in 1992. Subsequent to the completion of the Commission in 1992, the Province moved to establish the Waterfront Regeneration Trust as the vehicle for co-ordinating regeneration efforts and, in particular to help build the Waterfront Trail.

And thus, the idea of a Waterfront Trail was born. A trail that would connect the many existing parks, pathways, natural areas and activity areas along the waterfront. That would provide a place for recreation close to home for the 3 million people who live near the lake. That would help waterfront visitors understand the interconnections, both natural and cultural, that are so vital to the health and vitality of the lakeshore. That would celebrate the progress made already in regenerating the waterfront, and encourage further progress where necessary.

In all those ways, then, the Waterfront Trail becomes a symbol for a changed view of the waterfront as a whole. Rather than the derelict backyard of yesteryear, the waterfront has become the front yard for communities, a place of pride, a testament to and for the future.

LEARNING FROM THE LANDSCAPE...

As you leaf through this Guide or travel along the waterfront, we hope that it will add to your enjoyment, and to your understanding as well. With the aid of the Guide, you should be able to read the landscape as well. There are many fascinating stories hidden there in the waterfront landscape, and many lessons.

You will see that the character of waterfront communities today is not simply accidental. They are the result of strong personalities and strong communities, as any local history book will tell you. But they are also a product of a distinctive natural environment, and the way people have acted within, as part of, that environment. Understanding that we humans are part of waterfront ecology, not something separate, is fundamental to its regeneration.

The waterfront is an area of constant change. Much of that change is the result of natural forces – the action of waves cutting into shoreline bluffs in some areas for example, and building beaches elsewhere. But much of the change is also culturally-related, as human activities leave their stamp on the landscape. But these forces of change, both powerful in their own ways, almost always act together to produce the communities and features we see along the waterfront today.

Look at the city of Toronto, for example. Why did it develop in this location, rather than elsewhere along the lake? To answer that deceptively simple question, it is helpful to know that the Toronto area has been home to native settlements for over 10,000 years, since shortly after the glaciers withdrew. Why here? In part because the lake currents here created a spit (now Toronto Islands) with sheltered water behind. This bay was fringed by extensive marshlands, with ducks and swans and muskrat that served as a ready source of food and furs. The light sandy soils on the tablelands nearby provided easy cultivation for the corn, beans, and pumpkins of later native cultures.

Equally important were the rivers, especially the Humber and the Rouge, which provided easy capture of spawning fish at their rapids and links to portages into Lake Simcoe and the upper Great Lakes beyond. Whoever controlled these portages controlled the trade of furs and other goods in a large area, a strategic advantage not overlooked by native groups. When the Seneca tribe pushed into southern Ontario in the late 1600s from New York State, for example, they established villages near the mouths of both the Humber and the Rouge rivers.

These trade links were so important they even gave the later city its name – from the Toronto Portage, referring originally to the narrows at the top of Lake Simcoe to the north.

Those same strategic advantages in controlling trade led the French to establish Fort Rouillé as an outpost on what is now Exhibition Place in Toronto. And as European settlement grew, the same natural advantages – a ready-made harbour, rivers for waterpower for early mills, fertile farmland – were adapted to different uses. The selection of York (now Toronto) as the capital of Upper Canada was not just a desire to be somewhat removed from the hostile American border, but also a recognition of the town's natural advantages.

In other parts of the waterfront, early transportation decisions had a major influence in the landscape patterns you see today. Why is it, for example, that town centres developed around the harbour areas in Bronte, Oakville, and Port Credit, while to the east the towns are several kilometres inland from their corresponding harbours? This "twinning" pattern is especially obvious in Whitby, Oshawa, Bowmanville, Darlington, Grafton, Colborne and Brighton.

The answer lies in transportation connections. When the Danforth Road (now Highway 2) was constructed to link waterfront communities, it stayed near the shore in the Peel and Halton areas, and the previous harbours were reinforced as nodes of economic growth. But to the east, the road, and later the railways, were routed inland to drier ground, and the lure of wheeled transport quickly won out.

One other example shows the links between landscape and human endeavour. As you drive along the QEW across Halton Region, and again on Highway 401 from Cobourg most of the way to Trenton, there is a ridge of hills close by to the north, running parallel to the road. Is this simply coincidence? Not really – that ridge is the former shore bluff of glacial Lake Iroquois, a higher stage of Lake Ontario from the period shortly after the glaciers. As well as creating the bluffs, the lake created sandy beaches in the shallow waters at their toe, just as Lake Ontario does today. Highway engineers, knowing a good thing when they saw it, routed the road bed along that flat, easily-worked beach sand for miles at a time.

These three stories are but a small sample of the connecting links that weave together to form the landscapes you see today along the waterfront. This Guide will introduce you to many other places where natural elements and human energies have intermingled. Often it will tell of past changes in waterfront communities, in the hope that you will begin to see that those changes are not random, but rather the result of the environment in which they are set, the temper of the times, and the character of the humans involved.

Your job, as you guide yourself along the waterfront, is to keep asking why. Why are there so many apple orchards in Northumberland but not elsewhere? Why do some parts of the shoreline have sand, and others cobble? Why are some bathing beaches regularly closed, and others not at all?

This Guide will help you with some of the answers, but not all. In other places, it may just help direct you to some of the right questions, and you will have to look elsewhere for answers. But as you look, and as you come to better understand the waterfront, my hope is that you will also come to a deeper commitment to the potential of its regeneration.

A STRATEGY FOR REGENERATION...

If the Waterfront Trail is a symbol of changing attitudes to the waterfront, is there something of substance behind that symbol as well? The answer lies in the Lake Ontario Greenway Strategy, a document developed by the Lake Ontario Greenway Strategy Steering Committee. The Committee is made up of municipalities, conservation authorities, community groups, private sector representatives, all levels of government, and the Waterfront Reneration Trust.

The Greenway has been described as "a fat trail", but in fact it is far more than that. It includes the lands along the shore from Burlington to Trenton, inland some 2-5 kilometres to the first rise in elevation, and the adjacent shallow waters. This corridor, which provides the setting for the Waterfront Trail, recognizes that the shoreline is greatly affected by the people and land uses of the waterfront area. In turn, the Greenway also recognizes that the lake strongly influences the adjacent lands – by moderating the climate, for example, and by providing historic sources of food and transport that influenced economic and community development.

The Greenway Strategy is based on the involvement of municipalities and government agencies, expert studies and the "on-the-ground" wisdom of local residents. It sets out to address the challenges facing the Lake Ontario waterfront today – providing access to the shore for a growing population, reversing environmental degradation, fostering economic renewal, managing urban growth, improving the decision-making process, and balancing competing objectives for a limited land and water base.

The core of the Greenway Strategy is a series of five objectives, with a range of action steps identified for each. These objectives are to:

1. Protect the physical, natural and cultural attributes of the waterfront

The first step in regeneration is protecting the best of what we have now. The Strategy identifies 92 significant natural habitats which deserve protection, and 35 valley corridors connecting the waterfront to other natural habitats on the Niagara Escarpment and Oak Ridges Moraine. These habitats are vital to the diversity and movement of wildlife along the waterfront. As well, natural shoreline processes need protection, so that armouring the waterfront with concrete or breakwalls does not destroy fish habitat and cut off the sand supply to beaches. Protecting archaeological and historic sites and landscapes is also vital to maintaining our connections to the past.

2. Restore degraded areas along the waterfront

In many parts of the waterfront, we need to re-build environmental quality, to reverse past damage to habitats and communities. Much progress has been made already in some areas – controls on phosphorus in detergents, for example, and improved sewage treatment have brought lake-wide nutrient levels below the restoration target level since 1986. Declining levels of toxic contaminants in Lake Ontario waters and fish have resulted in a striking recovery of some fish-eating birds such as cormorants. There is a long way yet to go in restoring near-shore water quality, particularly in the four designated Remedial Action Plan areas in Hamilton Harbour, Toronto, Port Hope, and Bay of Quinte, but we have shown clearly that determined effort can yield results.

Another area where the Greenway Strategy process has been active is the restoration of former industrial sites with contaminated soils or groundwater. Re-development of these sites into housing or parkland uses can provide a vehicle for their recovery, but new remediation methods and improvements to the framework of regulations are essential to allow progress.

Restoration of natural habitats is another priority, especially in valley corridors and in shallow waters. And in many places the human habitat could benefit greatly by strengthening of community identity and landscape character, to highlight traditional connections to the waterfront.

3. Promote awareness, recreational use, and community participation

People who make frequent use of the waterfront are much more likely to support its renewal. Completing the Waterfront Trail, and providing other appropriate forms of access such as boat launch ramps, help to encourage public use and to develop community participation in waterfront projects. Waterfront festivals and celebrations are another popular way of attracting waterfront visitors. A range of interpretive facilities, from signs to major interpretive centres, will be developed. We also need to recognize the importance of changing populations in planning waterfront recreation –

waterfront residents are becoming older on average, and are showing a greater mix of ethnic origins.

4. Promote compatible economic activities and employment on the waterfront

The waterfront, especially in harbour areas, has long been a focus
of economic activity. While the nature of that activity is changing,
with goods-producing industries often moving elsewhere, the
waterfront will remain an important economic force. The Strategy
emphasizes the need to enhance these economic and employment
opportunities, and to direct them to urban core areas where
re-development can provide a compact form and environmental
and community benefits.

Tourism and recreation are growth industries with
special potential along the waterfront, and the Strategy identifies
10 primary and 12 secondary destination areas. Development of
new waterfront attractions and joint packaging and marketing of
themed waterfront experiences will help to create a critical mass
of tourism facilities and services to attract and hold visitors. This
development should be clustered in destination areas with the
ability to support large numbers of visitors, and away from natural
areas and quiet neighbourhoods.

5. Reduce gridlock and increase sharing of resources and coordination

Too often, government policies overlap or conflict with one
another, and beneficial waterfront projects can become snared in
red tape. Through a recently-approved set of comprehensive
Provincial policies, this jurisdictional gridlock will be partly resolved;
the Greenway Strategy suggests better coordination in the applica-
tion of other waterfront legislation as well. The use of "round-table"
approaches to decision-making, which has been employed by the
Waterfront Regeneration Trust to address difficult issues, has much
promise as well to improve decisions.

The Strategy also recognizes the need to coordinate
the allocation and timing of funding to waterfront projects, and to
encourage private as well as public investments. By working in part-

nerships, much faster progress can be made in waterfront regeneration activities.

There is no quick fix for waterfront challenges. The Waterfront Trail will continue to evolve and improve over many years to come. Progress on water quality, wildlife habitats, economic renewal, and community development will often seem frustratingly slow and uneven. But we will make progress. We will learn from the successes, and from the failures, of our own and other communities. We will persist in the face of inertia and ineptitude, and innovate in the face of obstacles. We will leave our children a healthier, more attractive waterfront than the one we inherited.

So welcome to a new waterfront. Not yesterday's waterfront of neglect and decline, but tomorrow's waterfront, full of bright promise.

David Crombie, 1995

HOW TO USE THIS
Guide

◀ ···

There are two kinds of information in this book: the very factual
first-you-turn-left-then-you-turn-right data (as thorough, concise,
and accurate as the work of dozens of people could make it).
Second, there are brief descriptions of things, places, and people:
the overwintering habits of butterflies; the first distillery in Upper
Canada; the sculptor whose lion welcomed a Queen to the
waterfront.

Along the way, there are small excursions into history
and politics: the definition of a "United Empire Loyalist"; the meaning of the phrase "Responsible Government". These are not
designed to be definitive, but only to give visitors to the Lake
Ontario waterfront some context in which to understand what they
see. The hope is that these vignettes and asides will either satisfy
people's appetite – or whet it.

The guide is laid out from west to east, an admittedly
arbitrary decision, but one that has been used in all the publications
of the Waterfront Regeneration Trust.

Below you will find a brief explanation of some terms
and reference tools used in this book.

ON-ROAD AND OFF-ROAD

An on-road section is one actually on the road surface, not
separated from it by a physical barrier such as a boulevard.

Cycling lanes along paved shoulders are considered
on-road; however, they may not be suitable for some Trail users or
modes of transportation because of the surface type or the close
proximity to vehicular traffic.

An off-road section is separated from a road surface by a physical barrier such as a boulevard; these are generally considered safe for non-vehicular traffic but, because of the surface, may not be suitable for Trail users.

TRAIL SURFACES

There are various types of surfaces used on the Waterfront Trail. These include:

- natural footpath
- grass
- wood chips
- boardwalk
- granular materials, including limestone screenings
- asphalt
- concrete

Natural foot paths may not be suitable for cyclists or in-line skaters and may also be difficult for people in wheelchairs. The same is true of sections covered by wood chips and granular materials. Limestone screenings, which are hard-packed fine gravel, are not appropriate for use by in-line skaters and may be difficult for some people in wheelchairs.

MAPS

Maps show the route of the Waterfront Trail for each municipality. The deep green lines (whether solid to indicate on-road sections or broken for off-road) represent the Trail's main route, while the lighter shade is used for selected side trips that can be made from the Trail. When you're on a side trip, remember that the on-road/off-road designation does not apply: it is used only in relation to the Trail itself. Areas in the faintest green colour are the perimeters of parks and green spaces.

PUBLIC TRANSPORTATION

You will find public transit "side bars" in the left margin in each chapter; these list phone numbers for local transit and VIA Rail. GO Transit information is also provided, including the GO station locations relative to the Trail. Those using hearing impaired devices (TDDs) may wish to call 1-800-387-3652 for GO Transit information.

GO Transit is an excellent way to travel to many points along the Trail. Bicycles are permitted on the trains, except during rush hours.

ICONS

Illustrations or "icons" in the left margin refer to some of the uses for which the given area is most noted, but do not attempt to identify all amenities or all locations where a particular activity can be enjoyed. They include:

Art Gallery or
Museum

Formal
Gardens

Lighthouse

Public Boat
Launch or
Public Marina

Tourist
Information
Centres

Birding

Camping

Canoeing

Fishing

Hiking

In-line
Skating

Picnic

Look Out

Shopping

Swimming

Information that may be of interest to people in wheelchairs is also identified with an icon. As with the other icons, this is not a comprehensive inventory of amenities and activities.

MATRICES

Matrices, summarizing the amenities and attractions in each municipality, follow the Trenton chapter. These offer practical information such as the location of washrooms, snack bars, and public telephones.

LOCAL BUSINESSES

While every waterfront community offers many services to the Trail user, this book focuses on those local businesses, such as bed-and-breakfasts and antique shops, that lie along the Waterfront Trail. Local tourist information offices or Chambers of Commerce can provide information about other nearby places of interest.

TRAIL ETIQUETTE

Here are some common sense suggestions to help everyone enjoy the Waterfront Trail:
- respect the privacy of people living along the Trail
- don't litter
- leave flowers and plants for others to enjoy
- keep dogs on a leash, especially near farmland
- protect and do not disturb wildlife
- take nothing but photographs
- alert any slower-moving Trail users to your presence and then slow down and proceed with caution as you pass them (usually on the left)

THE TRAIL OF THE FUTURE

As you follow the Waterfront Trail you may encounter areas where the signed route does not coincide with the directions that are given in the book. Such instances are a reflection of the evolutionary process that the Trail will enjoy over time.

The goal is to bring the Trail closer to the lake in places where it is now some distance away, and to have the route aligned off-road wherever possible. As a result, the route will change where bridges are constructed over rivers and creeks, pathways extended, cycling lanes created, or voluntary agreements with major land owners provide better waterfront access.

In areas where the route has changed since the publication of this book, watch for signs bearing the Waterfront Trail logo.

KEEP IN TOUCH

This is the first of many guides to the Waterfront Trail. It is our intention to reprint approximately every two years to reflect ongoing trail improvements and changes along the waterfront. Because people enjoy the Trail in so many different ways, we will also publish other books, such as a birders guide.

To keep up to date on happenings, you may wish to receive the Waterfront Trail newsletter, a quarterly publication of the Waterfront Regeneration Trust.

A guidebook like this works best when its readers are involved. Your thoughts and dreams for the Lake Ontario waterfront are important, and we want to hear and learn from them. Please send your comments and suggestions to the Waterfront Regeneration Trust, 207 Queen's Quay West, Box 129, Toronto, Ontario, M5J 1A7 (fax: 416-314-9497).

After *more than a century of industrial growth, Hamilton is on the verge of yet another major change, re-establishing once – abundant natural and aesthetic resources*

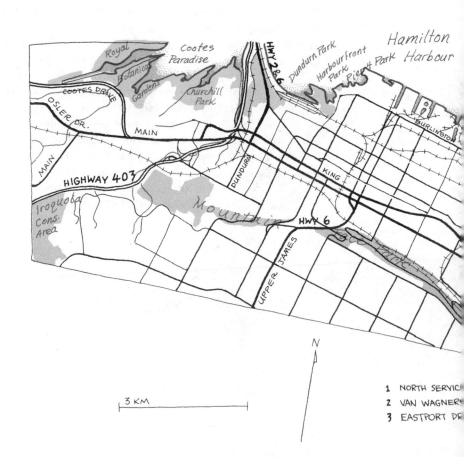

1 NORTH SERVIC
2 VAN WAGNER
3 EASTPORT DR

Hamilton

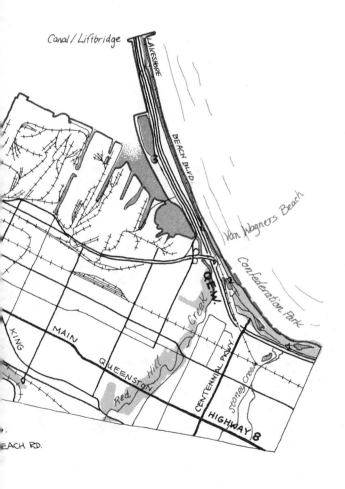

Canal / Liftbridge

LAKESHORE

BEACH BLVD.

Van Wagners Beach

Confederation Park

Q.E.W.

KING

MAIN

QUEENSTON

Red Hill Creek

CENTENNIAL PKWY.

Stoney Creek

HIGHWAY 8

BEACH RD.

N THE TIME BEFORE history, there was a lake so immense that it covered a substantial slice of what became North America, north and east from what is now Manitoulin Island, south and west to Wisconsin. We call the remaining shoreline of that long-gone lake the Niagara Escarpment, and if you stand on its rim overlooking Hamilton Harbour, you will find that it encapsulates the journey you are about to begin. In the foreground is the harbour, with its freighters briskly heading in and out, its smokestacks looming, and its environmental challenges.

But farther west, you can also see Cootes Paradise, slowly being returned to its natural state, its marshlands bursting with energy and life.

This is a good introduction to Hamilton and, in fact, to the Waterfront Trail across its length: a history of nature and humans, one so durable, the other so frequently uncomprehending but working now to heal what was wounded, protect what remains, and right past wrongs.

For more than six centuries Hamilton has been home to people: the first were natives, the Neutral Indians, who, from 1350, centred their territory on Burlington Bay. There they made use of the food and water around them – plentiful marshes and forests, full of bear, wolves, snakes, fish, and waterfowl. Although French explorers had visited First Nations peoples in the area as early as 1615, it was not until 1669 that René Robert Cavelier de La Salle, became the first European to set foot on the shores of the bay.

After the Revolutionary War, those Americans who remained loyal to the Crown began to move north, and they received lands in the Hamilton area, as elsewhere in the province, throughout the late 1700s. Population increases slowed during the War of 1812, and it was not until 1823 that Hamilton began to grow as transportation routes, such as the Burlington and Desjardins canals, were established.

In 1846, the City of Hamilton (population 6,832) was incorporated. Shortly thereafter, the Great Western Railway came to

PUBLIC TRANSIT

Local Transit
(905-527-4441)

GO (905-527-8187)
• CN Station – James
at Murray St., 1 km
north of Pier 4 Park

town, and Hamilton began to make its mark as the province's largest industrial city; in 1895, several local companies combined to form the Hamilton Iron and Steel Company (now Stelco), and Hamilton achieved its status as Canada's Steel City.

Over the next 70 years, Hamilton's face was changed forever as an increasing number of people – responding to the rise and then the gradual decline of agriculture and to rapid industrial expansion – replaced the bay's natural features with farms, housing, and commercial developments.

In the early 1970s, environmental concerns in the Hamilton area began to coalesce around water quality in the bay. In 1985, in response to these water quality concerns, Hamilton Harbour was designated an Area of Concern by the International Joint Commission and in 1992 a plan known as the Hamilton Harbour Remedial Action Plan was completed; it calls for improved sewage treatment facilities, industrial clean-up, controls on stormwater, habitat rehabilitation, and improved public access.

In 1994, the Regional Municipality of Hamilton-Wentworth was recognized by the United Nations as one of 21 locations around the world testing new ideas on sustainable development. After more than a century of industrial growth, it would seem that Hamilton is on the verge of yet another major change, moving ahead by looking to the past and trying to re-establish once-abundant natural and aesthetic resources.

While in time it may extend into the Niagara area, the Waterfront Trail now starts in easternmost Hamilton, at Confederation Park, and comprises roughly two sections. The first is along Van Wagners Beach Road and the second on Beach Boulevard as far as the municipal boundary with Burlington.

You may get to Confederation Park by car from the Queen Elizabeth Way (QEW), exiting at Highway 20, the Centennial Parkway; follow it north to the lake. At the stoplights at the North Service Road, turn left onto what becomes Van Wagners Beach Road and proceed; the road is also accessible from the North Service Road and from Beach Boulevard.

Areas of Concern in the Great Lakes basin are locations where beneficial uses are impaired because of contaminants in the water, sediment, plant, aquatic and terrestrial life. There are 42 Areas of Concern in the Great Lakes basin. The Remedial Action Plan (RAP) identifies the actions we have to take to restore environmental health to these areas. These plans involve citizens, industry, and government at all levels. There are four RAPs along the north shore of Lake Ontario: Hamilton Harbour, Metro Toronto and Region, Port Hope, and Bay of Quinte.

VAN WAGNERS BEACH

The Trail stretches 2.6 kilometres (1.6 miles) along Van Wagners Beach Road, from the North Service Road at Centennial Parkway to Beach Boulevard. It is fairly quiet, suitable for bicycles, and in-line skates, as well as for pedestrians. However, those on foot might prefer to walk along the asphalt Trail at the lakefront, a 3-kilometre (1.8-mile) promenade running the length of the beach behind Confederation Park; it is suitable for pedestrians, in-line skates, bicycles, and wheelchairs. It is accessible from the back of Hutch's Restaurant in Confederation Park.

CONFEDERATION PARK

The Hamilton Region Conservation Authority's 83-hectare (205-acre) Confederation Park includes the many attractions along Van Wagners Beach; it is open year-round, and offers picnic areas with both sunny and shaded tables, as well as a concession stand. A large children's area, which is accessible to those with special needs, was generously donated by the Kinsmen Club of Hamilton. The park also has a campground with serviced sites for recreational vehicles and unserviced sites for tents; it is open from May 1 to the Thanksgiving weekend. Serviced sites should be booked in advance, especially for the month of July, the busiest time. For information or reservations, phone 905-578-1644.

Wild Waterworks in Confederation Park is accessible to people in wheelchairs; it is open from June through Labour Day, weather permitting. The waterpark features a wave-action pool, two waterslides, an Action River ride, and a children's wading pool. For information about fees and hours, call 905-561-2292.

Confederation Park also has an Adventure Village that includes Canada's largest 18-hole mini-golf course. Visitors will also find batting cages, a 30-game arcade, and a basketball court. It is open daily and charges admission. For further information, phone 905-549-9444.

Continue west along Van Wagners Beach Road and turn right after you leave Confederation Park's main gates. Further along the winding beach road on your right are a couple of well-known restaurants.

Baranga's on the Beach

The word *baranga* is derived from the Greek word for shed. This restaurant is located in the old Van Wagners schoolhouse, which was built in 1905 and closed in 1961. The restaurant operates a casual outdoor deck in good weather, from which two beach volleyball courts are accessible. Baranga's is open daily from April 1 to Labour Day. Call 905-544-7122 for information about fall and winter hours.

Hutch's Dingley Dell

Beyond Baranga's is Hutch's Dingley Dell Restaurant, a Hamilton Beach landmark; formerly a snack bar and changehouse, it was built in the early 1960s to cater to visitors to the beach. The restaurant is noted for its french fries, spectacular lakefront view, and the sports memorabilia, featuring local hockey and football heroes, that line its walls. Hutch's is open year-round; for further information, phone 905-545-5508.

West of Hutch's, near the parking lot, is a plaque commemorating the site of the former King's Head Inn. This "Government House" was the first building south of the canal, though its precise location is unknown. As the link between the settlements at Niagara and York, the King's Head Inn was important to both the government and the military. The plaque was erected thanks to the efforts of local residents.

Van Wagners Ponds

Across the road from Hutch's Restaurant, a trail formed by the abandoned railway embankment leads to Van Wagners Ponds, a noteworthy natural area. From June to August, you will find common, Caspian, and black terns feeding in this provincially significant Class 1 wetland. In June, look for painted turtles sunning themselves on the embankment. During the winter months, the frozen ponds provide an outdoor skating rink.

If you follow the trail from Hutch's, it leads back to Confederation Park. Either retrace your steps through the ponds or follow Van Wagners Beach Road back to Hutch's.

Wetlands are "lands that are seasonally or permanently covered by shallow water, as well as lands where the water table is close to or at the surface. In either case the presence of abundant water has caused the formation of *hydric soils* and has favoured the dominance of either *hydrophytic* or water tolerant plants. The four major types of wetlands are swamps, marshes, bogs, and fens." (Ontario. Ministry of Municipal Affairs, 1995)

Wetlands are classified from 1 to 7 based on their biological, social, hydrological, and special features values. Classes 1, 2, and 3 are provincially significant, classes 4 to 7 are locally significant.

Continue along Van Wagners Beach Road to Lakeland Community Centre, on your right.

LAKELAND COMMUNITY CENTRE

Operated by the Hamilton East Kiwanis and Woodward Beach Community Council, the Lakeland Community Centre offers various recreational services: from Canada Day to Labour Day, its pool, a popular attraction, is open daily, weather permitting. The Community Centre also boasts volleyball and basketball courts, and a children's play area. Lakeland has washrooms, open during park hours, that are fully accessible to people in wheelchairs. The centre has an admission charge; for more information, call 905-547-1814.

Next door there is another summer attraction, Lakeland Go-Carts; for further information on this 0.8-kilometre (0.5-mile) track, call 905-544-3951.

The beach at Lakeland has been eroding over the years, and now consists mainly of stone and rock. As a result, the Trail follows the sidewalk at this point, but joins up with the continuous lakefront Trail behind Hutch's, Baranga's, and through Confederation Park.

From Lakeland, continue along Van Wagners Beach Road to the intersection at Beach Boulevard; turn right to continue on the Waterfront Trail.

WINDERMERE BASIN/TOLL GATE PONDS

If, instead of turning right from Van Wagners Beach Road onto Beach Boulevard, you proceed through the lights and under the overpass, you will come to Eastport Drive. At the next lights, turn right onto Eastport Drive and cross to the bay side of the road on the paved shoulder. There is ample parking for viewing the wildfowl in Windermere Basin.

During May and June, one of the largest colonies of common terns along Lake Ontario (in recent years, nearly 1,000 pairs) take up residence in Windermere Basin, while the colder months are a good time to watch for snowy owls and such overwintering waterfowl as scaup and mergansers.

Farther along Eastport Drive – about 2 kilometres (1.2 miles) – is another birding spot, the Toll Gate Ponds. Looking toward the harbour from Eastport Drive, note the large colony of birds on the berms along the ponds' perimeters; from May to July, double-crested cormorants, black-crowned night herons, Caspian terns, herring gulls, and ring-billed gulls nest here. Note especially the cormorant nests in the cottonwood trees. During the spring and fall months, the Toll Gate Ponds provide a stopover area for a great variety of migrating waterfowl.

To continue along the Waterfront Trail, return to the intersection of Van Wagners Beach Road and Beach Boulevard (left at the lights), and turn left onto Beach Boulevard at the second set of lights.

FORMATION OF THE BEACH STRIP

Beach Boulevard is popularly known as "the Beach Strip", but it is actually a baymouth barrier. One source describes the formation of the beach between Lake Ontario and Hamilton Harbour this way:

> The formation of a baymouth barrier occurs over thousands of years. Initially a submerged bar is formed from sand deposited by waves breaking in deep water off-shore. As the process continues, a dune is gradually developed which rises above the water level. Other isolated bars emerge and eventually join together to form a continuous strip. The water behind the barrier becomes a bay. A second submerged bar forms on the lake side and rises above the water to form a primary dune. Over time the trough between the dunes is filled by windblown sand and the formation of the baymouth barrier is complete. (Middleton, 1971)

Before the commercial and residential development that began toward the end of the 19th century, the sandstrip was a functioning natural ecosystem. A description from the *Ghent Papers* (c. 1890) notes that:

> When the Beach was first seen by white men it was exceedingly beautiful and picturesque. It was overgrown with immense Basswood, interspersed by large oaks and

willows throughout the Beach. And the wild grapes luxuri-
ously wound its thongs among them. (McCowell, 1981)

Apart from a native trail that ran along the length of
the beach, there was little evidence of the presence of humans. In
the present century the area has been altered considerably by the
fill used in constructing the Burlington Skyway, the Queen
Elizabeth Way, and the Canada Centre for Inland Waters (CCIW).
However, as part of the Hamilton Harbour Remedial Action Plan,
three islands are being built on the bay side (adjacent to CCIW) in
order to improve conditions for the diverse populations of fish and
waterfowl that still inhabit the area. When they are completed, a
trail and look-out towers will offer prime views of such nesting birds
as common and Caspian terns, black-crowned night herons, double-
crested cormorants, and herring and ring-billed gulls.

HISTORY OF THE BEACH COMMUNITY

Once dubbed "Hamilton's Playground", the Beach Strip first
received widespread attention as a recreational area in the late
1800s. With the construction of the Ocean House, a large luxury
hotel, in 1875, and the Royal Hamilton Yacht Club in 1892, the area
began to draw wealthy summer vacationers eager to enjoy its clean
air and waterfront attractions. The advent of the inter-urban railway,
the Electric Radial, in 1896, made a weekend trip to the beach popular for working-class Hamiltonians as well.

Demand for land for cottages and summer homes sky-
rocketed, and the beach continued to attract huge crowds,
especially for events such as Victoria Day fireworks and the Annual
Beach Fête. As the beach became increasingly residential, many
prominent Hamiltonians built ostentatious summer homes on the
bay side of the beach, near the former site of the Royal Hamilton
Yacht Club, not far south of the canal. The homes that remain give
the beach a unique architectural heritage: the "cottages" were primarily built of wood, rather than the brick of the typical
late-Victorian homes in Hamilton. In fact, 33 of the houses along
Beach Boulevard are listed in Hamilton's Inventory of
Architecturally and Historically Significant Buildings.

BEACH BOULEVARD

The Waterfront Trail travels 3.7 kilometres (2.3 miles) along Beach Boulevard from its start at Van Wagners Beach Road to where the road ends at Eastport Drive. While there are sidewalks for pedestrians and people using wheelchairs, cyclists are asked to follow the wide lanes of the road. Those who want to gain access to the lakefront beach can turn right onto any of the cross streets along Beach Boulevard: most dead-end at the beach. Access may also be attained through some of the vacant lots, which are the property of the Hamilton Region Conservation Authority.

The first lake access point on Beach Boulevard is the Skyway Playground, a small parkette that provides picnic tables and children's swings.

Hamilton Beach Rescue Club

Farther along Beach Boulevard on the left are the headquarters of the Hamilton Beach Rescue Club; the rescue unit is a volunteer organization begun in 1941 as the Burlington Beach Fire Department. The original club house was built in 1952 on the site of a former ice rink; when Hamilton annexed the Beach Strip and the Hamilton Fire Department took over in 1957, the volunteers formed the Beach Rescue Unit to monitor Confederation Park.

With the Beach Commission office no longer in use, the building was moved from the canal to its current site, and attached to the original structure. All of the approximately 30 volunteers of the Beach Rescue Unit are members of the Coast Guard Auxiliary, and use their two boats to participate in search-and-rescue operations for the Region of Hamilton-Wentworth. They patrol Lake Ontario from the canal to Fifty Point at the Fifty Point Conservation Area in Winona at 1479 Baseline Road.

Dynes Hotel

Beyond the Beach Rescue Club is another beach landmark, the Dynes Hotel. This lakefront restaurant is one of the many taverns and inns constructed in the mid-19th century to attract holiday visitors; it is the oldest operating tavern in Ontario. Established in 1846 by John Dynes, it burnt down in 1882, but was rebuilt and has hosted many gatherings since then. The restaurant's large patio and outdoor bar operate between May and October; live entertainment, pool tables, euchre, and cribbage games provide year-round entertainment. Telephone 905-549-2588.

Kinsmen Park

One block past Dynes is Kinsmen Park, comprising 0.8 hectares (2 acres), with direct access to the beach; it features a wading pool, swings, a basketball court, and nets. There is a children's supervisor on duty; washrooms are open in July and August. The park is on the site of the former Hamilton Spectator Fresh Air Camp, which operated during the 1930s and 1940s, providing a place where needy Hamilton children could spend a couple of weeks enjoying the beach and sunshine.

Beach Bungalow School

Just past Kinsmen Park, also on your right, is the Bell Cairn Staff Development Centre, the site of the former Beach School. An original one-room schoolhouse, built to serve neighbourhood children in 1916, it was expanded over the years. In 1952, after the school suffered extensive fire damage, it was rebuilt and renamed Bell Cairn School in recognition of the bell presented to the Beach School in its inaugural year by Colonel Grafton, one of the first members of the Beach Commission.

By 1981 only 88 children were attending classes at Bell Cairn, and it was closed. The building is currently occupied by the Ministry of the Solicitor General and Correctional Services' Bell Cairn Staff Development Centre.

As you continue along Beach Boulevard, you will see several of the historically significant houses wealthy Hamiltonians built a century ago.

The Moorings

Located at 913 Beach Boulevard, this shingle-style Queen Anne house was built for Francis Kilvert in 1891. Kilvert, a noted lawyer, was the mayor of Hamilton from 1877 to 1878 and later served as a Member of Parliament. His two-storey beach house, which he called "The Moorings", has been designated under the Hamilton Local Architectural Conservancy Advisory Committee (LACAC) as a heritage property. The current owners also had the house designated under the Ontario Heritage Act so they could obtain a grant to replace asphalt shingles with wood-shingled roofing, the type used in the original house.

Sweetheart House

Built in 1898 by the Dexter family, this charming house is named for the broad, heart-shaped trim on the verandah encircling it. Located at 935 Beach Boulevard.

Cahill's Castle

This majestic summer home was built in 1891 for Charles Murton, a coal merchant, and remained in his family until 1945. Though the focal point of the 20-room Queen Anne house is its impressive corner tower, it also boasts a wide verandah, a bathhouse, and servants' quarters. This "cottage" is now owned by Bud Cahill, from whom it takes the name Cahill's Castle. Located at 957 Beach Boulevard.

Tuckett's Villa

The Gothic Revival "Tuckett's Villa" was built in 1890 for George Tuckett, a former mayor of Hamilton and president of the Tuckett Tobacco Company. Located at 1008 Beach Boulevard.

Galbraith

"Galbraith", the first of the original summer homes on the beach, was built for Newton Galbraith, a successful Hamilton businessman and avid art collector. The original house had ornamental arches on its upper balcony, which have since been removed. The large wooden verandahs, as well as balconies on some homes, were a representative feature of the lakeside architecture of the time. Located at 1117 Beach Boulevard.

Beach Marine

From April to October, canoes can be rented at Beach Marine, 1127 Beach Boulevard. Because of the often treacherous conditions on the water and the unpredictable nature of the weather, the staff at Beach Marine rarely allow boaters to launch into Lake Ontario. Instead, they recommend exploring calmer waters such as Cootes Paradise, Sunfish Pond, or Hamilton Harbour at Pier 4 Park, all of which are at the west end of the harbour; Beach Marine will supply equipment needed to transport the canoes, as well as life jackets for all passengers. Beach Boulevard ends at Eastport Drive, just past Beach Marine. Phone 905-545-4745.

The Hamilton section of the Waterfront Trail ends at the canal and lift bridge; when commercial shipping on the lakes was in its heyday, this was an excellent spot for watching the schooners, steamboats, paddle-wheelers, and barges that sailed into the inner harbour; there was no bridge, and scows ferried wagons, animals, and people.

In 1876, a large iron bridge was built to accommodate the Hamilton and Northwestern Railway. By 1897, a radial electric railway line had been constructed and there was a second bridge crossing the canal. The coming of the railway ended the pastoral quiet of the beach as iron giants deposited large crowds in the area. Buildings sprang up to accommodate visitors; electric radial cars became a link with outlying streets. By the early 1900s, dirt roads were gradually being paved over as motor cars began to replace horses.

If you intend to continue on the Waterfront Trail into Burlington, follow the signs. But if you're interested in another bit of Hamilton history, look to your left, to the old lighthouse.

LIGHTHOUSE AND LIGHT KEEPER'S HOME

Made of stone, this was built in 1858 to guide ships into the bay. It replaced an earlier wooden lighthouse which, with the ferry dock and light keeper's buildings, burned to the ground in 1856 when sparks from a government supply steamer started a fire. The new Burlington Bay Imperial Light Station was built of limestone brought by John Brown from his quarry in Thorold; the lamps there were the first in Canada to use coal oil rather than whale oil as a fuel source.

George Thompson was the first person to operate the new lighthouse; he had served as light keeper for Burlington Bay since 1846, and continued in that capacity until 1875. In 1961, the Burlington Bay light station was retired from service and subsequently recognized as a federal heritage building; however, its main light was placed atop the lift bridge to help guide ships through the canal. Ever since Thompson's days, there have been rumours of ghosts haunting the lighthouse.

BURLINGTON CANAL LIFT BRIDGE

The first small swing bridge was installed in 1830; damaged by ships, it was soon unuseable. The problem was resolved in 1876, when the railway line was constructed. Two years later, the first trains crossed the canal on an iron swing bridge. A second bridge was constructed in 1897 to accommodate the electric radial; it, too, was replaced in 1931 by the Bascule Bridge. After extensive damage to the Bascule Bridge from the U.S. sandboat *W.E. Fitzgerald* in 1952, the present vertical lift bridge was built.

TRAIL NETWORKS

The government agencies and non-government groups in Greater Hamilton Area have been safeguarding the Niagara Escarpment, Cootes Paradise, and the Dundas Valley by buying land in the area and maintaining it in its natural state, with a network of connecting trails. In turn, they link up with the Bruce Trail, which extends from Queenston on the Niagara Peninsula to Tobermory on the Bruce Peninsula.

Information on trails and the best places in the Hamilton area for viewing wildlife can be found in the Hamilton Naturalists' Club's *Naturally Hamilton: A Guide to the Green Spaces of Hamilton-Wentworth*. It can be ordered by phoning 905-547-5116.

Bruce Trail

The Bruce Trail is for hiking only; cycling and other uses are not permitted. For information call the Bruce Trail Association at 1-800-665-HIKE (4453).

The Hamilton leg of the Waterfront Trail in Confederation Park has the most direct access to the Bruce Trail; the 3-kilometre (1.8-mile) route that reaches the Bruce Trail's Iroquoia section follows city streets. From the park, take Centennial Parkway south towards the city to King Street. Turn left at 77 King Street West, and right into Stoney Creek Battlefield Park. A 300-metre (984-foot) side trail in Battlefield Park leads to the main Bruce Trail. Drinking water is available in the park, and washrooms are open from Victoria Day to Labour Day.

Rail Trails

Because of its location at the western end of Lake Ontario, the Hamilton area historically served as a place where all types of transportation routes, north-south and east-west, converged.

At the turn of the century, entrepreneurs developed one of the most successful inter-urban electric radial networks in the country; today, some of these lines are being converted to rail trails, thereby expanding the hiking/cycling possibilities radiating from Hamilton. For example, the Dundas Valley Rail Trail extends from West Hamilton to Jerseyville; for details, contact the Hamilton Region Conservation Authority, 905-525-2181.

The Escarpment Rail Trail goes from the bottom of Wentworth Street to Stonechurch Road in Hamilton; for more information, contact the Hamilton Culture and Recreation Department, 905-546-2750.

HARBOURFRONT AND PIER 4 PARKS

These two City of Hamilton parks are on the shores of Hamilton Harbour in the city's northwest end. Pier 4 Park has a children's play area featuring an old tugboat and look-out piers that provide a view of surrounding marinas, parkland, and vistas of the bay. Harbourfront Park has 1,800 metres (5,906 feet) of shoreline integrating fish habitat, native vegetation, and park facilities that

BICYCLE ROUTE MAP FOR HARBOURFRONT AND PIER 4 PARKS

include a sandy beach, circle trail, and public boat launch. The parks are also used for a variety of summer festivals and concerts. The Hamilton-Wentworth Regional Cycling Committee has published a bicycle route map for this area (see above) and other maps can be obtained by calling 905-546-BIKE (2453).

DUNDURN CASTLE

Not too far from Harbourfront Park, overlooking the city and the bay, is Dundurn Castle, located in Dundurn Park at 610 York Boulevard. Built between 1832 and 1835, this 35-room mansion has been restored to its original splendour. It was the home of Allan Napier MacNab, the prime minister of pre-confederation Upper Canada. Admission to the grounds of Dundurn Castle is free but there is an admission fee for castle tours and special events held throughout the summer and late fall. For more information call 905-546-2872.

OTHER ATTRACTIONS IN THE HAMILTON AREA

The Tourism Information Centre at 127 King Street East (recognized by its blue awnings) in downtown Hamilton offers information on a wide variety of attractions in the Regional Municipality of Hamilton-Wentworth; phone 905-546-2666.

Hamilton Museum of Steam and Technology

The Hamilton Steam Museum, at 900 Woodward Avenue in the historic Hamilton Waterworks Pumping Station, was built in 1859. The museum is open to the public Monday to Saturday from 12 p.m. to 4 p.m; phone 905-546-4797.

As Hamilton expanded, suburbs grew up around it. One of the most vital is Burlington, the next stop on the Waterfront Trail.

THOMAS BAKER MCQUESTEN

The inscription that honours architect Christopher Wren ("If you would see the man's monument, look around") might aptly describe the contributions Thomas Baker McQuesten made over his lifetime – from 1882 to 1948 – to Ontario.

The first McQuesten in Hamilton was Thomas's grandfather, Calvin, a doctor who arrived in 1839, and developed an association with the Massey family. The McQuestens lived in Whitehearn, now a historical site that is often used as a movie set.

Thomas seemed dedicated to the creation of public works of striking beauty.

He was a cabinet minister in the 1940s, at a time when politics was considered a noble profession, and individual ministers had much more power in making and implementing policies. He was involved in creating such landmarks as the Royal Botanical Gardens, the Queen Elizabeth Way, and Trans-Canada Highway, as well as bridges such as Sarnia's Bluewater, the Rainbow at Fort Erie, Ivy Lea at Gananoque, and the Burlington Skyway.

As chairman of the Niagara Parks Commission, he strongly influenced the architecture and parks along the Canadian side of the Niagara River. Always active in developments in his home city, his work there culminated in the creation of the Royal Botanical Gardens. Frances Loring's lion in Toronto (see page 99) and the Greek ship in St. Catherines are also the result of his efforts to beautify Canada's first highway.

Although highways have long since become more functional than beautiful, Tom McQuesten's efforts remind us that function and beauty are part of a tradition that is worth following.

The *Brant Museum, Cootes Paradise, old churches, and aboriginal burial grounds – a treasure of both the natural and built environments*

2 KM.

Burlington

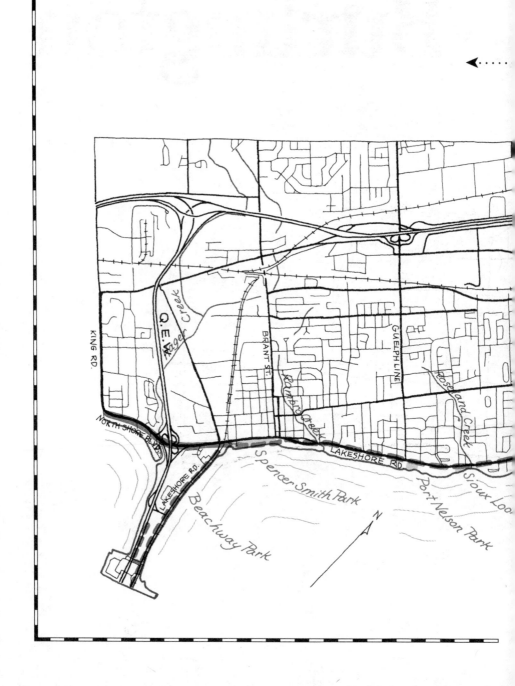

Burlington

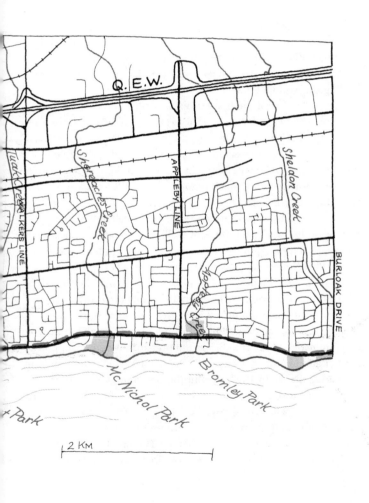

Q.E.W.

Walkers Line

Shoreacres Creek

APPLEBY LINE

Sheldon Creek

Appleby Creek

BURLOAK DRIVE

McNichol Park

Bromley Park

Park

2 KM

LTHOUGH MUCH OF this area's forest was felled more than a century ago, the fortunate wildlife enthusiast can still glimpse deer browsing in nearby woodlands; even coyotes have been sighted in the sanctuary of the Royal Botanical Gardens. Home to such historical sites as the Brant Museum, Cootes Paradise, old churches, and aboriginal burial grounds, the Burlington-area Waterfront Trail is a treasure of both the natural and built environments.

Before the War of 1812, many settlers were United Empire Loyalists, lured here by land grants. Europeans joined the Loyalists (although not on free land) and helped clear the forest. But they might have trouble recognizing today's bustling City of Burlington, with its 130,000 residents.

One of the first European settlers was George Chisolm, who began farming at Indian Point on Lake Geneva (now Burlington Bay) in 1791. By 1802, Joseph Brant had built his house at what is now the intersection of Lakeshore Road and Maple Avenue, although it is thought that Brant lived there even before he received his land grant; much of today's City of Burlington is on land granted to Brant.

Downtown Burlington was once called Wellington Square (in honour of the Duke of Wellington) and became an important shipping port for locally grown fruit, vegetables, and wheat. Port Nelson, located on the lakeshore at Guelph Line, and now a part of Burlington, was also a busy port. When the villages of Wellington Square and Port Nelson amalgamated in 1873, the new town, with a population of 750, was given the name Burlington.

In the early 1900s, Burlington was a small but thriving community: in addition to farms and orchards, the town supported lumber and planing mills, as well as basket factories and other manufacturing plants. In 1903, the Burlington Canning Company opened a factory on the lakeshore (current site of the Venture Inn).

Not surprisingly, there have been a number of interesting historical finds in the area, perhaps the most important of which was unearthed in 1892 by Samuel Thomas, Jr. on the old Wellington Square town site. The trove included a medal weighing about two ounces (57 grams); a large skeleton with two ivory rings through the nose; and a scalping knife, tomahawk, pipe, and hunting knife. Historians have speculated that the medal, which bears the date 1764, a relief of King George III, and the words "Happy While United", was bestowed at a First Nations council held at the mouth of the Niagara River. The award may have been presented to chiefs of the Six Nations Tribes to honour their bravery and loyalty to Britain during the Pontiac War.

PUBLIC TRANSIT .

Local Transit
(905-639-0550)

VIA Train
(905-522-7533)

GO (905-527-8187)
• **Aldershot –**
Waterdown Rd. at Hwy.
#403 (2 km from
LaSalle Park)

• **Burlington W. –**
Fairview St. at Brant St.
(2 km from Spencer
Smith Park)

•**Appleby - Fairview St.**
at Appleby Line (2 km
from Lakeshore Rd.)

GETTING TO BURLINGTON

There are two places to enter the Burlington section of the Waterfront Trail. The main Trail begins at the Burlington Canal Lift Bridge just across from the City of Hamilton, where it leads to Beach Boulevard. Alternatively, you may begin at the Royal Botanical Gardens; the two routes meet at the intersection of Highway 2 and Lakeshore Road.

BURLINGTON CANAL/BEACHWAY PARK

Following the Trail from Hamilton along Beach Boulevard (see page 7 for more details) you will reach the Burlington Canal; once across the canal, signs direct you to the lake where the Burlington portion of the Waterfront Trail begins. The land surrounding the canal is federally owned and is used for maintaining the canal and lift bridge. In time, the grounds, now off limits to the public, will be redeveloped and incorporated into the park.

Today, large sailing vessels navigate the Burlington Canal to enter and exit Hamilton Harbour; however, until 1832, the canal was a narrow, silt-filled passage that was difficult for ships to navigate. In that year, a wider canal was completed, and later a small swing bridge was built.

Around the turn of the century, Beachway Park was a very popular spot for waterfront cottages; some 240 lined the eastern shoreline, 80 of them directly on the beach. Since 1987, the Halton Region Conservation Authority (HRCA), the City and the Region have been acquiring some of the leasehold properties and demolishing the cottages. Today, all but a few are gone, making way for redevelopment for recreational use.

At the southern end of Beachway Park, you will find one of the few sand dunes along the north shore of Lake Ontario. Efforts to preserve this significant natural beach area and stabilize the sand dunes are underway. This is a popular location for beach volleyball, swimming, windsurfing, and remote-control model aeroplane enthusiasts.

The newly constructed deck and walkway, running from the canal to Spencer Smith Park (see page 32), is on the site of abandoned railway tracks. In the days when it was a summer cottage community, owners travelled by train to Burlington from Toronto, Niagara Falls, and upstate New York to spend summers along Lake Ontario's sparkling waters.

This section of the Trail has a limestone screening surface that is not suited for in-line skating, but cyclists and walkers can use it easily. Follow this path, which runs parallel to Beachway Park, and you will come to the Joseph Brant Museum.

JOSEPH BRANT MUSEUM

The Joseph Brant Museum, 1240 North Shore Boulevard East on the southwest corner of the intersection of North Shore Boulevard East and Highway 2, provides an excellent opportunity to explore Ontario's heritage. Joseph Brant, whose aboriginal name was Thayendanegea, was leader of the Six Nations Indians and is regarded as the founding father of Burlington.

Less well known, but a leader in her time, was Molly Brant – native name Konwatsi'tsiaiénni: "Someone Lends Her a Flower" – Joseph's older sister. One Six Nations leader described her "influence [over her people] which is far superior to that of all their chiefs put together". Although there are at least two full-length paintings of Joseph, one by the great English portraitist George Romney, there is not a single image of Molly. All we know of her comes from snippets of diaries, legal documents, and contemporary reports.

The museum is a replica of the two-storey house Brant lived in from about 1802 until his death in 1807. It contains a variety of household artifacts, costumes, and exhibits of the Iroquois and of Burlington's early years.

The museum holds one of the finest Canadian clothing collections outside the Royal Ontario Museum. The clothing and textiles, dating from the 1800s to the early 1900s, are displayed in the museum's Costume Gallery. There is a gift shop and a reference library with photographs and other documents available to researchers. One portrait shows the daughter of Joseph Brant, Elizabeth Brant, who married the Burlington Canal Commissioner, William Johnson Kerr.

The museum is open Tuesday to Sunday. For hours and other information phone 905-634-3556. The ground floor of the museum is wheelchair-accessible, but there is no elevator to the upper floor and the washroom.

Royal Botanical Gardens

There is another starting point for the Trail, in the Royal Botanical Gardens at the Cherry Hill Gate, located at the northwestern end of the Rose Garden parking lot on Spring Gardens Road.

These world-renowned gardens were created to develop, preserve, and – in particular – to conserve plants and natural habitats for the people's enjoyment. The Waterfront Trail covers only a fragment of nearly 1,100 hectares (2,700 acres) that make up one of North America's largest botanical gardens. Visitors can enjoy a wide variety of habitats: cool woodlands, wildflower meadows, a shallow lake, an escarpment face, and marshland with its fascinating microscopic life. Walking enthusiasts will find more than 50 kilometres (31 miles) of hiking trails.

Although cycling is not allowed on Royal Botanical Gardens property, bike racks are provided at the RBG Centre. Wheelchair access is good throughout the cultivated garden areas, but the Waterfront Trail portion includes rugged and hilly terrain: visitors may find it difficult to manoeuvre in a wheelchair. There are no washroom facilities on the Trail itself.

The dream of a botanical garden began to take form in the 1920s, when the old Kerr's Gravel Pits were acquired; the foundations of the Rock Garden were laid in November 1929. A year later, King George V gave permission for the gardens to use the designation "Royal".

Each season has its own unique attractions: in spring, 125,000 daffodils, tulips, hyacinths, and other flowering bulbs create masses of colour. May is a good month to visit when the exceptional lilac collection provides a fragrant and beautiful display. From June to October the Centennial Rose Garden delights the eye and perfumes the air. The Rock Garden, Scented Garden, Queen Beatrix Collection, and the edible borders and herb garden are just a few of the special areas where you can enjoy hours of relaxation and find gardening and landscaping ideas.

RBG Centre

The Royal Botanical Gardens Centre at 680 Plains Road West is a good place to begin your journey. Take some of the excellent free literature; the maps offer an orientation to the gardens and the various trails. The Hendrie Valley Trail Guide is particularly useful in showing the lay of the land through which the Waterfront Trail passes.

The centre, a contemporary structure of concrete, glass, and steel, harmonizes with the topography and provides a warm and inviting ambience. During the year, it offers a variety of events and space for private and public functions. You will also find a new restaurant, the Gardens' Cafe, which provides good food in a pleasant setting.

Just a few steps from the cafe is the Floral Art Shop, where you can browse through an interesting collection of small plants, dried floral arrangements, artwork, glassware, and books on gardening and birdwatching. The centre also includes a greenhouse and conference room where exhibitions and floral competitions are held.

In the winter, snow lends a pristine beauty to the trees and shrubs, and a visit to the indoor Mediterranean Garden (open year-round) is an antidote to the winter chills. The garden is laid out on two landscaped patios within the centre. Although there is an elevator to the upper level of the Mediterranean Garden, a number of stone steps limit wheelchair access.

However, washrooms and telephones are barrier-free and accessible to people in wheelchairs. Other accessible washrooms and water fountains are available at the Arboretum, Laking Garden, the Rock Garden, Hendrie Park, and the Teaching Garden.

Admission is charged for the gardens, but those walking only the Waterfront Trail can avoid paying the entrance fee by gaining access to the Trail from Cherry Hill Gate in the Rose Garden parking lot on Plains Road, west of the centre.

Waterfront Trail through the RBG

The Waterfront Trail follows a footpath that hairpins through the woods to Hendrie Valley and Grindstone Creek where, in season, salmon swim upstream to spawn. Hendrie Valley has been a crossroads for centuries; aboriginal footpaths criss-crossed the valley and people frequently travelled what is now Plains Road. Some historians speculate that the valley may also have served as a link between the bay and Iroquois villages above the escarpment.

Eventually, there will be a bridge across the creek, and a regeneration program to provide healthier environments for animals, birds, and plants. The area contains a mix of northern and Carolinian trees in which you may catch a glimpse of a goldfinch, pine warbler, or blue-grey gnatcatcher. North of the pike-spawning dam, which is part of the fish regeneration program, a boardwalk cuts across the floor of the valley, providing a wonderful observation deck for viewing marsh wildlife.

Red-winged blackbirds nest in the cattails and wood ducks, geese, and other waterbirds forage the wetland for food. This is a serene place, where salamanders or midland painted turtles sun themselves on rocks. Fox, coyote, muskrats, voles, rabbits, and deer make their home in and around the valley.

Crossing Grindstone Creek, the Trail makes its way west, passing Laking Garden as it parallels the creek and ultimately connecting with Grindstone Marsh. Laking Garden, named for Dr. Leslie Laking, the gardens' director from 1954 to 1981, stands on a peninsula overlooking the lower reaches of Grindstone Creek and includes the Heritage and Rock gardens and the herbaceous perennial collection. There are lovely borders of aster, coneflowers, lungwort, roses, and, from June to October, the slender spires of monkshood.

The area is also home to 200 kinds of wild iris; Japanese irises grace the Rock Garden pools in June and an extensive collection of bearded irises can be found on the lower terrace. Refreshments are available in the Rock Garden Tea House, which is open from May to August; it is wheelchair-accessible and offers a wonderful view of the gardens.

The Botanical Gardens section of the Waterfront Trail ends at Sunfish Pond, a traditional fishing spot where anglers spend leisurely hours fishing for pike or salmon. It is popular year-round. From this point, the Trail continues up-valley along Spring Gardens Road to Plains Road. For information on the Royal Botanical Gardens, its hours of operation, education programs, fees, and details of special events, call 905-527-1158.

COOTES PARADISE

Cootes Paradise is well worth a short loop west. Its verdant marsh was once home to a wide variety of plants, animals, fish, and birds. The marsh is named for Captain Thomas Coote, who found a hunter's paradise there, and visited whenever he was on leave from guarding the Canadian border at Niagara.

The marsh began to decline as settlers moved into the Dundas Valley and cleared the forest. In 1837, erosion became more rapid as Spencer Creek was dredged to form Desjardin Canal as a way of accommodating sailing vessels. The inadvertent introduction of carp in 1896 compounded the problem. Plants died, salmon and other fish were driven away or died out, and wildlife found other feeding grounds.

Today, Cootes Paradise, which is administered by the Royal Botanical Gardens, is on the long road back to recovery, with help from a variety of sources, including a hard-working contingent of volunteers. Adult carp are being kept out of the area and new marsh plants are being introduced; water quality is improving; and new trails are being created for the enjoyment of visitors. Cootes Paradise may never return to its original, pristine state, but it is far from dead.

The South and North Shore Trail guides, available at the nearby Royal Botanical Gardens Centre, are particularly useful for people arriving here for the first time. On the north shore, Captain Cootes Trail begins at the Nature Interpretive Centre on Arboretum Road, and winds down to the marsh boathouse and along the north shore. The walking trail, which is 2.9 kilometres (1.8 miles) from start to finish, is moderately difficult.

Both trails give evidence of the regeneration work that is under way: there are observation towers, boardwalks that enable people to view wildlife in its natural habitat, and walking trails. Improved waterways will be home to pike, bass, perch, ducks, mink, muskrat, and turtles. This is a birdwatcher's paradise, with more than 248 species either in residence or passing through during migration. The visitor may spot sandpipers, herons, terns, and osprey in their natural habitat.

Leaving the fascinating terrain of the Royal Botanical Gardens and Cootes Paradise, the Waterfront Trail continues along Plains Road West (Highway 2). Not far past the Holy Sepulchre Cemetery, it turns south onto Gorton Avenue. This quiet residential street leads to North Shore Boulevard West, which marks the beginning of a lengthy stretch of Burlington's waterfront.

Bicycles are best suited to this excursion; there are no sidewalks along the moderately hilly and winding route, so caution is urged. Cyclists will find considerable traffic along this scenic route and should proceed carefully. Follow the signs along North Shore Boulevard to LaSalle Park.

LaSalle Park

This historic park is located on Burlington Bay at LaSalle Park Road and North Shore Boulevard. The land was purchased in 1915 by the Hamilton Parks Board and called Wabasso Park; the name was changed in 1923 to honour the French explorer René Robert Cavelier de La Salle, who set out from Montreal in 1669 to find a passage to the southern sea but landed on the shores of Lake Ontario, at what is now Burlington Bay.

Today, the 23-hectare (57-acre) park is still owned by the City of Hamilton but leased to the City of Burlington, which assumes all maintenance and management responsibilities. Towards the lake, a short flight of stairs down a wooded hillside leads to a short path along the shore. LaSalle has a lovely wide view of the lake and marina from the elevated lookout at the south end of the park. The marina provides seasonal boating slips and is a popular sailing dock. On a spring day, the park is a pleasant place to sit and listen to the waves on the shore, or watch Canada Geese and white swans skimming across the water.

Just-off shore an island is being created as part of the Remedial Action Plan's project to recreate fish and wildlife habitat in the area. A footbridge will connect the Waterfront Trail to this island.

LaSalle is an active park with long picnic benches for community gatherings, while its rolling landscape forms a wonderful playground for children. Most of the park is wheelchair-accessible: the washrooms and water fountains are barrier-free and there is a ramp into the LaSalle Pavilion's lower concourse.

When cyclists exit the park, they can enjoy a short section of off-road trail that cuts through the north end of LaSalle Park along an asphalt path east and connects with North Shore Boulevard.

The Trail weaves its way along tree-lined North Shore Boulevard where old estate homes shelter behind fieldstone walls and picket fences. The sparkling lake shimmers in the distance and can be seen easily, especially at Bayshore Park, a small greenspace about 1.6 kilometres (1 mile) east of LaSalle. On a quiet day this greenspace offers a place to rest and a chance to catch your breath.

Continue along North Shore Boulevard, following the QEW underpass to the intersection with Lakeshore Road. There you will find the Joseph Brant Memorial Hospital, built in 1961. This was once the site of the Hotel Brant, which was built by A.B. Coleman, a prosperous mill and construction company owner who was responsible for building many of Burlington's finest homes, as well as three Ontario landmarks: parts of the Canadian National Exhibition, the Fort Erie Race Track, and the University of Toronto's Convocation Hall.

TO FEED OR NOT TO FEED

In recent decades, feeding the waterfowl that frequent Lake Ontario's shores has become a popular pastime. Perhaps because of its stately bearing and handsome colouring, the giant Canada goose, in particular, has been the object of our affections. Many of us can remember tossing chunks of bread to an ever-eager beak, or mustering up enough courage to let a bird snap its reward from our nervous fingertips.

Today, many people continue to share their food and even derive a sense of satisfaction from supposedly helping these magnificent creatures plump up before winter comes. Not so. In fact, there are several reasons why such feeding is creating a nuisance and could cause long-term trouble for these birds.

First, bread has very little nutrient value and is low in fibre; this often results in digestive problems for these birds. Second, they foul the areas where they congregate and as recreational areas become heavily soiled, the cost of maintaining parks and facilities rises. Furthermore, fecal matter in such quantities upsets the natural balance of delicate wetlands and water systems by over-fertilizing plant life, causing fish to dwindle as populations are choked out of their habitats.

As well, the regular migratory pattern of many of these birds has been altered by: the abundance of food provided by humans, the presence of manicured lawns, and the moderate microclimate of urban areas. The result is that large numbers of geese remain in the southern Ontario area instead of flying south for the winter.

Remarkably, the idea of feeding Canada geese dates only to the 1960s; before then, most people in southern Ontario were content to merely watch in admiration as migrating flocks, always in their distinctive V formations, flew to or from their summering areas. In December 1960 only a single Canada goose was sighted in the area between Hamilton and Oshawa; the summer population in Ontario is now estimated to be as high as 100,000 and what was once a pleasant visitor has, for many people, become a pest.

Astonishingly, this species, thought to be close to extinction in the early 1900s when it was being over-hunted, is now estimated to be increasing by about 30 percent a year.

You can help by remembering that the idea of feeding the geese is strictly for the birds!

For 15 years, the Hotel Brant flourished, until it was appropriated by the federal government in 1917 for use as a military hospital for casualties of WW I. The hotel building burned down in 1923.

The Hotel Brant's rival, the Brant Inn, was east of the Beach Strip along Lakeshore Road. Because the hotel was "dry", guests with a thirst went to the Brant Inn. In its day, the inn attracted such stars as Ella Fitzgerald, Benny Goodman, and Lena Horne. In the years after WW II, a date at the inn was considered a sign of serious intentions – the kind that sent young women (then known as "girls") to their knitting needles to make a pair of argyle socks (another sign of a meaningful relationship). In time, however, the inn went into decline. It was torn down in 1969. Just to the east is Spencer Smith Park.

SPENCER SMITH PARK

Spencer Smith Park, named for a former president of the Burlington Horticultural Society, is on land once part of the block granted by the British to Joseph Brant. In 1810, a portion of that block was purchased by James Gage, whose land stretched from Lakeshore north between Brant Street and Rambo Creek. Gage, an early Canadian entrepreneur, built a wharf, a warehouse, a factory, and mills at the foot of Brant Street to provide goods for the new settlement.

However, there was no protection from storms and in bad weather Lakeshore Road was frequently under water; at one point, two streets and several buildings were swallowed by the lake. In 1939, the federal government built a protective seawall; at about that time, the Burlington Horticulture Society began cleaning up the shoreline just west of the foot of Brant Street. From 1965 to 1969, the city worked on the parkland as a Centennial project.

The Waterfront Trail follows the shoreline, providing opportunities to observe shorebirds or to photograph passing freighters. The concrete pedestrian Trail is about 6 metres (20 feet) wide, making it well suited for all users. Information can be obtained at the Burlington Visitors and Convention Bureau; call 905-634-5594 or visit the bureau, which is close to the entrance to the parking lot, open in summer and early fall. Visitors will find washrooms, picnic areas, children's play area, a first aid station, water fountains, and telephones. Refreshments are available at the concession stands. The park is barrier free and suitable for people in wheelchairs.

Near the inland edge, observing the passing traffic, is a statue of a sailor, a tribute to those who fought and died in WW I. In a willow grove at the east end of the park is a gazebo where public events and festivals are held.

Travelling east from Spencer Smith Park along Lakeshore Road, pedestrians will enjoy the sidewalk, while cyclists travel the adjacent cycling lane.

DOWNTOWN BURLINGTON

Burlington has many cultural and recreational facilities and hosts a number of festivals and special events throughout the year; these include a children's festival at Spencer Smith Park, a multicultural festival in June, and the Beachway Park Summer Opening, also in June. Across from the park, visitors will find the Burlington Art Centre with its collection of the work of Canadian and European artists. Music lovers will be interested in the Sound of Music Festival, which has been held every June for more than a decade. There are a variety excellent restaurants and cafés within a short distance of the waterfront. The historic Estaminet restaurant, is now home to two restaurants, Water Street Cooker and Emma's Backporch, which offers the only waterfront patio east of the Venture Inn. For more information, call Burlington City Hall's Department of Parks and Recreation at 905-335-7704.

PORT NELSON

The Trail continues for about 3 kilometres (1.8 miles) to the next window on the lake; Port Nelson is located at the foot of Guelph Line and has a wide view of the lake and Skyway Bridge. There is a short gravel path that leads from the parking lot toward the waterfront; it does, however, end before reaching the shore and the uneven grass on which you must continue may pose a problem for people in wheelchairs. No washrooms or other facilities are available.

SIOUX LOOKOUT PARK

Sioux Lookout Park is approximately 1 kilometre (1.6 miles) east of Port Nelson; the route goes east on an asphalt path that can be used by cyclists and pedestrians. Atop a bluff overlooking Lake Ontario, Sioux Lookout is a popular destination for those who want to get away from the office for lunch. Parking is limited but there is easy access to the water along a gentle path down to the shingle beach, where a creek spills into the lake.

While there is another window to the lake at the end of Walker's Line, you will want to delay seeing it so that you can walk through the grounds of the old McNichol Estate; they are hidden behind tall trees adjacent to Shoreacres Creek valley.

McNICHOL PARK

From this magnificent mansion you can conjure up scenes of a time when the elite mingled in magnificent mansions set amidst lush park-like settings. Back then, the melodies of Strauss or the Black Bottom filled the night air and crystal chandeliers illuminated the dance floors of private ballrooms. Guests would arrive at private docks by yacht to sip champagne and nibble hors d'oeuvres as they sat by the pool.

Those days are long gone, but a leisurely walk around the grounds of McNichol Park brings them momentarily to life. The three-storey house was built in 1931, its design incorporating elements of a French country estate. It is an excellent example of the lavish homes built in the '30s, even as the majority of Canadians tried to cope with a catastrophic Depression.

The property itself has a long and varied history and was once part of a tract of land granted to Laura Secord by King George III in 1809, in recognition of her service during the Revolutionary War. After passing through numerous hands, the land was sold to W.D. Flatt and Cyrus A. Birge in the early 1900s. Flatt, a developer, created some of the most luxurious residential communities along Burlington's lakeshore. Birge was a founding

Information about Burlington's heritage houses can be found in A *Driving Tour of Rural Burlington*, published by the Local Architectural Conservation Advisory Committee (LACAC). This and other useful publications are available from the Burlington Visitors and Convention Bureau at 1340 Lakeshore Road in Spencer Smith Park. For information call 905-634-5594.

SHINGLE BEACH

Between the cities of Hamilton and Etobicoke, both the main body of the lakebed and the shore are made up of sedimentary shale bedrock, material formed when muddy clay-rich sediments were deposited on an ancient sea floor during the Ordovician age, more than 400 million years ago; these were later compressed to form shale. Near Oakville, the bedrock changes from the red shales of the Queenston Formation in the west, to the grey shales and limestones of the Georgian Bay Formation in the east. These formations are the source for the shingle beaches found along this part of the shoreline; the shingles are created when the thinly bedded shales are eroded from the bedrock. These are smoothed by waves and deposited as stacked plates of rock, forming the shingle beach.

The shales and limestones of the Georgian Bay Formation are rich in fossils, and you may see some as you walk along the waterfront.

In other areas along the Waterfront Trail, small beach deposits can be made up of other materials; for example, the gradual erosion of the sand and gravel shore in the Cobourg area provides a source for sand and gravel beaches. ·

board member of the Canadian Screw Company (now Stelco). After Birge's death in 1929, his daughter Edythe MacKay used her inheritance to build Shoreacres. It was later called the McNichol Estate after Edythe's daughter, Dorothy McNichol, who inherited the property in 1960.

The City of Burlington acquired the estate in 1990 and has committed 4 hectares (10 acres) to public park use. While restoring the magnificent old house would preserve much of its original stately grandeur, it is not open to the public now and its future is under discussion. However, the formal gardens have been restored; on the west side of the house, nestled among a stand of trees and tall ferns, is the "doll house", once used as a play area. You can see the nearby remnants of a private tennis court and swimming pool.

The lot has 275 metres (900 feet) of lake frontage, with a retaining wall and 100 metres (330 feet) of cobble and sand beach. The eastern part of the estate is a wetland surrounding Shoreacres Creek, which is a migratory stopover for a variety of birds. All this is being left in its natural state in order to allow regeneration of habitats and provide a home for deer, fox, and many species of birds; eventually, a boardwalk will be built for pedestrian use.

The lakeshore here, as elsewhere, is subject to erosion; steps are being taken to minimize or prevent further damage, not only to protect the shoreline, but also to preserve fish and wildlife habitats.

As you leave McNichol Park, turn right and head east along Lakeshore Road as it passes over Shoreacres Creek. The off-road path continues for those walking, on bicycles or in-line skates.

East of Shoreacres you pass through a residential neighbourhood along Lakeshore Road, which is part of the Heritage Highway. Here, century homes and estates still stand amidst new developments. Beyond stone walls and wrought-iron gates, it is possible to catch glimpses of private gardens with their ancient oak trees and winding pathways.

BURLOAK WATERFRONT PARK

Some 5 kilometres (3 miles) from McNichol Park, you will find Burloak Waterfront Park. Work is now going on according to a master plan developed in 1986 for the 4-hectare (10-acre) site, unique in that it has an exposed natural Queenston shale bluff and shoreline. The park ends at a steep bluff overlooking the lake and the land nearby slopes gently to a short shingle beach at the water's edge. In summer, many people use this area to go windsurfing. There is a playground, and parking. At this point of the Trail no washrooms are available and wheelchair access is limited. A local mall is directly north of the park.

Burloak Park marks the end of the Burlington section of the Waterfront Trail. As you cross Burloak Drive you enter the Town of Oakville.

Oakville *is known for its two historic harbours, lovely parks, ravines, woodlots, and trails* ◄·····

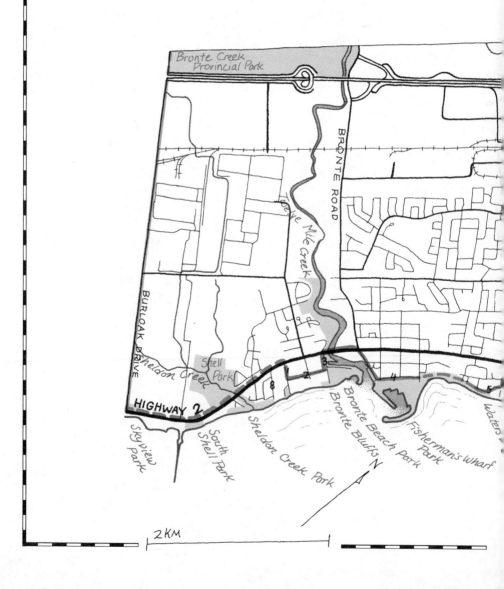

Bronte Creek Provincial Park

BRONTE ROAD

Twelve Mile Creek

BURLOAK DRIVE

Sheldon Creek

Shell Park

HIGHWAY 2

Skyview Park

South Shell Park

Sheldon Creek Park

Bronte Bluffs Park

Bronte Beach Park

Fisherman's Wharf Park

Waters

N

2KM

Oakville

1 WEST STREET 5 WATER'S EDGE
2 SENECA DRIVE 6 OLD LAKESHORE RD.
3 WEST RIVER 7 BELVEDERE
4 ONTARIO STREET 8 CUDMORE ROAD

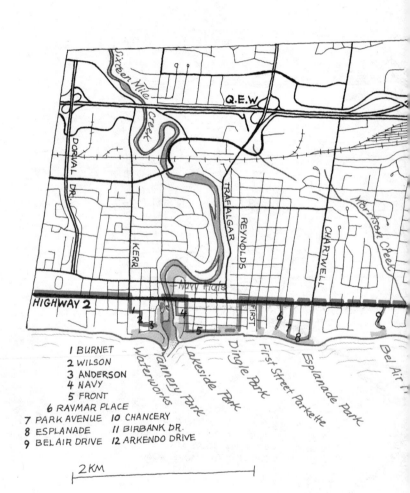

Q.E.W.

Sixteen Mile Creek

DORVAL DR.

KERR

TRAFALGAR

REYNOLDS

CHARTWELL

Morrison Creek

Navy Flats

HIGHWAY 2

FIRST

1 BURNET
2 WILSON
3 ANDERSON
4 NAVY
5 FRONT
6 RAVMAR PLACE
7 PARK AVENUE   10 CHANCERY
8 ESPLANADE   11 BIRBANK DR.
9 BELAIR DRIVE   12 ARKENDO DRIVE

Waterworks
Tannery Park
Lakeside Park
Dingle Park
First Street Parkette
Esplanade Park
Bel Air P.

2 KM

Oakville

AKVILLE IS KNOWN FOR its two historic harbours, lovely parks, ravines, woodlots, and trails and, with as many as 3,000 trees planted annually, has one of Ontario's most comprehensive urban forestry programs. Beautiful flowerbeds, stately old trees, and manicured lawns are common here.

The land on which Oakville sits is rich in history. Aside from its waterfront location, three centuries ago it was laden with dense forests of white pine and oak. Several swift creeks flowed into the lake. Mississaugas, members of the Ojibwa Nation, farmed, hunted, and fished around two of these large creeks: Nassagaweya (Sixteen Mile Creek) and Esquisink (Twelve Mile Creek). The newer names do not describe the length of the creeks, only their distance from Burlington.

In the early 1820s, William Chisholm, an enterprising young merchant and shipbuilder who travelled from Wellington Square (Burlington) to York (Toronto), envisioned a productive port and village at the mouth of Sixteen Mile Creek. Chisholm's dream became a reality in 1827 when he purchased 388 hectares (960 acres) of land there and founded the village of Oakville.

Established later than Burlington and Mississauga, it was a place with a difference – not a pioneer community, but a commercial harbour and a source of timber; in fact, Oakville was the first privately owned harbour in Upper Canada.

In 1962, the boundaries of the Town of Oakville were enlarged to incorporate many smaller surrounding villages and towns, including Bronte, Palermo, and Sheridan.

Nature lovers visiting the Oakville area may want to begin by taking a trip to Bronte Creek Provincial Park. While not part of the Waterfront Trail, it is an interesting detour. Turn left from Lakeshore Road West as you enter Oakville and go north on Burloak Road for almost 3 kilometres (1.8 miles) to the park entrance.

PUBLIC TRANSIT

Local Transit
(905-815-2020)

VIA Train
(416-366-8411)

GO (416-869-3200)
• **Bronte – Wyecroft Rd. at 3rd Line and Spears Rd. (3 km from Water Edge Park)**

• **Oakville – Cross Ave. at Trafalgar Rd. (2 km from Dingle Park)**

Side Trip
BRONTE CREEK PROVINCIAL PARK

You will find this provincial park combines natural and built elements that, together, create an outstanding recreational facility.

Open year-round, Bronte Creek Provincial Park offers a wide variety of activities including summer hiking, swimming, fishing, and picnicking, as well as winter skating, tobogganing, and cross-country skiing. There is a delightful children's farm that includes a playloft and opportunities for kids to visit many friendly farm animals.

The park's natural beauty focuses on the deep winding ravine of Twelve Mile Creek (also known as Bronte Creek), which runs through the park. From the Half Moon Valley or the Ravine Trail, both of which are heavily wooded, you can see the creek. Although the park is in a deciduous forest region, it also has the plants found in Carolinian forests and in prairie areas; these species are of regional, provincial, and national significance.

Part of the visible history at Bronte Creek Provincial Park is Spruce Lane Farm, a pretty Victorian house built in 1899. Costumed interpreters demonstrate how tasks typical of turn-of-the-century homemakers were carried out. The farm's outbuildings, complete with animals, include a main cattle barn, horse barn, piggery, fowl houses, icehouses, and a woodshed; all of these have been restored on their original foundations. What were once the orchards surrounding Spruce Lane Farm are now large picnic areas with grazing pastures for the farm animals.

The park is home to many species of wildlife, including such common mammals as chipmunks, grey squirrels, woodchucks, and European hares. While visitors may not see them as often, there are other, warier residents: white-tailed deer, red fox, coyotes, and raccoons. Among the kinds of birds are woodpeckers, scarlet tanagers, hawks, blue jays, blackbirds, and sparrows. Twenty types of amphibians and reptiles dwell in the park, as do more than seventy species of moths and butterflies and 125 insects, including a rare type of katydid.

The facilities at Bronte Creek Provincial Park include a recreation complex with a 0.6-hectare (1.6-acre) swimming pool, designed for both children and adults. In the winter, it becomes a spectacular skating rink. The rooms used for changing in the summer become heated rest areas in the winter. Nearby are eight flood-lit tennis courts and a court area for basketball, volleyball, and shuffleboard.

Bronte Creek Provincial Park has a visitors' centre; if you want more information about the park and the many programs there, call the Bronte Creek Provincial Park office at 905-827-6911. ▩

You can return to the Waterfront Trail by going south on Burloak Road until you reach Lakeshore Road (Highway 2). This is the main lakefront access into Oakville.

The first park you come to on the south side of Lakeshore Road, 0.8 kilometres (0.5 miles) east from Burloak Road, is South Shell Park.

SOUTH SHELL PARK

There are picnic tables shaded by large pine trees and, at the east end of the park, a huge climber children will enjoy. A large rectangular fountain, framed by birch trees, is especially striking at night, when it is pleasantly lit. Just a short distance away, on the north side of Lakeshore Road, is Shell Park – also well worth a stop.

SHELL PARK

A small stream with weeping willows on its banks, Sheldon Creek winds through the park. Larger than South Shell Park, this amenity has a delightful rose garden, where well-placed benches and the sense bath offered by the flowers create an ideal spot for quiet meditation. The variety of rose and tree species is sure to delight gardening enthusiasts.

There is an attractive play area for children, complete with swings, a slide, and a few "forts". There are washrooms, a water fountain, phone booth, and lots of parking. This park also has four major soccer fields and a baseball field and can be a busy place in summer.

Directly across from Shell Park, on the south side of Lakeshore Road, is Shelbourne Place, a residential street that gives you access to the lakefront at Shelbourne Promenade. Keep to the right and you will find a sign that directs you to the small path leading to the lakefront.

This is a long thin stretch of land running along the water's edge behind some large homes. A gravel path leads you to Sheldon Creek Park.

Sheldon Creek Park, a stunning window to the lake, which ends at Cudmore Road, marks the place where Sheldon Creek empties into Lake Ontario. You can gain access to it directly from Lakeshore Road on a wooded path that follows the creek's course.

To continue on the Waterfront Trail, you have to go north back up to Lakeshore Road West. Once you're there, you will find that the Trail continues east one block, turns south onto West Street, and follows it to the Lake.

The end of West Street provides another window to the lake. Set in a residential area amid large oak and pine trees, it has a fine view of the Bronte pier to the east. Just to the right, you will see the Pioneer Cemetery. This is the final resting place for members of many pioneer families in Bronte: the Sovereigns, Trillers, Williamses, and Ribbles, among them.

From the Pioneer Cemetery, the Trail takes you back up West Street and east on Seneca Drive. Continuing along this residential street will bring you to West River Street and Bronte Bluffs Park, the most westerly of a series of parks that make up the Bronte harbour area.

BRONTE HARBOUR WATERFRONT PARK

The existing five public park areas and the new outer harbour park, situated on both sides of Twelve Mile Creek, have been designated as the Bronte Harbour Waterfront Park. This designation recognizes the regional significance of this public waterfront area and the importance of a harbour to both the former village of Bronte and the Bronte of today.

During the mid-1800s, the Bronte community formed at the mouth of Twelve Mile Creek; it had been Mississauga land until 1820 and was officially designated the Village of Bronte in 1834. However, some native people remained in the area for many years thereafter. According to Bronte folklore, a Mississauga chief haunts the mouth of Twelve Mile Creek atop a majestic white stallion.

Bronte Bluffs Park

In the park, a gravel walking path leads you to a historic home set in a natural woodlot. The main part of the house dates from about 1825 and is one of the oldest surviving dwellings in Halton Region. When restoration, a project of the Bronte Historical Society, is complete, this will become the Sovereign House/Mazo de la Roche Heritage Display Centre.

Sovereign House was the home of a founding father of Bronte, Charles Sovereign. Later, novelist Mazo de la Roche lived here (between 1911 and 1914), and began her writing career with *Possession,* a novel about small-town Ontario based on her time in Bronte. Today, de la Roche is probably best remembered for *The Whiteoaks of Jalna* and the other Whiteoaks chronicles.

If you walk along the Bronte Bluffs, they will lead you to a set of stairs that descend into Bronte Beach Park, or proceed north on West River Street until you go down a small hill and turn east on Bronte Park Road, which will lead you into Bronte Beach Park.

Bronte Beach Park

Bronte Beach Park is a large recreational area with a beautiful sandy beach. There is a public launch ramp for boats; in the warmer months this is a busy marina area. Amidst a grove of large willows there are barbecues, picnic tables, public washrooms, and a telephone. This is a favourite spot for picnicking, boating, and fishing, and is a great place to windsurf.

Because the only way to cross Twelve Mile Creek is via the bridge on Lakeshore Road, you have to follow Bronte Park Road back up to West River Street and north to Lakeshore Road West.

C. Volkes Memorial Park

Immediately west of the bridge and Bronte Harbour Yacht Club, on your right, is C. Volkes Memorial Park. The park, which overlooks the inner marina, is the setting for a memorial that pays tribute to Canadians who died in two world wars and the Korean War.

From C. Volkes Memorial Park, head south on Bronte Road and you are on the east side of Twelve Mile Creek, surrounded by boutiques, restaurants, and shops.

Fisherman's Wharf

This is a delightful tourist area that is suited for those with strollers and people in wheelchairs. Walk south on the west side of Bronte Road to a boardwalk that takes you to the wharf and outer harbour area; along the way there are well-placed benches, and washrooms which are wheelchair-accessible. Please note that bicycles are not permitted on the boardwalk. Parking is free where allowed. Across the road, there is a restaurant, Stoneboats, in a historic building made from the lake stone brought up by stonehookers. Beside it is an attractive, centre-gabled building, an early Bronte post office, now Bronte Harbour Fine Arts.

Bronte began to take its place among important ports on Lake Ontario when the first harbour was completed in 1856 by the Bronte Harbour Company. The early commerce of Bronte was shipping of wheat and timber, but this was gradually replaced by fishing, boat building and stonehooking (see page 75).

Today, if you turn to the southeast, you are looking out over the area of the new outer harbour and park framed by two breakwaters built in 1991 by the federal government. The Region of Halton is co-ordinating the work in this area with senior government and others. The 5.6-hectares (14-acre) parkland area is scheduled to be completed by 1996, 140 years after the first harbour in Bronte was built. Subsequent development will provide a 450-slip marina and related facilities in keeping with the adjacent village character and providing docking and major parkland amenities for boaters, tourists, and residents alike.

Bronte Harbour is one of the sites of the Oakville Waterfront Festival each June; on Canada Day, it offers dazzling fireworks displays. (See the section on Coronation Park for more information about the festival.)

If you continue east you will be in Vista Promenade Park, which extends along the south side of Ontario Street, which used to be the old Lake Road from Hamilton to York (Toronto). This area is the northern limit of the new Bronte Harbour Waterfront Park.

Vista Promenade and Water's Edge Park

This section of trail through Vista Promenade and Water's Edge Park represents the longest section of the Trail that is right on the waterfront.

As you continue along this area of manicured lawns, Vista Promenade Park has many benches that make it an ideal stop for enjoying views of the outer harbour – an area that is always home to geese, ducks, and swans.

Large rocks mark the section where the Trail enters Water's Edge Park, stretching along the shoreline to Water's Edge Drive; the Trail then continues east to the Third Line. Travel north on Third Line and turn right onto Old Lakeshore Road, which immediately joins Lakeshore Road West. On the south side you will find one of Oakville's largest greenspaces, Coronation Park.

Another route along the water's edge that also enters Coronation Park involves walking or cycling on Old Lakeshore Road until you reach Belvedere Drive and go south to the waterfront to Bayview Parkette. Continue east on the path in Bayview Parkette to Coronation Park.

CORONATION PARK

As you continue on the Waterfront Trail, you enter Coronation Park from the west, near a beautiful new stage built to showcase community entertainers (the "Stars of the Stage" summer series), as well as big-name acts during the annual Oakville Waterfront Festival each June. The park is also home to the annual Civic Holiday picnic in August.

Coronation Park was opened in 1954 on land that was originally the Wilsons' family farm. The old barn, now the office of the Oakville Waterfront Festival, was constructed more than one hundred years ago, of stones from the nearby beach.

Family fun is guaranteed at the Oakville Waterfront Festival. With the help of 1,000-plus community volunteers, over 100 corporate sponsors, lots of goodwill and community spirit, the fourth annual Oakville Waterfront Festival sparkles up the waterfront with Canadian headliners, fireworks, a sailing regatta, children's activities, a craft show, and more. Visit the festival during the third week in June. For more information call 905-845-5585.

Coronation Park has a huge play area for children of all ages, a water spray pad, as well as a drinking fountain, washrooms that are accessible to people in wheelchairs, barbecues, and large picnic areas. There are many shade trees and a sandy beach stretching the entire length of the park. Parking is provided on an internal road that runs through the park.

In 1995, Cornation Park underwent a number of improvements including additional trails, expanded play facilities and skating area, beach volleyball courts, improved lighting, the addition of drainage tile in the low-lying grass area, and shoreline protection work.

From the park, the Waterfront Trail is aligned with Lakeshore Road West for 1.9 kilometres (1.1 miles) to Appleby College. After you cross over Fourteen Mile Creek, there are several large private homes, Appleby College, and residential areas on what was once the site of great estates. These are what remain from the early part of this century, when Oakville was a fashionable summer retreat and the well-to-do built their homes along Lakeshore Road. Continue for another kilometre (0.6 mile) and you will pass St. Jude's Cemetery.

Continue east along Lakeshore until you get to Kerr Street, turn south and this will take you to Waterworks Park. This waterfront park goes east all the way to the Oakville Harbour at Sixteen Mile Creek. It involves climbing a large staircase and therefore can be used only by pedestrians. If you are cycling, turn east on Burnet Street (from Kerr Street) to Chisholm Street and then south to Walker Street and east into Tannery Park. Parking is available in the harbour area.

OAKVILLE HARBOUR AREA

This is the second of Oakville's two harbours, and like the Bronte harbour area, this area also comprises a number of smaller parks.

Tannery Park

Situated on a hill, you will find striking views of the lake, the harbour, the town, and Toronto's skyline. It is a good spot for a picnic as you will find a drinking fountain, picnic tables, benches, and public washrooms.

The park was named for one of Oakville's most prosperous businesses between 1856 and 1926; the tannery stood on the site, which had originally been the location of Oakville's first brewery. The rock cairn in Tannery Park honours the officers and crew of the HMCS Oakville.

Shipyard Park

Walk north through Tannery Park and you arrive at another area with a few picnic tables and a bench, Shipyard Park, once the site of the shipyard owned by Oakville's premier boat-builders, Captain James Andrew and his brother John. At the time, shipbuilding was a thriving industry and an important factor in the local economy.

Shipyard Park is now the site of Lyon's Log Cabin, built in the 1820s and originally located on Trafalgar Road near Upper Middle Road. Behind the cabin, on the grounds of the Oakville Yacht Squadron, is the Oakville Lighthouse.

Built circa 1889 and moved here in the 1950s, the hexagonal structure replaced the first lighthouse, which was destroyed in 1886 during a storm so severe that it is said to have destroyed every lighthouse between the Credit River and Burlington.

Continue north up the hill toward Forsythe Street and the Lakeshore Road Bridge over Sixteen Mile Creek. Once on the east side of Sixteen Mile Creek, the Waterfront Trail continues south on Navy Street to Lakeside Park.

From the intersection of Lakeshore Road and Navy Street you have a couple of options rather than immediately proceeding south on Navy Street. You can either go north through

Centennial Plaza to Navy Flats Park and Busby Park or, if shopping or dining are the first priority, head straight on Lakeshore Road East into Old Oakville's charming downtown.

The quaint main street is lined with well-preserved 19th-century buildings. Much of the new architecture pays tribute to the past and most new buildings are no more than three storeys high. Flower planters line the sidewalks, and there is a picturesque town square a few blocks east; it is the venue for the annual Jazz Festival each July. This main street has been used as the backdrop for many movies, including the hit The Santa Clause.

If you decide to stroll north from the intersection of Lakeshore Road and Navy Street, there are charming gardens throughout Centennial Plaza; to your left is the main branch of the Oakville Library and, at the north end, the Oakville Centre for the Performing Arts. If you continue down the stairs on your left and walk north you arrive at Navy Flats Park.

Navy Flats Park and Busby Park

The site of William Chisholm's shipbuilding yards was located at the north end of Navy Street, where Sixteen Mile Creek turns sharply. It is now home to the Burloak Canoe Club and the Oakville Power Boat Club.

There are docks along the creek, and the fall colours make this an especially lovely scene; if you arrive by car, you will find several nearby municipal parking lots. If you head south on Water Street you will arrive at Busby Park.

As unlikely as it seems, this pretty creek-side greenspace, with its inviting benches and picnic tables, was built on the town's dumpsite. Busby Park is also home of Oakville's medal-winning canoe club. Continuing south on Water Street, you will find the old stone granary on your left; now an office, this handsome building was constructed in the 1850s.

Follow Water Street, and you pass the Oakville Club on your left, which dates from 1908; past it, you will connect back to the Waterfront Trail when you get to Navy Street just north of the lawn-bowling greens, at the Civic Park. As you look around Navy Street, you will notice how rich it is in historic homes. You are now

in the Old Oakville Heritage District, where these treasures are preserved by their conscientious owners.

Civic Park

This was once the site of the Market Building (town hall), a two-
storey brick structure opened in 1862, which housed a lock-up
(jail), council chambers, and a large main-floor hall. Today it is surrounded by trees and shrubs, and there are benches and picnic
tables overlooking the lawn-bowling greens; these greenswards have
been used for that purpose since 1903. At the end of Navy Street,
you reach the exquisite Erchless Estate.

Erchless Estate

When he founded Oakville, William Chisholm claimed the property
overlooking the lake on the east side of Sixteen Mile Creek. He had
one of Oakville's first brick buildings constructed in the early 1830s,
which served as a customs facility and warehouse.

Chisholm deeded the property to his son, Robert,
known as R.K. who built a handsome red-brick custom house in
1856 and, beside it, Erchless, a Georgian-style family home
constructed in 1858. Erchless (pronounced with the soft "ch" of
"loch") is named in honour of the Chisholms' clan seat and castle in
Scotland; it comes from a Gaelic word meaning "on the stream".

At about the turn of the century, R.K.'s son Allan
began beautifying the estate. The lodge, constructed on the north
end of the property, included a gardener's cottage, stables, and carriage house. Allan Chisholm designed the original wooden gates,
now copied, at the north entrance onto King Street. He laid out the
long curving carriage path bordered by large flowerbeds, terraced
the lawns, and planted extensive gardens. Today the carriage path
remains as a narrow footpath through the gardens.

An avid sailor and sportsman, in 1908 Allan Chisholm
helped found the Oakville Club, which is still going strong. He died
in 1918, and the Erchless Estate was purchased by his cousin's
widow, Emelda Beeler Chisholm. A beautiful rock garden was laid
out and the terraces were replaced by sloping lawns. The gardens
you see today at Erchless were recreated from photographs taken

in the 1920s. A wide variety of flowers bloom continuously from spring to fall.

Inside, Erchless is restored to its 1920s look, recalling the time Emelda lived there; many of her furnishings of that period grace its interior. Today the estate, which covers 1.6 hectares (4 acres) at the end of Navy Street, is the home of the Oakville Museum and the Oakville Historical Society. The museum is open afternoons from Tuesday to Sunday; there is ample free parking. For information call 905-845-3541.

Right across the street from the Erchless Estate is Lakeside Park.

Lakeside Park

Lakeside Park, at the foot of Navy Street, is an attractive treed space with a large climber for children, well-placed benches, washrooms that are accessible to people in wheelchairs, and a water fountain. There are a number of walkways; at the west end of the park you can stroll onto the Oakville pier and survey the harbour and the lake.

There is a bandstand at the top of a gently sloping grass hill leading to the water's edge, making it an ideal setting for wedding photos and outdoor concerts. Lakeside Park is another venue of the Oakville Waterfront Festival each June, and the Jazz Festival each July.

The park is the site of Thomas House, which was built in 1829, with an interior that was later restored to that period; the house is operated by the Oakville Historical Society. Beside it is the Old Post Office, 1835, which is part of the Oakville Museum and has been partially re-created as a 1850s post office. Both are open to the public from May to September, and on some special days.

The Waterfront Trail leads from Lakeside Park east along Front Street (one-way eastbound) past George St. Park, a window to the lake where a bench is provided for a quiet stop before you arrive at Dingle Park.

The natural path through Dingle Park provides a country-like setting which takes you to Reynolds Street. This thin stretch of parkland along the water's edge has picnic tables, benches, and some parking. Many beautiful historic homes back onto this park.

Continue north on Reynolds Street and the Trail again links up to Lakeshore Road East. Lakeshore is a busy road; however, the Trail alignment is off-road as it takes you past some magnificent waterfront mansions.

The Trail user now has a choice to continue east along Lakeshore Road East for 6.3 kilometres (4 miles) directly to Gairloch Gardens or choose any number of mini side trips to one of the waterfront parks.

The first park along this stretch is First Street Parkette. Follow First Street to the end, where you will find an inviting bench for you to sit and enjoy the view. To return to the Trail go north to Lakeshore Road East.

Cycle or walk south at Raymar Place; this attractive street is the site of a large Oakville estate of the past, Raymar. Now beautiful homes line this winding dead-end street. Raymar Promenade at the end of Raymar Place allows public access to the waterfront for another view of the lake. Return to Lakeshore Road to continue east on the Trail.

A short detour south on Park Avenue leads to the Esplanade Waterfront Park. Large homes back onto this long stretch of lakefront park. This open space is ideally suited to brisk walks and has benches along the way. At the end of this park, exit north on Chartwell Road and then east again onto Lakeshore Road East.

The last park before you reach Gairloch Gardens is Bel Air Promenade, which is located at the end of Bel Air Drive. Return to the Trail by going north, back to Lakeshore Road East and head east until you reach Gairloch Gardens.

GAIRLOCH GARDENS

On the grounds of this handsome 4.5-hectare (11-acre) estate stands a Tudor-style residence, built in the 1920s and strongly influenced by the Arts and Crafts movement. Gairloch Gallery and Gardens is owned and operated by the Town of Oakville, thanks to the generosity of James Gairdner, a wealthy broker and artist who lived in the town from 1918 until his death in 1971. In 1949, he took early retirement from business and pursued his other passion, oil painting.

Gairdner purchased Gairloch from the estate of Colonel William MacKendrick, an engineer and writer, who had designed and built what he called Chestnut Point. After he bought the property in 1960, Gairdner renamed it Gairloch, which means "short lake" in Gaelic.

The quaint studio, where Gairdner painted, had been built to his own specifications and moved from his former residence. With its knotty-pine panelling, fieldstone fireplace, and skylight, the studio is now the site of the Oakville Galleries' Studio gift shop. For more information call Oakville Galleries at 905-844-4402.

Gairloch is surrounded by aromatic gardens dotted with intriguing sculpture, and the grounds offer a variety of stunning shrubs and flora (especially a spectacular formal rose garden), many species of birds, and a wonderful view of Lake Ontario. In addition, there are duck ponds which are also home to elegant trumpet swans.

Continue east along the Waterfront Trail on Lakeshore Road East for approximately 2 kilometres (1.2 miles), and if you wish to walk or cycle the following side trip to one of Oakville's linear waterfront parks, turn south at Chancery Lane. Follow it to Carrington Place, which will give you access to Carrington Promenade.

Carrington Promenade takes you east to Birkbank Drive. Head north to Lakeshore Road East at this point and you will soon arrive at Arkendo Park. From here you may wish to go south on Arkendo Drive to take in Arkendo Waterfront Park.

ARKENDO WATERFRONT PARK

As you venture along the lakefront through Arkendo Waterfront Park, you are almost at the Oakville town limits. At this point, Joshua's Creek runs through the park and empties into the lake.

Travel north through Arkendo Park to Lakeshore Road East. Proceed east over the Lakeshore Road bridge crossing Joshua's Creek and you will link up with the Mississauga Waterfront Trail section.

Side Trip

JOSHUA'S CREEK TRAIL

 This beautiful natural trail, which winds its way north into Joshua Valley Park, is 2.1 kilometres (1.3 miles) long.

The Joshua's Creek Trail system was developed in 1983; it is suitable for hiking or cross-country skiing and hikers are encouraged to use it year-round. The trail surface is made of woodchips; in areas prone to erosion, limestone screenings have been used.

Joshua's Creek was named for Joshua Leach, who bought Lot 3, Third Concession in 1822 and built a sawmill powered by the creek. The area was dense with white pine and white oak trees, at a time when massive white pine trunks were being shipped to England for use as ships' masts and oak was a valued building and carpentry material. Not surprisingly, Leach's three sons became skilled carpenters and built many of the homes in the area.

The Joshua's Creek Trail starts at the Waste Water Treatment Plant on Lakeshore Road East, marked by a white sign. If you travel north along the fence about 30 metres (100 feet), you come to the start of the woodchip trail. At the edge of the woodlot there are sumacs which turn a brilliant red in autumn. Once inside the woodlot, you will see a wide variety of trees, including sugar maple, black cherry, hemlock, white ash, red maple, yellow birch, and beech.

There is a fork in the Creek Trail: if you go south, you return to Lakeshore Road East; if you decide to travel north, you pass through an area of weeping willow and black locust trees, which are rapidly taking over abandoned farmland.

The trees that grow on the valley floor are different from those in the woodlot; here, the soil is shallow and subject to flooding – conditions that enable willows and green ash to thrive; you will also find a broad range of ferns and wildflowers.

You come to another fork in the Joshua's Creek Trail; it goes north, crosses the creek on stepping stones, and rejoins the main trail a little further along. (The stepping stones are not passable when the water level is high.) In this area, there are mountain maples, a species not usually found in Oakville, which have the characteristic maple leaf, but can be identified by their brownish-yellow twigs, which turn brownish-red on more mature bark.

Take the next right, which leads you to the Roselawn Orchards dam, constructed during the 1940s to supply water to the Roselawn apple orchards; the paved trail across the dam connects Devon Road on the south with Deer Run Avenue on the north.

Keep to the left and the Joshua's Creek Trail winds through an area of tall grass known as Phragmites. A bit farther along there is what was once the dam floodplain; once dominated by cattails, the land is now being regenerated with willow, shrub dogwood, poplar, and ash trees. Once you pass under the power lines, you are in the vicinity of Joshua Leach's sawmill, but it is very hard to find any trace of the once thriving industry in what is now an area of black walnut, green ash, and willow.

The main Trail bends to the left (south) and the next bend, which is to the right, leads to Cedarberry Court. If you continue along through the white elm you cross a small bridge over the creek. If you branch to the left, the Trail leads to Maplegrove Arena; if you continue straight ahead to the grassy area, you will have reached Brookmill Road and the end of the Joshua's Creek Trail. ■

The *woodlot is one of those rare places that, while surrounded by the noise and bustle of the Big City seems indelibly part of the country*

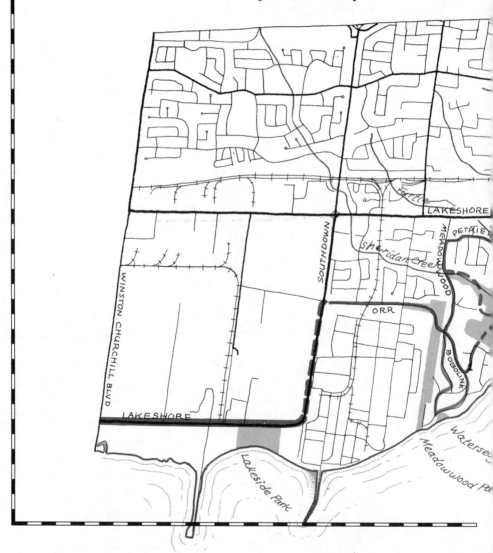

Mississauga

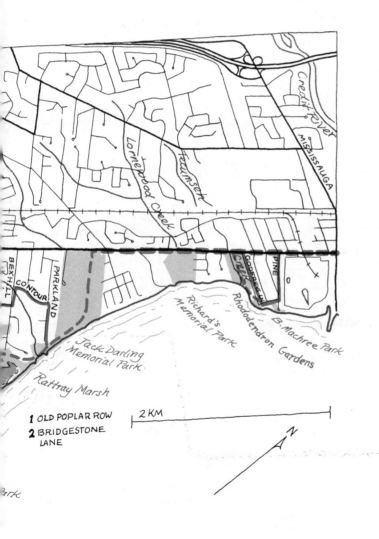

1 OLD POPLAR ROW
2 BRIDGESTONE LANE

2 KM

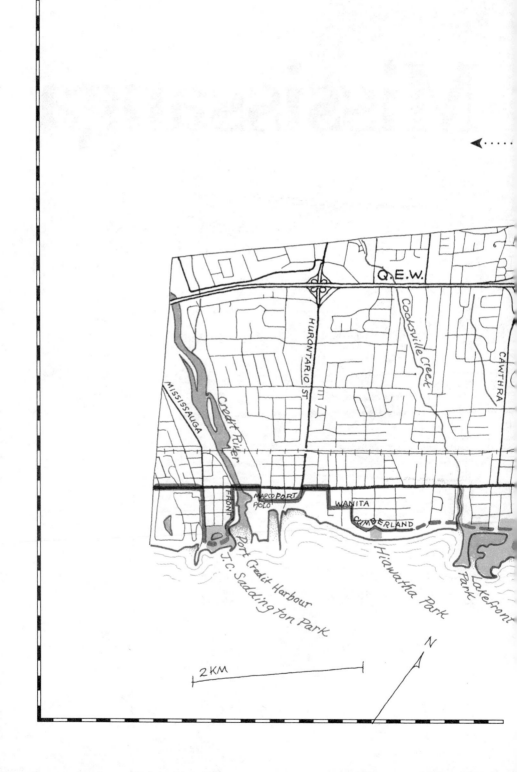

Mississauga

NCE THIS WAS DENSE FOREST known only to the Mississauga, members of the Ojibwa nation, who had made their way from Northern Ontario to the Credit River Valley in the late 1600s. A nomadic people, they relied primarily on fishing and hunting and, later, on commerce with settlers, principally French fur-traders. By the early 19th century, the Mississauga had sold much of their land to the British, but they retained authority in the area until 1847, when the British uprooted them. (The native people moved to the Grand River Reserve in southwestern Ontario where, to this day, their descendants live.)

In time, the area was incorporated as Toronto Township, covering several villages and hamlets, some of which are now remembered only in the names of highway exit signs: Dixie was a farm service centre, while Erindale and Meadowvale were millsites. By 1968, the township had outgrown its role as a Toronto satellite and, looking to the original inhabitants of the area, it took the Town of Mississauga as its name.

The Mississauga portion of the Waterfront Trail offers many delights, especially for people who enjoy parks and wildlife, as well as for those interested in early architecture and in industry. Travelling from west to east, the first part of the Mississauga section of the Trail, approximately 2 kilometres (1.2 miles) long, follows Lakeshore Road West from Winston Churchill Boulevard, the Oakville/Mississauga border.

Once the site of native trails, by the beginning of this century Lakeshore Road West was the only major surface route along Lake Ontario's north shore. In 1918, it became the first paved road in the entire province. This section is best suited for car or bike travel: it's a busy road, without sidewalks, where large trucks thunder by, travelling to and from such companies as St. Lawrence Cement, Holderbank, Alcan, Westroc, and Ontario Hydro's Canadian Centre for Fusion Fuel.

What seems to be a walkway across Lakeshore is actually a St. Lawrence Cement conveyor belt used to transport limestone (see page 271 for information on the company's operations in

PUBLIC TRANSIT

Local Transit
(905-279-5800)

GO (416-869-3200)
• Clarkson – Southdown
Rd. at Lakeshore Blvd.
just north of HWY 2
• Port Credit – Queen
St. at Hwy 10 and
Lakeshore Rd. W.
just north of St.
Lawrence Park

Cramahe Township, the source of the material used here) from ships docked at the company's pier to the plant, where cement powder is produced.

As you continue east along Lakeshore Road, the Trail brings you to a park with a unique beach.

LAKESIDE PARK

Brick manufacturing was once a major industry across the Mississauga shoreline and the unusual red "rocks" that comprise this park's beach were formed when one of the clay tile companies backfilled its property with defective and surplus product. Over the years, the waters of Lake Ontario have smoothed the surfaces and created the unusual formations you see.

This quiet, passive park contains picnic tables and a small playground, making it a good place to rest. There are two piers, one east of the park, owned by Petro Canada and one west, the property of St. Lawrence Cement. International freighters visit both frequently – a reminder that the lake is, as it has long been, a highway for waterfront industry.

PETRO CANADA LUBRICANT CENTRE

Just east of Lakeside Park you will find a surreal maze of silver-coloured steel. With the look of the next century about it, this is actually Petro Canada's Lubricant Centre, which produces millions of litres of "white oil". Crude oil is first refined at the company's Oakville plant before being further treated here and blended into specialty oils for automotive, industrial, and pharmaceutical use.

Lakeshore Road ends at this point, with the Trail going north for 1.5 kilometres (1 mile) along Southdown Road, parallelling the Petro Canada plant. There is an asphalt surface 3.5 metres (11 feet) wide, marked for both pedestrians and cyclists. Turning right onto Orr Road takes you off busy streets for a while as the Trail heads east along Orr Road. There is a sidewalk along the north side, for pedestrian use only.

At this point, the Trail runs parallel to Petro Canada's northern border and passes by the Lewis Bradley Pool, where the public can swim between 1:30 and 5 p.m. and between 6 and 8 p.m.

every day from mid-June to Labour Day. For further information, contact Mississauga Parks and Recreation at 905-896-5382 or the Lewis Bradley Pool at 905-823-5720.

The gateway of trees ahead of you defines the sharp contrast between the industrial nature of the past few kilometres and the stately residential community up ahead. A good way to begin this part of the journey is to step back in time with a visit to the Bradley Museum.

BRADLEY MUSEUM AND ANCHORAGE

The Bradley Museum, 1620 Orr Road, dates back to the 1830s and was built in the salt-box style typical of Atlantic architecture of that time. Once the home of United Empire Loyalist settler Lewis Bradley and his family, the building, which was originally located on the lands now occupied by the Petro Canada Centre, was moved to this location and restored as a public museum in 1967. The furnishings are authentic and reflect the life of families, many from the United States, who chose to remain loyal to the Crown and who settled here; Lewis Bradley, for example, came from Georgia.

The museum, which is operated by the City of Mississauga, is open Tuesday to Friday from 1 to 4 p.m. and on Saturday and Sunday from 1 to 5 p.m., from April to December. Because of special exhibits, regular hours of operation may be interrupted; it is best to call the museum at 905-822-1569 or 905-822-4884 for more information on special events, hours of operation, and admission charges.

The Bradley Museum shares its site with an Ontario Regency-style cottage known as the Anchorage. Built in 1839 as the retirement home of Captain John Skynner, a British officer who lived in it until his death in 1846, its name comes from Captain Skynner's own words: "Here is my anchorage; here I will take my rest."

Open year-round, the Anchorage features fashions and artifacts of the 1800s and includes a gift shop and tea room. Afternoon tea is served from 2 to 4 p.m. every Sunday.

East of the museum, Orr Road links to Meadow Wood and Bob-O-Link roads, where a number of route options await. A right turn onto Meadow Wood Road begins an enjoyable loop through a beautiful area of estate homes known as Merigold's Point; the name is taken from the Merigold family, who came from New Brunswick in 1809 and were among the area's first settlers. Follow Meadow Wood south to Country Club Crescent and turn right. From there, Country Club winds its way down to Watersedge Park, a quiet window on the Lake.

MEADOWWOOD PARK

Don't overlook this thin parcel of land north of Watersedge Park. Its 14 hectares (34.5 acres) are leased to the City of Mississauga by Petro Canada as a buffer between the refinery and the residential area. But it is much more: hidden among its trees are a playground, tennis courts, and an ice rink. (You can get to these directly off Meadow Wood Road.) You may even be fortunate enough to see some of the white-tailed deer that make their home in the park's natural woods and meadows. The park also contains a re-naturalized area along the west side (see page 72 for more information about naturalized areas).

On the return portion of the loop, turn right onto Watersedge Road which will take you to Bob-O-Link Road. Turning left onto Bob-O-Link will take you back to the intersection of Orr, Meadow Wood, and Bob-O-Link roads, which is where you began the 4-kilometre (2.5-mile) loop. While only parts of the loop have sidewalks, the asphalt surface is suitable for pedestrians and in-line skaters as well as cyclists. If you are travelling on foot, you will want to turn onto Old Poplar Row (which runs off Bob-O-Link before you get back up to Meadow Wood Road); it brings you to the western entrance of the Rattray Marsh Conservation Area. Cyclists will have to complete the loop and then head north on Meadow Wood Road.

Follow this hilly section of Meadow Wood Road north to Petrie Way, and turn right. Head east on Petrie to Silver Birch Trail; make a left and then a quick right onto Bridgestone Lane. Bridgestone leads to Bexhill Road, where a right-hand turn will bring you south to another entrance to Rattray Marsh Conservation Area. This one is especially important to people in wheelchairs

◀ · · · 65 · · · ▶

because it is the only wheelchair-accessible point for entering the Rattray Marsh boardwalk trail.

Turning left onto Bexhill will take those travelling by bicycle up to Lakeshore Road where a short distance east is the main entrance to Jack Darling Park.

RATTRAY MARSH CONSERVATION AREA

Situated at the mouth of Sheridan Creek, this is the last natural waterfront marsh of its kind between St. Catharines and Oshawa. There are other wetlands along this stretch; however, the shingle beach at Rattray Marsh makes it unique. A Class 2 Provincially Significant Wetland (see page 5 for more on wetland classification), it is a poignant reminder that, in times gone by, the area overflowed with wildlife, with birdsong, and with the rush and stillness of natural life. Once slated to become a housing development and marina, the marsh is a tribute to the tenacity and determination of the concerned citizens who rallied to save it. Its approximately 37 hectares (91 acres) are a crucial area for fish and migrating birds. More than 200 species of birds have been sighted here, and it is home to a wide variety of wildlife and plants (some specific to the area). In all, there are 3 kilometres (1.8 miles) of path, a portion of which is boardwalk, with the remainder consisting of gravel and natural surface.

One of the trails leads to the shingle beach that serves as a natural barrier protecting the marsh; it also offers a spectacular view over the lake to the Toronto skyline. You should allow yourself at least an hour to cover the entire signed trail system. For further information, contact the Credit Valley Conservation Authority at 905-670-1615.

Please note that, because of the sensitive nature of the marsh, cycling is prohibited and dogs must be kept leashed. For those travelling by bike, the nearest racks are located in the south-west corner of Jack Darling Park, in the children's play area; access to the marsh can be made on foot from this corner. This is also the exit for those who have followed the Trail through the marsh from one of the entrances.

JACK DARLING PARK

After extensive redevelopment, completed in the fall of 1994, Jack Darling Park is now considered one of the jewels of Mississauga's park system. There are two new viewing decks near the beach, lovely spots, particularly as the sun sets and city lights begin to animate the sky. It has all the amenities: modern washroom facilities, ample and well-lit parking areas, a new playground and picnic area. Access to the largest public beach in Mississauga has been made easier for those in wheelchairs, thanks to the construction of wide, gently inclined concrete ramps.

Windsurfers will find this a popular spot for riding the crest of a wave, while cyclists, in-line skaters, and pedestrians will be pleased with the new asphalt pathway on the east side of the grounds, which parallels the shoreline.

If your particular interest is environmental or ecological, you will be pleased that extensive shoreline stabilization and alterations have been made and that a naturalization/planting program is under way.

To continue east along the Trail you head up the asphalt path which will bring you back onto Lakeshore Road.

RICHARD'S MEMORIAL PARK

This small park is dedicated to the memory of 14-year-old Richard Wolniewicz, who died in 1971 and whose heart was donated to Robert W. Speck, then the mayor of Mississauga. Two years later, the City decided to honour the youngster by naming this park for him. Stop to read the touching memorial plaque just inside the entrance, which many visitors say inspires reflection on the importance and fragility of life.

Richard's Memorial Park is a link in the chain of Mississauga's waterfront greenspaces; it has seasonal washroom facilities which are wheelchair-accessible, a playground, and a large picnic area that includes a barbecue (which should be reserved ahead of time). Contact the Mississauga Community Services Department during regular business hours, Monday to Friday, at 905-896-5384.

A short distance east along Lakeshore Road are the
Rhododendron Gardens (see the vignette, *Creating Tranquillity*).

On the east side of the gardens, tiny Godfrey's Lane
connects Lakeshore Road to Ben Machree Drive. If you're travelling
by bike, use this lane to connect back to the Trail.

BEN MACHREE PARK

This window to the lake is named after the first reeve of Mississauga.
At the lake's edge you will see, first-hand, two approaches to shoreline management. First, there is the armourstone, paid for by
residents and installed to shore up and protect their backyards. Just
to the east, you will see the second type, a shingle beach (see page
35 for description), a fine example of natural shoreline protection.

Ben Machree Drive runs into Pine Avenue, which is
the Trail alignment until the route can be continued along the
waterfront across land that belongs to Imperial Oil and was once
the site of a Texaco refinery.

Imperial Oil has agreed to build a berm along the
Trail's north side which will allow the Trail to continue along the
water's edge, linking directly to J.C. Saddington Park. However,
until the Trail and berm are completed, the route goes north on
Pine Avenue, east on Lakeshore Road, and then south on
Mississauga Road South to connect with J.C. Saddington Park.

J.C. SADDINGTON PARK

A popular spot for shore fishing, this community park has two path
systems to accommodate walkers, in-line skaters, cyclists, and
runners. There are washroom facilities and ample parking, as well
as a soft-drink machine and a large picnic area with tables and several barbecues. The barge you see just offshore serves as a
breakwater for the Port Credit Harbour.

If you want a glimpse of the province's early history,
walk along Front Street South, where a number of buildings date
back to the mid-1800s. The log house at number 21 was built near
Orangeville circa 1830 and was dismantled and moved to its present
location in 1967 as part of a Centennial project sponsored by the
Port Credit Rovers. Today it serves as their clubhouse and headquar-

CREATING TRANQUILLITY:
A Lakeshore Garden Is Born

Mississauga's Rhododendron Gardens, once called Cranberry Cove after the bogs that were prominent in the area, are a tribute to the generosity and botanical expertise of the late Dr. Joseph Brueckner. When the Cooksville Creek was re-channelled a few years ago, Dr. Brueckner, an authority on rhododendron hybridizing and a retired scientist, was forced to relocate his rare rhododendrons. He donated many beautiful shrubs to this lakeshore garden, which he believed had the perfect micro-climate.

Dr. Brueckner became interested in the evergreen plant when he lived in New Zealand; when he moved to Canada in 1957, he was intrigued with warnings that rhododendrons would never flourish in Canada's severe climate. But, as a scientist, he knew that rhododendrons thrive in extreme temperatures – from the Arctic to the Equator. So he began hybridizing rhododendrons with exotic tropical flowers with hardier, northern types. Today, his carefully reared plants thrive in many Canadian gardens.

When he became involved in the Mississauga garden project, the city had more than three hundred parks in its boundaries, but no official garden. Dr. Brueckner took on the long and demanding task of gaining support for a by-law that would protect the integrity and physical properties of a garden once a site was developed.

Dr. Brueckner envisioned a garden, not a park, a place of beauty, peace, and reflection. "A charming and lovely garden is a blessing," he said. "[The] city needs a place where people can go to find peace and a rest from their daily worries, an island where they can find harmony and beauty." His solution: "...rare and interesting plants that are botanically and aesthetically pleasing, and skilled personnel to take care of them."

The garden he helped create is marked by the beauty and rarity of many of its plants, but they need protection against nature, animals, and people. Sadly, vandalism and theft have robbed the garden of many rare plants.

The picturesque, well-manicured gardens, with their mature trees, are perfect for a quiet stroll or for people who want to read quietly or just enjoy the view from one of the lakeside benches. Because they are evergreen, rhododendrons are in leaf year-round, however from mid-May to mid-June, these beautiful plants are in full bloom. Bicycles are forbidden; there are bike racks, washroom facilities, and a soft-drink machine near the parking lot, which is off Lakeshore Road.

ters for the Salmon Masters Tournament, which has replaced the annual Toronto Star Salmon Hunt.

The Wilcox Inn at 32 Front Street South was built in 1850 and offered food and beds for sailors, harbour workers, farmers, and travellers; it is now used for offices.

Abram Block, Jr., captain of a stonehooker (see page 75), built the home at 42 Front Street in about 1850.

PORT CREDIT HARBOUR

The Credit River has always been vital to development in the Mississauga area. The river takes its name from the winter supplies French settlers gave natives ("on credit") to be exchanged for furs in the spring. Of all the rivers in Ontario that once boasted populations of native Atlantic salmon, this is one of only two in which the native species have been successfully reintroduced. (The other is Wilmot Creek in Clarington.)

Mississauga plans a facelift for the quaint Port Credit Harbour. Over nine years, it will reconstruct the harbour, build a new marina and restaurant, and build a pedestrian bridge beside the one now used for vehicular traffic. For more information on Port Credit, contact the Port Credit Business Association at 905-278-7742.

East of Port Credit Harbour, the Trail continues along Port Street. Notice the small brown brick building at the corner of Port and Lakeshore Road. Built in 1932 during the Great Depression to house the administration offices of the St. Lawrence Starch Company, it stands as a reminder of desperation. The company's own employees had to act as labourers during construction.

This heritage building is all that remains of the original facilities; demolition in 1994 of the once prominent water tower and smokestack sparked a great deal of controversy among those who wanted the property preserved in its original form. Discussions are under way among St. Lawrence Starch, citizens of Port Credit, and the City of Mississauga to develop the land as a mixed residential and commercial area.

The Trail now makes its way through a residential area along Cumberland Drive before it reaches the maple woodlot that leads to the Adamson Estate. The woodlot is one of those increasingly rare places that, while surrounded by the noise and bustle of the Big City, seem indelibly part of the country. During the spring bird migration, this woodlot serves as a resting area for yellow-rumped and many other warblers.

ADAMSON ESTATE

Originally the Grove Farm, the estate was acquired from architect Anthony Adamson by the Credit Valley Conservation Authority (CVCA) in 1975. A decade earlier, Adamson had worked with Marion MacRae to produce *The Ancestral Roof,* a proud and loving look at early Ontario houses that first made the general public aware of the province's architectural heritage.

The estate consists of the main house (circa 1920), a folly, a barn, a garden, and a maple woodlot. The CVCA more recently acquired the Derry House (circa 1934), which sits on the same property and was designed by Adamson as his residence.

The City of Mississauga entered into a long-term lease for passive use of the grounds as a public park; in 1989, Council granted the Royal Conservatory of Music permission to use the main house as a teaching facility. So, if your timing is right, you may hear the strains of a Chopin étude flowing from behind the curtains.

Stop – at least for a moment. Look about you at the grounds and you may decide to stroll toward the lake. The barn was converted into a theatre by Anthony Adamson. To the south lies the pet cemetery and nearby is the folly, built in 1904 and believed to be the only wooden structure of its kind in Canada. Southwest of the main house are the remnants of what was once a circular swimming pool; there are plans to restore it as a reflecting pool with an adjacent seating area.

A paved pedestrian/bike path winds its way through the woodlot, out of the estate. Follow Ritchey Crescent over the Cooksville Creek Bridge into Lakefront Promenade.

LAKEFRONT PROMENADE PARK

This 42-hectare (103-acre) park, with its 11 kilometres (6.8 miles) of trails, was completed in 1994. Created from lakefill, it consists of three headlands, one named for R.K. McMillan, which is mainly natural areas; A.E. Crookes, where you can enjoy boating and fishing; and Douglas Kennedy, where you will find playgrounds and picnic areas.

The three are linked by a paved path and boardwalk bridge that offer convenient access to abundant picnic and recreational areas. The path is well suited for walkers and runners, as well as for in-line skaters and cyclists.

R.K. McMillan Headland

Only recently have parks been designed and developed to acknowledge the environmental importance of wetlands and natural areas. To this end, an extensive portion of the R.K. McMillan Headland is being allowed to regenerate naturally. The mowing, pruning, and landscaping usually carried out in city parks do not take place and nature is allowed to take its course. The naturalized areas slow run-off into the lake and provides habitat for a variety of wildlife.

A.E. Crookes Headland

For the avid or weekend angler the wide boardwalk provides a popular spot for shore fishing; its new fish-cleaning station is a convenient place to prepare the catch of the day.

If you would rather relax close to the water, watch the boats sailing in and out of the Port Credit Yacht Club from the public marina and launch ramp. The marina has a waterside patio that is another favourite spot for people and boat-watchers.

The marina is open until the early fall and you can enjoy ice cream, a hot dog or cold drink (including beer from the licensed snack bar). There are public phones and washrooms in the building, which also houses the Harbour Master and Peel Police Marine Unit.

Between the A.E. Crookes and Douglas Kennedy headlands is a basin being used as an experiment in wetland regeneration. Native trees, shrubs, cattails, and other wetland plants have been extensively planted along the east shore of the basin; over the years, as these plants mature, they will cleanse water flowing through the basin into Lake Ontario and become a habitat for wildlife.

Douglas Kennedy Headland

This is an especially attractive place for families with small children. There is a spray pad where sensors designed to control water consumption allow the kids to play. The play structure has been built to look like a 20-metre (65-foot) ship, and is named the HMCS Lakefront Promenade; it is guaranteed to delight small pirates. The fact that it is cypress wood, particularly resistant to fire and weather, and that it contains no chemicals, makes it equally appealing to their parents. In-line skaters will also find a haven here. In-line skates, as well as bicycles, are available on a rental basis.

You may notice that the asphalt of the main parking lot is very porous. This is experimental "popcorn" asphalt, designed to absorb more water and prevent the hard-surface run-off that carries salt, pesticides, and other contaminants into the waters of the Great Lakes.

LAKEVIEW GENERATING STATION

Directly beside Lakefront Promenade are four huge concrete stacks, affectionately referred to by some as the "Four Sisters". Towering some 146 metres (480 feet), they are part of the Lakeview Generating Station located at the foot of Hydro Road. This is a coal-burning generating station owned and operated by Ontario Hydro, used to supply electricity during peak consumption periods. Construction of the eight-unit station began in 1958, and was completed ten years later, with the first unit producing power in 1961. The "Sisters" also serve as a navigational aid to pilots, boats, and ships.

The plant produces electricity through a process in which coal is ground into a fine powder and then fed into the furnace. Water circulating through tubes surrounding the furnace is converted into steam at a temperature of 538 degrees Celsius (1,000 degrees Fahrenheit), which rotates a turbine which in turn drives the generator. This mechanical energy is converted into electrical power for distribution through Hydro's high-voltage transmission lines.

Water from Lake Ontario is used to cool the steam after it has done its work so that the cycle can be repeated. As a safeguard for life in nearby waters, the cooling water is returned to the lake at a temperature no more than 11 degrees Celsius (50 degrees Fahrenheit) warmer than it was at the beginning of the process. One benefit created by the slightly warmer water is the presence of a year-round fishing spot on the Port Credit side of the generating station.

As part of its commitment to the environment, Hydro recently overhauled four of the plant's eight units. The remaining four units have been shut down. This has resulted in a reduction of acid gas emissions of up to 50 percent, and virtual elimination of emissions to the lake.

The coal on the east side of the plant is expected to provide enough fuel to meet the plant's needs until 1997. The coal is brought by rail and ship from Pennsylvania and West Virginia. To help reduce the amount of coal dust, the pile is regularly sprayed with a water-based sealant. Public tours of the facility can be arranged by calling 905-274-3461.

After cutting across the north side of the Lakeview Generating Station site and Hydro Road, the trail runs north to Lakeshore Road. If there's a slight wind, you may feel that you're being saluted by the flyers who crossed this same ground at what was Canada's first aerodrome, built in 1915. Here, to the north and east of the Lakeview Station, three hangars and an airfield accommodated the Curtis Aeroplane Company's flight training program in WW I.

LONG BRANCH RIFLE RANGE

Just east of the aerodrome grounds, on lands that are now part of the Lakeview Water Pollution Control Plant, you will find several wooden walls and a large concrete one. Although these appear to be randomly scattered and oddly out of place, they are, in fact, the remains of the Long Branch Rifle Range. The wooden walls served as baffles to deflect sound and absorb ricocheting bullets; the concrete structure, which was the backdrop for targets, still bears the scars of off-line shots.

Built in 1891 by the Ontario Rifle Association for practice and competition, these facilities were later taken over by

STONEHOOKING

In the early days of the province, it seemed a painless trade-off: The sailing ships that were Canada's first transports required ballast, while building foundations and walls needed stone. Answer: Gather the loose rock from beaches and shallow waters and deliver it to shipping and construction companies. Soon there was a thriving fleet along the Lake Ontario shore, their crews using stonehooks. Large forks, tines bent at right angles, they looked as if they had been forged from King Poseidon's best dinner set. These tools hooked and lifted stone from the lake's bottom and, by the 1830s, they were carrying away as much as 43,000 tonnes (47,000 tons) of it annually.

What was unrecognized at the time was the reason the stone was at the lake bottom in the first place: not to keep ships upright or build walls, but as armour for the lake's bottom and shores. Once the stones had been carted off, erosion of the lakeshore accelerated. Farmers watched their shorefront property begin to wear away and, in 1857, successfully urged the legislature to pass what was known as the three-rod law. It prohibited stone-hookers from operating within three rods (15 metres) of the shore, but the law came too late for fish habitat that had been destroyed, and shorelines and farmland that were damaged or lost.

Canada's Militia Department and were the site of annual competitions, with members of the militia competing. By the end of the 1920s, the ranges were also used daily by the Toronto Police Department for target practice.

The last annual rifle competition was held in 1957; soon after, the bungalows in which the militia had once lived were torn down and the guns silenced.

The asphalt path leads to the southwestern end of Marie Curtis Park (which is shared with the City of Etobicoke), revealing beautiful open spaces and a great view across the water of the Toronto skyline to the east.

A collage of wildlife preserve, residential community and public recreation areas

EVANS

Q.E.W.

Etobicoke Creek

BROWNS LINE

KIPLING

ISLINGTON

HIGHWAY 2

LAKE PROMENADE

47th

Marie Curtis Park

Len Ford and Long Branch Park

Col. Samuel Smith Park

Rotary Peace Park

LAKESHORE DR.

Prince of Wales Park

2 KM

Etobicoke

1 LAKESHORE DRIVE
2 SECOND STREET
3 FIRST STREET
4 FIFTH STREET
5 PALACE PIER COURT

TRETCHING FROM Etobicoke Creek east to the Humber River, Etobicoke's waterfront spans almost 11 kilometres (6.8 miles) along the shore of Lake Ontario; it is a collage of wildlife preserve, residential community, and user-friendly public recreation areas.

The land was originally populated by natives who found a fertile hunting ground in the area between the Humber River and River Tobicoke; they named the territory 'Wah-do-be-kaug', an Ojibwa term meaning "the place where the black alders grow". However, early settlers had trouble pronouncing and writing the word, which was rendered as Adobe-Keg, Tobicoak, and Toby Cook. In 1795, Lieutenant-Governor John Graves Simcoe took the matter into his own hands and officially declared the name of the township and its spelling as Etobicoke.

Like many settlements along the Great Lakes, Etobicoke was sparsely populated, with 84 people forming its first European-based community. As news of the land's agricultural gifts spread, more settlers came to make Etobicoke their home. In January 1850, the township held its first municipal election, and by 1871, the region was 2,985 citizens strong. Villages began sprouting up everywhere, including Mimico, Islington, Summerville, and a portion of Weston.

On January 1, 1967, the Village of Long Branch, Town of Mimico, Town of New Toronto, and the Township of Etobicoke merged to form the Borough of Etobicoke. On June 29, 1983, there was a celebration on the steps of City Hall where, at precisely 12:01 a.m., Mayor Dennis C. Flynn became the last mayor of the Borough of Etobicoke and the first mayor of the City of Etobicoke. Today there are more than 300,000 people living in the city.

MARIE CURTIS PARK

The Etobicoke section of the Waterfront Trail begins in the scenic Marie Curtis Park, which takes its name from a beloved reeve of the Village of Long Branch from 1953 to 1962. Sitting at the mouth of Etobicoke Creek, the park's current tranquil and picturesque setting belies its tragic beginnings.

PUBLIC TRANSIT

Local Transit
(416-393-4636)

GO (416-869-3200)
• Long Branch – Lake Shore Blvd. just west of Brown's Line just north of Marie Curtis Park

• Mimico – Royal York Rd. at Judson St. approx. 1 km north of Lake Shore Blvd W.

It was formally created as the result of Hurricane Hazel which, in 1954, struck here, killing seven people and leaving 365 homeless. In the aftermath of Hazel, when perilously high flood waters jeopardized properties, a consortium of local and provincial governments stepped in to provide flood protection by purchasing 164 lots and moving families to higher ground. These land purchases created a large area of public parkland; four years later the Canadian Progress Club (Lakeshore Branch) donated playground facilities, and the Lakeshore Business and Professional Women's Club provided drinking fountains.

Today, the parkland provides year-round recreation for thousands of people and is home to numerous species of wildlife. Twenty-three hectares (56.8 acres) in size, it unfolds into Lake Ontario and offers a playground area, a wading pool, and a baseball diamond. A 100-metre (328-foot) stretch of soft sandy beach, supervised by a Metro Police lifeguard in July and August, borders its south rim. Boaters will find launching ramps and moorings west of the beach. There are also a public telephone, and a concession building with seasonal, wheelchair-accessible washroom and change facilities. There is a snack bar on the grounds that is open from 10:30 a.m. until sunset each day from May 1 to October 31.

You can enter the park from the 42nd Street entrance south of Lake Shore Boulevard and from Lake Shore Boulevard itself, which leads to the main parking area. If travelling on foot or by bike, you can also enter Marie Curtis Park from the Mississauga section of the Waterfront Trail that traverses the woodlot found at the park's southwest corner.

Etobicoke Creek, which runs from the region of the Moraine Eskers north of Markham, essentially cuts the park in two as it rushes to empty directly into Lake Ontario. A two-metre (6.5-foot) wide pedestrian bridge links east and west banks and is accessible to walkers, joggers, bikers, in-line skaters, and people in wheelchairs. To the west is a wildlife habitat owned and managed by the Metropolitan Toronto and Region Conservation Authority (MTRCA). Small birds such as sparrows nest there, and the site is often used as a stopover by other migrating species.

The woodlot is one of the last of the lakeshore's original forests, dating back to the time before European settlement; it provides shelter for saw-whet, long-eared, and great horned owls.

In winter, large groups of Canada geese and gulls inhabit the frozen creek banks, unperturbed by people walking among them, and providing good opportunities to see the creatures up close. Feeding them is discouraged because it diminishes their interest and ability to forage for food in winter, when there are few visitors. (See page 31.)

If you would enjoy a side trip, try the Alderwood Environmentalist's Interpretive Trail: created a few years ago by a group of environmentalists from the nearby Alderwood community, it consists of an asphalt path, three metres (10 feet) wide and stretching 2.4 kilometres (1.5 miles) north alongside Etobicoke Creek. Signs at the parking lot in the south portion of Marie Curtis Park will show you where the Interpretive Trail is or you can find it directly on the east side of the creek. The path travels through 43rd Street Park, under the CP bridge, into a black willow flood plain area, then continues up through a valley alongside the creek and winds its way into Etobicoke Valley Park just south of the QEW, through some of the region's most beautiful wooded landscape.

The Alderwood group received a grant from the Shell Environmental Fund to pay for and build the ten interpretive signs that line the way and explain its features. The forest that thrives here is known as transitional: it hosts a mix of trees and vegetation of two different types, those of the Great Lakes/St. Lawrence and the Carolinian forests. The result is an ecosystem of great diversity, supporting many species of plant and animal life normally found in one or the other type of forest. Migrant birds are known to use it as a resting place before the long journey south; if you go very early in the morning, you may spot deer and fox wandering through.

For more information on the Alderwood trail or the group that brought it into being, contact Metro Parks at 416-392-8186.

In Marie Curtis Park, the Waterfront Trail is a smooth asphalt path, three metres (10 feet) wide and almost a kilometre (0.6 mile) long, stretching through the woods at the park's western edge to the pedestrian bridge on the east bank of Etobicoke Creek.

The Trail exits Marie Curtis Park at its southeast corner, 42nd Street and Lake Promenade, and continues east 3 kilometres (1.8 miles) along Promenade. This wide, winding road with a speed limit of 40 kph (25 mph) travels through a residential community with no sidewalks; while it is possible to travel here by bicycle, on foot or in-line skates, wheelchair passage can be a little difficult. At 36th Street the road dips south past the residential community and is once again aligned with the water.

LONG BRANCH

A half-kilometre (0.3 mile) farther down the road is Long Branch Park, between Long Branch Avenue and 31st Street. The apartments that front the park were built on what was the grounds of the Long Branch Hotel. The area was first established as a resort more than one hundred years ago, in 1884, when Thomas Wilkie and a consortium of investors launched plans to create a community of prestigious Victorian cottages, with a nearby hotel, and named it Long Branch.

Because of its ideal location overlooking the water, Long Branch quickly became a favourite summering place for Toronto's wealthy. However, all that changed in 1916, when Lake Shore Boulevard was paved to accommodate the increasingly popular motor car.

Access was much easier and the local population quickly grew. Many residents elected to stay, and converted summer homes for year-round use.

Some original cottages remain and can be seen between 33rd and 35th streets along Lake Promenade, or you can take a quick side trip to look at those still standing between Lake Promenade and Lake Shore Boulevard. Wandering through the area is like a visit to the pages of a history book: one of the first cottages in the area, built in 1886 and known as Idle Wyld, is at 262 Lake Promenade; it was originally owned by architect Richard Ough.

Otherwise, the area has been transformed: apartment buildings dominate the view to the left of the Trail while, to the right is a portion of illegal lakefill created in the 1950s to hold more apartments; the plan failed when Etobicoke stepped in and expropriated the land, turning it into landscaped park. Benches line the sides and there is a playground in the middle of Long Branch Park.

A gazebo, that airy shelter so favoured by the Victorians, is an ideal place from which to imbibe intoxicating views of an open shoreline. The one in the park was built only in recent years, and is used for summer concerts organized by the Long Branch Historical Society and presented on the first three Sundays in July. Featuring everything from country music to barefoot Hawaiian dancers, the hour-long shows start at 6:30 p.m.; each July, the society also holds a one-day Strawberry Festival. For more information, contact Long Branch Historical Society member, Gloria Wilson, at 416-251-7052.

After you have traversed the Trail in the park, from its entry at Long Branch Avenue to its exit at 31st Street, you may continue along Lake Promenade for about one kilometre (0.6 mile), where you will find the R.C. Clark Filtration plant at 23rd Street. Its landscaped grounds are open to the public.

The Trail follows the driveway into the filtration plant and then moves on to a 3.5-metre (11.5-foot) wide asphalt path from the grounds in front of the plant to Colonel Samuel Smith Park.

COLONEL SAMUEL SMITH PARK

At this point, there are two possible routes Trail users can take: one skirts around the park's northern rim, which follows the natural shoreline. The other hooks south to cross a pedestrian promenade overlooking the boat basin. The northern path is paved, making it suitable for joggers, cyclists, in-line skaters, and people in wheelchairs; while the pedestrian promenade is a combination of asphalt, interlocking stone, and limestone screening areas.

The park is an Eden for nature lovers: in all there are more than 78 hectares (192 acres) of parkland, which includes the grounds of the former Lakeshore Psychiatric Hospital and the newly developed lakefill park.

The Trail along the promenade leads to the lakefill park which includes a wetland complex. The MTRCA has made the

R.C. CLARK
Filtration Plant

Named for Ross Clark, Metro's Commissioner of Works from 1956 to 1979, the plant converts raw water from Lake Ontario into the pure, safe drinking water that is pumped through Metro Toronto to consumers' taps.

The facility was built from 1962 to 1968, at a cost of approximately $21 million, on land that had previously been part of the Lakeshore Psychiatric Hospital. It was a huge project: nine major contractors worked for seven years, moving 322,000 cubic metres (420,000 cubic yards) of earth and rock, pouring 61,000 cubic metres (80,000 cubic yards) of concrete, and mobilizing 8,600 tonnes (8,500 tons) of steel, 385,000 bricks, and 250 major pieces of mechanical, electrical, and chemical equipment for the task.

As water from the lake filters into the plant's intake mouth, located 1,615 metres (1766 yards) from shore under 18 metres (59 feet) of water, screens remove the larger particles of debris, allowing the water to flow through with relative ease. Four large pumps lift the water into mixing chambers, after which the forces of gravity propel it through the rest of the plant.

The water is pre-chlorinated and Alum is added. Alum helps the settling process by forming a jelly-like material that joins to form large particles (known as Floc), which ultimately fall to the bottom and drag most impurities with them. Next, 24 sets of paddles and three mixers gently stir the water to encourage the formation of Floc. As the water passes slowly through three settling basins, the Floc settles to the bottom, carrying impurities with it.

The cleaner water at the top passes through 18 sand filters which remove most of the remaining impurities as well as some bacteria. Chlorine is added to remove the last of any renegade bacteria, and then fluoride is added. It is ammoniated to ensure the water remains pure as it makes its way through the distribution system.

environmental integrity of the park a priority and thus created this pilot project, which includes environmental gardens consisting of silver maples and trees of the Carolinian forest, as well as such ground cover as native grasses, wildflowers and perennials; fish habitats and spawning areas, as well as two snake hibernacula, winter quarters for such harmless snakes as garter and milk, and a sand bar where turtles bask.

In early 1995, The Citizens Concerned about the Future of the Etobicoke Waterfront (CCFEW), a local environmental group, received a grant of from Canada Trust's Friends of the Environment Foundation to help implement a self-guided interpretive trail system. This trail describes the habitat areas within the park, giving users the opportunity to see wildlife in its natural setting.

There are two ecosystem demonstration areas, the larger wetland in the north part of the park and the smaller one on the park's eastern edge, just south of the promenade. Both have areas where trout and bass feed, and where underwater reefs are visible in late summer and early fall, when water levels are lower. Each area has a boardwalk that overlooks the habitat; fishing is allowed during designated seasons.

Colonel Samuel Smith Park also has a small craft harbour with capacity for more than 530 boats; the 20-craft fleet of the Humber College Sailing Centre is located here and offers instructional sailing programs for people at all skill levels. The centre is located just beside the Lakeshore Yacht Club, a private facility with slips for more than two hundred boats.

The Waterfront Trail at the pedestrian promenade turns north at the eastern side of the park to meet up with the northern Trail route. From here, you can see the grounds of the former Lakeshore Psychiatric Hospital.

LAKESHORE PYSCHIATRIC HOSPITAL GROUNDS

Constructed in the late 1880s to ease overcrowding at Toronto's Queen Street Asylum, the hospital was built at a time when patients were thought to benefit more from a cottage-style village environment than from cold, clinical, centralized buildings. It was the first hospital of its type in the province, and was home to many people diagnosed as "incurably insane".

In keeping with the new philosophy, patients lived in cottages arranged around a central administration building. Gardening was a form of occupational therapy that resulted in the landscaped grounds still in evidence around the main building.

Many of the original structures are still standing and, in order to preserve the waterfront heritage buildings, the Ministry of Culture and Communications had the grounds declared provincially significant in 1986. Some of the buildings are being converted for use by nearby Humber College and are being incorporated into its campus.

Sandwiched between the filtration plant and the hospital is Humber College's south campus, located at the northern end of the grounds, on Lake Shore Boulevard. This is the site of the area's largest annual summer event, the Lakeshore Community Festival. Held the second Saturday in June, it features a variety of activities and events for the family, including arts and crafts exhibits, carnival rides, clowns, and face painting, as well as a live band and beer garden. According to legend, the weather must like the Lakeshore Community: since it began in 1973, the festival has never been rained out.

The Waterfront Trail continues east of the hospital grounds, exiting at 13th Street, and follows Lakeshore Drive, which winds through a residential community. There are sidewalks only on its north side; unfortunately these are only intermittent, making travel by foot or in a wheelchair somewhat problematic.

The Trail moves up 11th Street for a short distance, just skirting the edges of Rotary Peace Park (though, in time, it may cut through the park's northwest corner), then continues east once again along Lakeshore Drive.

At 9th Street, the road splits: be sure to stay on Lakshore Drive, which veers to the right, taking you to Cliff Lumsden Park, at 7th Street, which offers stunning unobstructed views of the water and shoreline, as well as an excellent panorama of the Toronto skyline. Once past Lumsden Park, the Trail travels north on 5th Street and then east again on Lakeshore Drive.

BIRDING IN THE CITY

You catch sight of them, often as they dodge behind trees. They lie motionless in the grass, their ears attuned to the slightest noise. Their eyes are hidden behind binoculars; they are always on the lookout. They are examples of a particularly interesting kind of urban dweller – the birdwatcher.

If cities were as barren of wildlife habitat as many people assume, there would, of course, be no birds. And if there were no birds, there would be no birdwatchers. But many of our cities are rich with birds: since the 1980s some 200 species have been recorded on or near Etobicoke's Colonel Samuel Smith Park alone.

Most birders enjoy the experience for its own sake, whether they are regulars or those who bird only once in a while or only at some seasons of the year. It requires equipment no more exotic than binoculars, comfortable shoes or boots, and a decent guidebook! The main requirement is patience; learning to understand bird sounds as well as sights, and delighting in even a quick glimpse of an Arctic snowy owl, or recognizing the still figure in the nearby tree as a hawk seeking prey.

Colonel Samuel Smith Park is an excellent site for urban bird-watching; some species make it their year-round home, others spend some seasons there, and still others use it as a stopover on their migratory flights north and south.

The park is also a popular destination for whimbrels. These large brown birds stop to rest on their long journey to the Arctic, and can most readily be seen in late May, when more than a thousand have been sighted in a single day.

In spring, the park and former Lakeshore Psychiatric Hospital grounds are alive with many colourful songbirds. The warming winds bring thousands of passerines, such as warblers, thrushes, and sparrows, after their night flights across Lake Ontario. Stopping on the north shore, they continue feeding and migrating by day, through the canopies of tall trees and low bushes lining Old North Creek. Among the species of birds that remain in the area to breed are the American robin, northern cardinal, red-winged blackbird, yellow warbler, Baltimore oriole, and several types of swallows.

As spring gives way to summer, double-crested cormorants arrive, their numbers having increased dramatically since DDT and PCBs were banned. Common terns that nest on the Leslie Street Spit (see page 120 for information on the Spit and Tommy Thompson Park) visit in order to dive for fish, occasionally accompanied by the larger Caspian terns that are rare in other parts of Canada but common in and around the Toronto lakefront.

Shorebirds or sandpipers, such as small "peeps" and yellowlegs, begin their migration in mid-July and can be seen feeding in mudflats along the shore until late fall. The mudflat habitats of fine soil and decaying vegetation are home to numerous invertebrates, including fresh-water shrimp and small molluscs. The shorebirds have been designed by nature to eat these creatures; each species has a bill that feeds at a specific depth on the various invertebrates living in the different levels of mud.

In order to keep these birds coming to our shores, the MTRCA has created mudflats in Colonel Samuel Smith Park – a reminder that urbanization has affected wildlife and that communities have to find ways of protecting it.

Along the shoreline and around ponds you can watch for several kinds of herons; the most commonly observed are black-crowned night herons, which are smaller than the great blue heron which can often be spotted in autumn.

Then there are the ever-present (and not always welcome) colonies of gulls, many of which seem to be noisy winged garbage cans, flocking wherever refuse can be used to feed their voracious appetites. But not all of those we see are "seagulls"; they may be any one of the 14 gull species reported in the Toronto area. These range from the very common ring-billed and herring gulls (the latter distinguished by its larger size and the absence of a ring around the bill), to the black-backed gull and, in the winter, to the uncommon glaucous gull.

Large flocks of common loons and mergansers often congregate offshore, diving for fish while the gulls hover watchfully above, hoping for a free meal.

With the arrival of winter, our Lake Ontario shore serves as a migratory route for most northern species of hawks, falcons, and eagles. Rather than crossing the lake's expanse, they follow the updraft air currents, usually in a west-southwest direction, that are generated along the old Lake Iroquois shoreline.

Throughout winter, the park is home to many species of ducks that do not migrate beyond Lake Ontario's open water, such as oldsquaw, common goldeneye, bufflehead, and scoters, which spend their summers in the Arctic and northern prairies but traditionally winter here. They pair and mate before flying north in summer, often to nesting sites they previously occupied. The greatest numbers of these diving ducks can be seen offshore, where they now dine on the zebra mussels that have concentrated on the lake's shale bedrock.

In fact, the relationship between the mussels and the ducks may offer us a prime example of environmental cause and effect. The presence of zebra mussels, a rapidly multiplying species that has invaded the Great Lakes in recent years, could explain why white-winged scoters, which normally spend the winter off the North Atlantic coast feeding on blue mussels, now remain in large numbers. While an estimated ten to twenty thousand winter in Burlington's lakefront area, many can be seen in Etobicoke's.

Dabbling ducks (those that tip up to feed) eat vegetation and are found closer to shore; species include mallards, gadwall, American black ducks, and American wigeon. Mallards and gadwall live here year-round, while the American black duck (numbers of which are rapidly declining) and American wigeon migrate from Ontario's northwest.

From November until the end of winter, look for the magnificent snowy owls on the tundra-like lakefill areas of the park. They tend to feel at home here, where the barren terrain closely resembles their habitat in the far north.

You may also find Arctic species of Canada geese, including the smaller-than-usual Brant and snow geese. As well, there are a few mute swans that nest east of Toronto in summer and move west along the waterfront in winter. (For more information – and a warning – about abundant Canada geese, see page 31.)

This necessarily brief catalogue of birds in and around just one area of the Trail is meant to encourage those who birdwatch and to persuade those who would like to but haven't tried yet. The fact that birding carries no guarantee – today you may see the most ordinary chickadee and tomorrow the most elusive owl – adds to its appeal. Your chances diminish when the park is crowded, especially on sunny days and on weekends; they increase when it is rainy, or foggy, or after a weather front has moved through the area.

Given that cities are filled with interesting and challenging cultural, artistic, and athletic opportunities, why bother birding? A vivid answer is supplied by author Michele Landsberg, an intermittent but enthusiastic participant, who says that:

There is the knowledge that only a few people share this experience of hidden beauty with you, of a secret world. It offers the delight of naming some of the creatures in our universe, of becoming familiar with the natural world that is around us but is mostly ignored.

In the spring and summer, for instance, when warblers, in all their roundness and beauty, go through here, you know they move quickly. But you recognize their song, you hear the rustle in the leaves, you see some perfect little being patterned in perfect colours. It gives you the pleasure of mastering a body of knowledge, of amassing experience. The quietness of bird watching – the need to be mentally alert but physically still, to concentrate on something other than work or daily troubles – this is refreshment; this is pleasure.

Just east of 3rd Street, you come upon the Prince of Wales Park, a 2-hectare (5-acre) community facility. The closer to Toronto, the faster the pace and, before you take the Trail north to busy Lake Shore Boulevard, this is a good place to rest for a moment. If you have your tennis racquet and want to "rest" actively, the park has four tennis courts, as well as playground equipment, an artificial skating rink in winter, a wading pool, change rooms and washrooms (not wheelchair-accessible), and a parking lot for 26 cars.

If you decide to carry on instead, take 1st Street north, which will bring you to Lake Shore Boulevard. You will find the next 3 kilometres (1.8 miles) of the Trail make their way east through an eclectic mix of stores and restaurants. This is a fairly busy area with parking on either side so it may be awkward for cyclists, but they are encouraged to walk their bikes in any event, because there are many interesting places to eat and shop.

As you move east along Lake Shore Boulevard, past Royal York Road, you will notice a number of large homes along the south side, fronting the lake. These are what remain of the former estates that used to line the entire waterfront of the former Town of Mimico. Originally a summer retreat area for some of Toronto's wealthiest families, Mimico evolved into a year-round community around the beginning of the 1900s, when the paving of Lake Shore Boulevard and the advent of the motor car made access to Toronto easy.

Stone walls were erected by the original estate owners to demarcate the boundaries of their lots. Just east of Royal York Road is the stone wall built by the Hayhoe family, successful tea merchants, whose stately French provincial home overlooks the lake. Further along you will see the impressive iron gates that surround the former McGuinness estate at 2603 Lake Shore Boulevard. Reputed to be bootleggers during the prohibition period, the McGuinesses went on to become respectable distillers; the building now serves as the Polish Consulate.

Farther along, past Lake Crescent, you will notice the stone wall of the former Hunter estate, built around 1885 and later sold to Harry Hornell, whose son David won the Victoria Cross in WW II and who was commemorated with the naming of the David Hornell School.

It was after WW II that the culture of Mimico started to change when these luxurious estates were sold to make room for low-rise apartments.

One is Amedeo Garden Court, which extends from Lake Shore Boulevard to the lake, west of Douglas Boulevard. Originally a 2.4-hectare (6-acre) summer estate built by A.B. Ormsby in 1906, the property was purchased by James Franceschini in 1925, who turned it into "Myrtle Villa", Mimico's largest estate at that time.

An Italian immigrant who had arrived as a penniless teenager, Franceschini amassed a fortune in the construction business, building everything from a road between Toronto and Hamilton, to the Dufferin Race Track and minesweepers for the Canadian navy in WW II. He also constructed the famous Toronto landmark hotel, the Royal York.

His stable of thoroughbred horses included white stallions rumoured to be a gift from Benito Mussolini. In 1940, Ottawa detained him on charges that he was involved in fascist activity – accusations that later turned out to be groundless. He left Ontario shortly after his release from detention in 1941 and

went to live in Montreal. However, traces of his life here remain:
the apartment complex includes the James Franceschini mansion,
the Leonard Franceschini house, which he built for his brother,
as well as formal gardens, servants quarters, and a garage that is
now a variety store. In fact, the initials M V (for Myrtle Villa)
can still be found on the wrought-iron gates looking out onto
Lake Shore Boulevard.

Other well known and influential neighbours in the
estates included Theodore Pringle Loblaw, the grocery merchant;
the Horwoods, architects whose designs included Simpson's on
Queen Street; Colonel Harry McGee, a vice-president of Eaton's;
and Louis J. West, founding member and one-time president of the
Toronto Stock Exchange.

As it continues east along Lake Shore Boulevard, the
Trail runs south down a laneway between the Grand Harbour and
Marina Del Rey condominiums. Look carefully for signs on the
right which indicate the turn-off; otherwise you may miss it. The
laneway will lead you directly into Humber Bay Promenade at the
end of the street, where the Trail links up with a wide concrete path
trimmed with ornamental brick binding. Although the Promenade
is not large (less than a hectare [2.4 acres] in size), it does provide a
sanctuary from the busy boulevard.

There is an inviting gazebo at the foot of the grounds,
and a nearby fountain with computer-controlled water levels that
make it summer fun for kids. The sea wall in front of the park
offers free space for daytime moorings, but boats must be gone by
nightfall. At this point, the Waterfront Trail follows the water's
edge and soon makes its way through Humber Bay Park West, the
next landmark.

HUMBER BAY PARK

Created by MTRCA with 5.1 million cubic metres (6.7 million cubic
yards) of lakefill, the Humber Bay Park peninsulas officially opened
in June 1984. Divided into east and west by Mimico Creek, which
runs through its grounds to empty into Lake Ontario, the western
portion has 26 hectares (64.2 acres) of waterfront parkland, and the
east 19 hectares (47 acres).

Humber Bay Park has a winterized washroom that is accessible to people in wheelchairs, as well as drinking taps, two public boat launches, the Humber Bay Park Boating Federation, and a mixture of open space, secluded coves, groves of trees and shrubs, and meadows. There is parking for 407 vehicles.

In Humber Bay Park West, the Trail winds along an asphalt path, crossing a two-way paved road that has a 30-kph (20-mph) speed limit and is fairly quiet but requires some caution. The Trail runs back to Lake Shore Boulevard from here, but you may prefer to spend a few minutes on the pedestrian path that goes south to the Metro Police Marine unit.

Trail users can also take the road that makes its way from Lake Shore Boulevard through the park to a turn-around point at the water; this road runs past the gates of the Mimico Cruising Club and the Etobicoke Yacht Club, down to a scenic lookout along the shore.

If you prefer to stay on the Waterfront Trail, the next section covers approximately 1.2 kilometres (0.7 mile) on Lake Shore Boulevard. It passes Humber Bay Park East, but you can detour into the park, if you wish, to a broad asphalt path that takes you to the middle of the park, where you will find three ponds.

The three ponds are the scene of many activities, including fly casting (which is limited to specialty clubs), and model boating. Jutting out into the water along the eastern side is a wheelchair-accessible pier for trout fishing.

From here the walkway is made of screened limestone and winds throughout the grounds, leading to various scenic look-out points along the water.

Humber Bay Park East, has 228 parking spaces; but, because there is no bridge crossing Mimico Creek, the only way to reach the eastern side is by Lake Shore Boulevard.

Sunbathers will enjoy the large, flat rocks provided by the armourstone. The beaches here have excellent skipping stones and beachcombers are often seen exploring the shores for "treasures".

THE MOTEL STRIP

The Trail continues east on Lakeshore Boulevard, passing the Motel Strip in an area once known as Humber Bay Village, established during the mid-1800s when a number of hotels were built along the water. While the Motel Strip's glory days have passed, this section of the Etobicoke Waterfront Trail has its own charms and historical significance. Among the landmarks were the Royal Oak Hotel, owned and operated by Scotsman Octavius L. Hicks, John Duck's Wimbledon House, which opened for business in 1872, and a hotel operated by the long-distance runner Charles Nurse.

Extensive redevelopment of this area is planned, consisting of residential, commercial, and recreational facilities, including a shoreline park.

The Trail dips at Palace Pier Court Road on the right, just before the Palace Pier condominium complex, and after The Playing Field restaurant.

The Palace Pier condominiums sit on the original site of what was once the Sunnyside Palace Pier project, first proposed in the mid-1920s. To cost $1.25 million, it called for an auditorium, a pier to rival the Steel Pier in Atlantic City, a dance hall, and a host of other amenities. Construction began in 1928 and went on for four years, but the market crash of 1929 and the Depression that followed put a halt to construction in 1932, when only 90 metres (300 feet) of the pier, which was intended to be 550 metres (1,800 feet) long, and the auditorium had been built.

The site finally opened in 1941 as the Strathcona Roller Rink and briefly became the Queensway Ball Room in 1943 before reverting back to the roller rink operation. In the 1940s and '50s, it was a popular place to catch the Big Bands of the era – Les Brown, the Dorsey Brothers, Duke Ellington, among others – but that all ended in 1963, when the building was gutted by fire.

At the southern end of Palace Pier Court is Palace Pier Park. Here the Trail splits; the concrete path is for pedestrians and the asphalt for cyclists. Both lead to the newly constructed Humber River cycling and pedestrian bridge that takes Trail users over the Humber River and across the boundary of the cities of Etobicoke and Toronto. ≋

Canada's *largest municipality – superb art galleries, ballet, opera, baseball, theatre, restaurants, and shopping.*

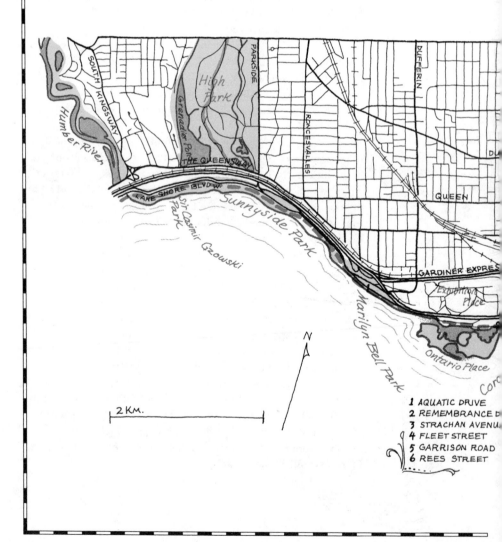

SOUTH KINGSWAY

Humber River

PARKSIDE

High Park

DUFFERIN

Grenadier Pond

RONCESVALLES

THE QUEENSWAY

LAKE SHORE BLVD. W.

Sir Casimir Gzowski Park

Sunnyside Park

QUEEN

GARDINER EXPRES

Exhibition Place

Marilyn Bell Park

N

Ontario Place

Core

2 KM.

1 AQUATIC DRIVE
2 REMEMBRANCE D
3 STRACHAN AVENU
4 FLEET STREET
5 GARRISON ROAD
6 REES STREET

Toronto

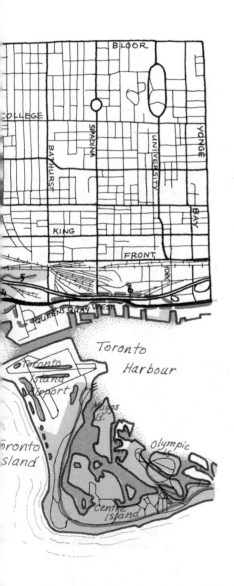

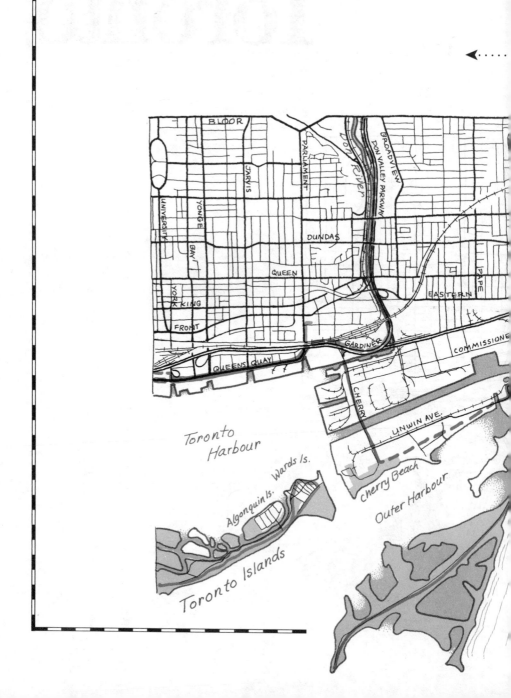

Toronto

VICTORIA PARK

Glen
Stewart
Park

COXWELL

KINGSTON ROAD

WOODBINE

QUEEN

LAKE SHORE BLVD.

Balmy
Beach

Kew Beach

Woodbine Beach

Ashbridges Bay
Park

Thompson Park

N

2 KM.

ERE IS THE 20th-century city, Canada's largest municipality, with all of the potential (and all of the problems) of urban life at its most concentrated: superb art galleries, ballet, opera, baseball, theatre, restaurants, and shopping.

The Toronto segment of the Trail begins with a 3-metre (10-foot) wide interlocking brick pathway in the final section of the Etobicoke Waterfront Trail, which leads to a magnificent new pedestrian bridge straddling the Humber River. The bridge is only the latest in a long series of highway, railway, and foot spans constructed over this historic waterway. The first was opened in 1809; by 1826, it was being used by the newly established York-Niagara stagecoaches.

The new steel arch suspension bridge, which soars some five storeys high, has become an instant landmark on the Lake Ontario shoreline, one that can be seen far away. Built to accommodate people in wheelchairs, as well as walkers, cyclists, and in-line skaters, the 6.5-metre (20-foot) wide structure was constructed on the east side of the Humber River and, with the help of a barge, moved into position in the fall of 1994. Once it was officially opened a few months later, it became possible for Trail users to get to the western beaches area without taking an on-road detour.

Not only are visitors struck by the beauty of the bridge, they are moved by the native Thunderbird motif that has been incorporated into its design. North of this bridge are highway spans, the oldest of which was built more than 50 years ago; in time, they will be replaced.

The Humber River was originally called the St. Jean River. It was named after pioneer fur trader Jean Baptiste Rousseau, whose house stood on the east bank of the river near its outlet into Lake Ontario. The St. Jean was also called the Toronto River because it formed part of the Toronto Carrying Place or Toronto Passage, an ancient "highway" used by native people travelling between the north country and Lake Ontario.

PUBLIC TRANSIT

Local Transit
(416-393-4636)

VIA Train
(416-366-8411)

GO (416-869-3200)
• CNE (seasonal only)

•Union – Bay St. and
Front St. just north of
Queen Quay

Danforth – Danforth
Ave. at Main St. I km
north of Kingston Rd.

HUMBER RIVER LOOP

Located a few kilometres upriver, on the site of the present Baby Point neighbourhood, was Teiaiagon, a large village established 300 years ago by the Senecas, an Iroquoian tribe. Among the explanations of the origin of the word Toronto is that it was derived from the name of that village.

The Humber River bridge marks the eastern terminus of the Queen Elizabeth Way, Canada's first four-lane highway. The first section, between Toronto and Burlington, was begun in the early-1930s and originally called the Middle Road; the last, comprising four lanes of pavement to Fort Erie, was completed only in 1956.

LION MONUMENT

Following the brick path east, the Trail passes the famous Lion Monument. However majestic, at first glance it appears to be somewhat out of place. The monument was designed by William Lyon Somerville and Frances Loring, and executed by her in Indiana limestone. Moved to Gzowski Park in 1974 when the highway was widened, it was decidedly less noticeable in its new location. However, its grand statement of welcome to Toronto has been restored, thanks to the nearby, handsome pedestrian and bicycle bridge recently opened across the Humber River.

Loring's Lion Monument was commissioned to honour the 1939 visit of King George VI and Queen Elizabeth (now Queen Mother) and the creation of the Queen Elizabeth Way.

As the Trail passes the monument, it bends to the north and connects with the Martin Goodman Trail.

MARTIN GOODMAN TRAIL

Named in memory of a young president of the *Toronto Star* who died in 1981 at age 46, the Martin Goodman Trail stretches from the City of Toronto's western border to its eastern end. In all, the Goodman Trail comprises 20 kilometres (12.5 miles) of 3-metre (10-foot) wide paved surface suitable for cyclists, pedestrians, in-line skaters, and people in wheelchairs.

THE SCULPTORS AND THE LION

While the parkette at Mount Pleasant and St. Clair is far from the Waterfront Trail, there is a connection between the two that makes it worth a visit when you're in north-central Toronto. The greenspace honours two women whose monumental sculptures are among Ontario's handsomest. Frances Loring and Florence Wyle, (referred to, affectionately, as "the Girls") worked in the popular beaux-arts style from the end of one world war until well after the second. The life-size heads in the tiny sanctuary – Wyle gravely looking west while Loring seems to be considering the traffic hurrying up Mount Pleasant Road – date from 1914; Wyle's is by Loring and Loring's is by Wyle.

In the City of Toronto, the Waterfront Trail follows this route, crossing the incredible diversity of areas and amenities along the Toronto waterfront. The first section passes the northern edge of Sir Casimir Gzowski Park.

SIR CASIMIR GZOWSKI PARK

A renowned engineer and businessman (from St. Petersburg by way of the United States), Gzowksi eventually built the Grand Trunk Railway between Toronto and Sarnia in the 1850s; he was later knighted by Queen Victoria for his services to Canada.

The park named after him has a children's play area with delightful climbing and swinging apparatuses, as well as a wading pool, ample room for flying a kite, and in-season, wheelchair-accessible washrooms, and drinking fountains.

GOVERNMENT BREAKWATER

You will notice the breakwall situated just offshore, which appears to go on forever to the east. In the early years of this century, the federally funded "Government Breakwater" was considered an outstanding triumph of engineering.

Built to protect the newly created western beaches, it was started shortly before the outbreak of WW I but, because of a lack of workers and materials, construction soon slowed. In fact, more than a decade would pass before the impressive structure – 5.5

kilometres (3.4 miles) in length – was completed. Stretching from
the mouth of the Humber River to the Western Gap, it is made of
30-centimetre (12-inch) squared timbers sunk to bedrock, hundreds
of tonnes of rock ballast, and dozens of precast concrete blocks.

As the Trail continues east, you will see the small,
architecturally distinctive gasoline station at the northwest corner
of Windermere and Lake Shore Boulevard, built in 1937 by the
Detroit-based Hercules Oil Company, later renamed Joy Oil. At one
time, there were 14 Joy stations around Toronto. The brand is long
gone and, with it, almost all the examples of chateau-style gas
stations for which it was best known.

High Park

A side trip into the city's largest park, which lies north of the
Waterfront Trail and can be reached by going north on Colborne
Lodge Drive, is well worth your time and trouble. It involves a loop
of almost 4 kilometres (2.5 miles), much of which is on road and
contains several very hilly areas that may be too difficult for many
cyclists or in-line skaters. However, it is a quintessential part of
Toronto and should not be missed.

While it now covers almost 162 hectares (400 acres),
the park began with 67 hectares (165 acres) of land owned by
pioneer architect and surveyor John George Howard (remembered
in Howard Park Avenue).

In the 1870s, Howard offered his property to the
City on condition that it pay a yearly annuity of $1,200 as long as
he and his wife lived. Although several aldermen felt the property
was too far away to be of any value, the more foresighted majority
approved Howard's offer. The arrangement ultimately cost the
City $20,000.

On summer weekends, the park is closed to vehicles,
in order to alleviate traffic problems that until recent years plagued
the park. In addition to the beautiful gardens, the park contains
public tennis courts, a swimming pool, significant wildlife habitats, a
small zoo, and the Grenadier Restaurant. There is also an outdoor
theatre where stage productions of Shakespeare are performed as
part of the Theatre in the Park series.

SUNNYSIDE

After completing the loop, back on the Trail heading east, you approach a once much-loved section of the waterfront – Sunnyside. As part of its plan for the western approaches to the city, the Toronto Harbour Commissioners (THC) had the waters of the old Humber Bay filled, and the reclaimed land groomed and manicured. An amusement park, complete with roller coaster, merry-go-rounds, hot-dog stands and dance pavilions, was added in 1922. There was a boardwalk where families strolled and looked across the water. Could that be the city of Buffalo in the distance? (Probably not, just nearby Toronto Island.) On especially hot summer nights in this innocent (and un-air-conditioned) time, entire families slept in Sunnyside Park. But in years when infantile paralysis (polio) seemed particularly threatening, the beaches, swimming pool, and grass were deserted by August, when spread of the disease was most common.

All that remains of the original buildings are the Bathing Pavilion, an elaborate changing room erected in 1922, which was recently restored in part, and the huge Sunnyside swimming pool. At the time it opened in 1925, this was the world's largest outdoor swimming facility, built to accommodate bathers who found the lake too cold. It was later renamed the Sunnyside-Gus Ryder Pool in honour of the late Gus Ryder, a famous Canadian swimming coach. (For more about Ryder, see the description of Marilyn Bell Park on page 103.)

Sunnyside Park contains a children's playground set amidst a grove of large willow trees. The dinosaur-themed play area features a wading pool; nearby are wheelchair-accessible washrooms and drinking fountains. A fast-food restaurant is open during the summer months and, as with other parks in the western beach area, this one has a large parking lot.

BUDAPEST PARK

The next greenspace on this continuous stretch of beach is Budapest Park, established by the City of Toronto on June 22, 1966, to commemorate the tenth anniversary of the Hungarian

Revolution. There are washroom facilities, ample parking, drinking fountains, and a playground for the kids.

A little farther east stands the Palais Royale, which opened in 1922 as Dean's Boat House and became *the* place for dancing, especially in the Big Band Era of the 1940s.

This is one of the most popular sections of the Martin Goodman/Waterfront Trail. A straight, continuous stretch with access to an abundance of recreational amenities and historic sites, it also offers excellent views of the lake and skyline.

It parallels one of the most historically significant roadways in the development of Toronto, Lake Shore Boulevard. The original plans for what was initially called Boulevard Drive, which were drawn up in the early part of the century by the newly established Board of Toronto Harbour Commissioners, called for a majestic thoroughfare that would sweep vehicles southeast over the Toronto Island chain and, in time, encircle the entire city. Building began in 1919 and, between then and 1925, the road was finished as far as the waterfront immediately south of the grounds of the Canadian National Exhibition.

The boulevard inched eastward and, in keeping with the THC's scheme, new wharves and slips were constructed, with the portion from Bathurst Street east known initially as Fleet Street. (In 1959, the name of the thoroughfare was consolidated as Lake Shore Boulevard East and West.)

On the lakefront, you will find the Toronto Sailing and Canoe Club. Originally known as the Toronto Canoe Club (TCC), when it was begun in 1880, it was said to be the world's largest such club in the early 1920s.

It stands next to the famed Argonaut Rowing Club, which was established in 1872.

MARILYN BELL PARK

Next to the rowing club is Marilyn Bell Park, which harks back to an athletic feat that excited Canadians, well before the creation of the hype and self-promotion of many sports today. In 1954, an American woman, Florence Chadwick, was paid to swim across

Lake Ontario, a feat that had been tried several times although
never successfully. But swimming coach Gus Ryder, who had urged
the sponsors to support Marilyn Bell, a 16-year-old schoolgirl
protégé of his, decided to go ahead even when his pleas fell on deaf
ears. (Obviously, no mere kid would be able to conquer the lake;
that was a job for an experienced pro!)

Undaunted, Bell, Ryder, and their team set off from
Youngstown, New York. After 20 hours and 57 minutes, at 11:07
p.m. on September 8, 1954, the teenager touched the breakwater
in front of the Boulevard Club. Chadwick had long since been
pulled from the chilly waters with their plentiful populations of
lamprey eels.

At that moment, Marilyn Bell was transformed into
"Canada's sweetheart", and so she remained when she swam the
English Channel in 1955 and the treacherous Juan de Fuca Straits
in 1956. In 1988, Aquatic Park was renamed in her honour.

EXHIBITION PLACE

On the north side of Lake Shore Boulevard stands Exhibition Place,
site of Toronto's celebrated Canadian National Exhibition (CNE),
as well as of numerous public events and trade shows. Although the
Trail does not enter the grounds of Exhibition Place, they are certainly worth a side trip.

A tour of the exhibition site enables you to see several
particularly handsome old buildings. A comprehensive map of the
grounds, prepared by the CNE's Archives, is available from the
receptionist in the Administration Office on the west side of the
Queen Elizabeth Building or can be obtained by mail from the CNE
Archives, Exhibition Place, Toronto M6K 3C3. While the best way to
see the interiors is during the annual fair, you will get a better view
of exteriors at other times of the year when foliage does not hide
some of the magnificent architectural detail.

The famous Princes' (often, mistakenly, referred to as
Princess) Gates are at the east end of the grounds. They were built
in 1927, as part of the celebrations of the Gold Jubilee of Canada's
nationhood, and known as the Confederation Gates. The name was
changed in honour of Edward, the Prince of Wales (later and for

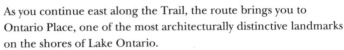

only a brief time King Edward VIII), and his brother Prince George, who dedicated the structure during a visit in August 1927. Atop the arch is the "Goddess of Winged Victory", sculpted by Charles McKechnie. Surrounding this beautiful figure are nine columns, representing the nine original provinces of Confederation. Just inside the gates is the site of the new trade centre.

ONTARIO PLACE

As you continue east along the Trail, the route brings you to Ontario Place, one of the most architecturally distinctive landmarks on the shores of Lake Ontario.

Ontario Place was opened in 1971 by Ontario Premier, John P. Robarts as a showplace for the province. Since its opening, it has become an internationally acclaimed cultural, leisure, and entertainment parkland complex and one of the top tourist attractions in North America with an average attendance of approximately 2 million visitors annually.

ONTARIO PLACE ATTRACTIONS

Designed to highlight excellence in leisure and entertainment, Ontario Place is home to Cinesphere, the first permanent Imax film theatre in the world. Other highlights include the new Molson Amphitheatre, a 16,000-seat outdoor concert venue, Atlantis, a year-round restaurant and entertainment complex, Sea Trek, a thrilling cabin simulator ride, the award-winning Children's Village, a 3-D theatre, the LEGO Creative Play Centre, Nintendo Power Pod, and a waterplay area.

Situated on a 38-hectare (96-acre) site, Ontario Place comprises three islands of reclaimed land, most of it clean fill excavated during construction of the TTC's Bloor-Danforth subway.

Located at the east end of Ontario Place is the HMCS Haida Naval Museum, a Tribal-class destroyer that served during the Korean War and Second World War. She was commissioned in 1943 and retired 20 years later. After being moored at the York Street slip, HMCS Haida was relocated to Ontario Place just before the facility opened in 1971.

CORONATION PARK

Just east of Ontario Place there is a Lancaster Bomber, like hundreds of the Canadian-built planes flown by Canadian air crews during WW II. This particular aircraft, FM-104, came off the assembly line at the Victory Aircraft plant in Malton in 1945 and, although it did not see action in war, was part of the search-and-rescue service until it was retired in 1964.

Coronation Park was officially dedicated in May 1937, on the day that King George VI was crowned at Westminster Abbey.

At this site, one english oak and 149 other trees were planted in honour of the 150 Canadian Expeditionary Force units who participated in WW I. During the royal couple's Toronto visit in May 1939, an additional 123 trees were planted, one for each of the city's public and separate schools. There is a new memorial – a circular amphitheatre around a large medallion inscribed with the word "Peace" in fifty languages – in the park, south of the Princes' Gates. Designed by artist John McEwen, it is a tribute to the "contribution made by all Canadians during World War II".

History buffs will be interested in the commemorative plaque, located in the park, which details the second invasion of the town of York, which was carried out by American troops on July 31, 1813.

The park has ample parking, which can be reached from Lake Shore Road, public washrooms that are open year-round, and three baseball diamonds.

Side Trip
FORT YORK

Now you can step out of the 20th century by visiting Fort York. To get there, head north on Strachan Avenue to Fleet Street, turn right, then make an immediate left through the gate. The road up the hill leads right to the entrance of the fort.

As the entrance road reaches the top of the hill and bends right, look to your left; there you will see a stone wall marking the Garrison Cemetery, holy ground that is the final resting place of several hundred men attached to the numerous military units that have been stationed in Toronto over the years. The first interments date from the 1830s; the most recent was in 1927.

Known officially as the Garrison at York, the fort was established in 1793 by John Graves Simcoe as a means of protecting the small community that had developed around the shipyard located at the harbour's east end. At a time when elements in the new nation to the south were becoming increasingly war-minded, the yard was producing the vessels needed to protect the colony from possible invasion.

The story of the fort, which was occupied by American invaders in April 1813, and its painstaking restoration, which was part of Toronto's centennial celebrations in 1934, are detailed in displays in several of the fort's structures. (And you can read about the many well-meant schemes that have endangered the fort over the years – everything from its use as housing to a scheme that would have plunked it in the middle of a superhighway cut-off.)

On holidays there are re-enactments of battles of the fort's early days (on the most special occasions, John Graves Simcoe and his remarkable wife, Elizabeth, have been known to drop by).

To return to the 20th century, retrace your steps to the entrance of Coronation Park and onto the Waterfront Trail. ■

As the Trail exits Coronation Park, it passes by the Naval Reserve Unit HMCS York, established in 1923 as the Toronto Half-Company. In 1941 the unit was renamed HMCS York (in honour of the Royal Navy's HMS *York*, which had sunk in the Mediterranean earlier that year).

To the east is the handsome Tip Top Tailors building opened in 1929. During the hectic years of WW II, Tip Top Tailors, which had been established in 1909, manufactured hundreds of thousands of military uniforms for Canadian personnel.

Watch for signs that direct you down the path along the western side of the Tip Top building and east across its south side; this path brings you to Stadium Road.

The name of Stadium Road reminds us that Maple Leaf Stadium once stood on the south side of Lake Shore Boulevard. At the time, the boulevard was called Fleet Street, which gave rise to the ballpark's nickname "Fleet Street Flats". From 1926 until the team's demise in 1967, the stadium was the home of the Toronto Maple Leafs baseball team of the International League. The following year, it was demolished.

Crossing Stadium Road, the Trail is now on Queen's Quay West, which will bring you to Little Norway Park, located just west of Bathurst Street.

LITTLE NORWAY PARK

This park was named in recognition of the Norwegian aviators and aircrew who lived in this area while training at Toronto Island Airport during the early days of WW II. Following the war, the buildings were used as emergency housing. Today, all that remains of the original site is the base of a flagpole that now stands near the commemorative plaque and a boulder brought here from Lista in Norway.

Located beyond the tiny main entrance is an extensive playground area that will no doubt delight kids. It includes an assortment of unique climbing and swinging structures, a slide in the shape of a lion, a wading pool, even a small maze. Facilities include seasonal washrooms and several water fountains.

At the northeast corner of Bathurst and Lake Shore is the former Loblaw's warehouse. Now, thanks to the company's generous support, the Daily Bread Food Bank (which has the sad distinction of being the largest such operation in North America) occupies part of the building.

Across the street, on the southeast corner, stands the former Crosse and Blackwell Building, with its distinctive glass crown and the C&B logo over the door. Built in 1927, it became Loblaw's head office in 1949 and is now occupied by CFMT, Toronto's multilingual television station.

A side trip to the foot of Bathurst Street leads to the point where people take either the Maple City or Windmill Point ferries across the 122-metre (400-foot) Western Gap, one of the shortest boat trips in the world, to Toronto Island Airport.

On the mainland side, at the east end of the gap, are the now-abandoned office buildings and elevators of Canada Malting. The company, established in 1900, moved here in 1928. Barley and other ingredients were converted into malt here for various breweries and distilleries and for a variety of food processors and pharmaceutical manufacturers. At present, the future of the complex, including its massive elevators, is uncertain.

At the intersection of Queen's Quay West and Bathurst Street, the Trail splits in two; cyclists cross to the north side and follow the asphalt path that travels under the Gardiner Expressway, while pedestrians travel along the sidewalks on either side of Queen's Quay West.

HARBOURFRONT

We come now to one of the most interesting, and most discussed, areas on the Toronto waterfront: Harbourfront. Sitting on some 40 hectares (100 acres) of reclaimed land, it was created by the federal government in 1972, and has been an exciting year-round venue for the performing and visual arts, educational programs, recreational activities, community festivals, and special events. Due to recent public funding cuts, Harbourfront's future operations are under review.

Bracketed by Stadium Road on the west and York Street on the east, Harbourfront is divided into distinct areas, some set aside for recreational and public uses and some for condos and office towers. Note the spectacular King's Landing condominium designed by Arthur Erickson; it stands on the north side of Queen's Quay, west of Spadina Avenue, on the site of a busy shipbuilding factory where 56 minesweepers were produced for the Royal Canadian and Royal navies during WW II. The Metro Toronto Police Marine Unit is at the foot of Rees Street; the historic Pier 4 complex of shops and restaurants is east of Rees Street. (In 1930, the pier was constructed as a simple storage shed in just 76 days, as a Depression make-work project.)

Antique Market

On the north side of Queen's Quay is Canada's largest permanent antique market. This 12,000-square-metre (40,000-square-foot) bazaar is open Tuesday to Sunday, year-round, as well as on holiday Mondays during the summer. The market features approximately one hundred dealers from across Canada, who offer everything from toys to jewelry to furniture. There is also a café, and ample public parking in the area.

Connecting York Quay and, farther west, John Quay, is the attractive Amsterdam Bridge, named in honour of Canada's twin city in the Netherlands.

Side Trip
CN TOWER, SKYDOME AND THE ENTERTAINMENT DISTRICT

Directly behind the Antique Market are two of Canada's most famous landmarks: the CN Tower and the SkyDome. For a side trip to these impressive facilities head north on Rees Street, which is just east of the Antique Market. You can cross the multi-lane, very busy Lake Shore Boulevard at the traffic lights.

The SkyDome is the world's first and largest multi-purpose stadium with a fully retractable roof, which can be opened or closed in 20 minutes. Officially opened in June 1989, it is the home of the Toronto Blue Jays baseball team, which won the World Series championship in 1992 and 1993, and the Toronto Argonauts of the Canadian Football League.

Towering over the SkyDome is the CN Tower; at 553 metres (1,815 feet), it is the world's tallest free-standing structure. In addition to being the best place to survey the city, the CN Tower was designed as a communications tower for TV, radio, and cell phones. Construction began in the fall of 1972 and the tower opened only three and a half years later, in June 1976.

Some of the attractions include the world's highest revolving restaurant, mini golf, and the Motion Simulator Theatre, which combines 70 mm surround-sound with full-motion flight simulation.

Perhaps the best way to experience the height is to visit the outdoor observation deck, where you can enjoy the 360-degree view. There is also a glass floor that allows you to look straight down to the ground from a height of 342 metres (1,122 feet).

To the north of the CN Tower lies Toronto's entertainment district where you can enjoy world-class theatre, concert halls, jazz clubs, restaurants, galleries, and shops. The district stretches south from Queen Street West to Lake Shore Boulevard, from Spadina to York Street. A walkabout reveals a wealth of architecture and public sculptures. You can get information about Toronto's entertainment district at Metro Hall, 55 John Street, 10th floor, phone 416-397-0815.

Just south of the SkyDome is Metro Toronto's John Street Water Pumping Station. This modern facility has been supplying Torontonians with more than 900 million litres (198 million gallons) of water daily since 1988. It replaced a station that was built, in the 1870s on what is now the SkyDome site. ∎

Railway Heritage

The Waterfront Trail provides many fascinating glimpses of Toronto's railway heritage. CPR's John Street Roundhouse, located south and east of the CN Tower, is particularly important because it is one of the last existing structures of its type in Canada. (The CN Roundhouse, just east of Spadina Avenue, was demolished when the SkyDome was built.)

Erected in 1929 (and enlarged in 1932), the facility served both steam and diesel locomotives until it was closed in 1986. As part of the expansion of the Metro Toronto Convention Centre, a portion of which will be built under the old structure, the Roundhouse will be partially restored and turned into a museum. The surrounding area will become a park, which will sit over the expanded Metro Convention Centre. Both the museum and park will be accessible from the Waterfront Trail.

Queen's Quay Terminal

At the foot of York Street is the imposing Queen's Quay Terminal, built in 1926-27. When Harbourfront came into being in the '70s, its board of directors spent months arguing about the structure and about the area in general. Some people wanted the terminal destroyed, others thought the space under the elevated section of the Gardiner Expressway should be filled with warehouses that would hold government records. Saner heads prevailed and the old building was renovated at a cost of several million dollars, to accommodate a complex of shops, condominiums, eateries, and offices, including those of the Waterfront Regeneration Trust.

Here you will also find the oldest building on the central waterfront – Pier 6. Erected much farther inland in 1907 as the Toronto Ferry Company's waiting room, it was moved several times as lake was filled in and the shoreline pushed farther into the bay. Today, the little building serves as an information centre for the THC and restaurant.

Because of its extensive amenities, wonderful shopping, and proximity to public transit, this area is an excellent starting point for Trail explorers. You can rent equipment (in-line skates, bicycles, paddle boats, canoes) from local vendors and tour either the western or eastern part of the Trail, or you may choose to board a ferry and enjoy the day on the Toronto Islands.

If you are on foot, you can walk from Queen's Quay Terminal to the ferry docks along the water's edge by following a new path down the east side of the condominiums at the foot of York Street. The round concrete sphere you see near the water is actually a sun dial; from this point follow the path east to the ferry terminal at the foot of Bay Street.

Those travelling the Trail by bicycle under the elevated Gardiner Expressway will pass two buildings of special note: the Toronto Harbour Commissioners Building and the former Post Office Building. While they can be glimpsed from Queen's Quay, much of the view is obstructed.

Toronto Harbour Commissioners Building

On the north side of Harbour Street stands the stately Toronto Harbour Commissioners Building, built at the water's edge as its headquarters. The body had been established in 1911 to develop and implement plans for improving and modernizing the Port of Toronto. Finished in 1918 at a cost of $245,000, the building was sited "to demonstrate the Harbour Commissioners' faith in the future of Toronto's waterfront". As the result of its own landfill and development policies, however, the THC's home is now cut off from the waterfront it was meant to celebrate by several hundred metres of transportation corridors, buildings, and parking lots.

Gardiner Expressway

The object blocking these and other sites from view is the Gardiner Expressway, named in honour of Metro Toronto's first chairman, Frederick Gardiner. Construction began in 1958 and was finished in 1964; once heralded as a triumph, in recent years this elevated road has been regarded as a barrier to the Toronto lakefront. There have been many discussions and countless plans have been suggested for hiding (perhaps burying) or removing the expressway without adding to existing traffic problems. If nothing else, the Gardiner stands as a prime example of how attitudes towards the accessibility and public use of Lake Ontario are shifting.

Side Trip
TORONTO ISLANDS

If you've never had the opportunity to do so, this is the perfect time to visit the Toronto Islands, a hook-shaped chain of more than a dozen islands, large and small.

Start at the foot of Bay Street and head for the ferry docks. As the boat leaves, imagine this same voyage in the 19th century. When the service first began to operate, in 1833, vessels were powered by two horses that walked on treadmills connected to a pair of sidepaddles by a set of gears.

While you're at the docks, pickup the schedules and maps, which have detailed descriptions of the islands' many events and attractions. For example, on sultry summer nights, you can circumnavigate the islands on chartered boats.

The islands were created over thousands of years, as eroded sand and gravel from the nearby Scarborough Bluffs were carried by the currents of the lake and deposited around the mouth of the Don River. Over time, the winds helped to shape the built-up sand ridge into a peninsula some 8 kilometres (5 miles) long. It began to separate from the mainland in 1852, when waves caused by a fierce storm began to break the sandy arm; in 1858 another gale struck and this time left in its wake a 150-metre (500-foot) gap. Within two years the gap had widened to about 1.2 kilometres (0.8 mile), creating a natural entrance into Toronto Harbour.

At the western tip of Hanlan's Point, named for rower Edward ("Ned") Hanlan, who was Canada's first internationally acclaimed athlete, you will find Toronto Island Airport (more formally, Port George VI Airport). When it was built, in concert with the construction of an airport in (then far-away) Malton, the plan was to use the Island Airport for passengers, Malton for cargo. But the Malton facility grew and, now named Pearson Airport, is Canada's busiest air traffic hub.

The Toronto Islands offer everything from beaches, carnival rides, tennis courts, and a wading pool, to formal gardens, wildlife areas, pedestrian and cycling trails, the charming homes and gardens of residential communities on Algonquin and Wards Island, as well as a public marina. A perfect place for a picnic, the islands also have snack bars and two licensed restaurants.

Centre Island, with its abundant recreational amenities, is the main island destination. For families with children, the Centreville facility is always popular, with its carnival atmosphere and rides.

The Gibraltar Point Lighthouse, on Centre Island, is well worth a walk or bike ride. Built in 1809, but no longer in operation, this is the oldest lighthouse on the Great Lakes. It is said to come complete with its own ghost, that of J.P. Rademuller. The first keeper of the lighthouse, he was reportedly murdered by drunken soldiers and now haunts the tower, seeking revenge. ■

ANNUAL CARIBANA FESTIVAL

Part of the annual Caribana festival, is held on the waterfront of the Toronto Islands. At the end of July, and culminating in a parade and street party on the long first weekend in August, Toronto becomes a northern extension of the

Caribbean islands. Dancers wearing costumes made equally of imagination and spangles would surely astonish the good burghers of yesteryear. The music, the food (and, very frequently, a co-operative weather system) are hot. Small wonder that the city welcomes thousands of visitors, most of them from the islands and the northern United States. By the time the steel drums have fallen silent and the elaborate raiments have been put away, the events have poured millions of dollars and hours of fun into the Metro area. For more information, call the Toronto Tourist and Convention Information Line at 416-203-2500.

On the trip back to the mainland, you will notice Toronto Fire Department Station 35, which is adjacent to the docks and is equipped with a fireboat, the *William Lyon Mackenzie*; named for Toronto's first mayor, a fiery Scot and revolutionary, it was launched in 1964.

If you would like more information about the islands or departure times and fares for the ferries, contact the Island Ferry Division at 416-392-8193. ∎

Back on the mainland, you reach Yonge Street, said to be one of the longest roads in the world (its northern terminus is near Thunder Bay, nearly 1,900 kilometres (1,180 miles) away. It was named to honour Sir George Yonge, King George III's Secretary of State for War from 1782 to 1794. While it is sometimes jokingly referred to as "Yon-jee", the correct pronunciation is "Young".

Beginning at Yonge Street, the Trail follows an on-road paved path along the north and south sides of Queen's Quay. As you travel east you will notice that the recreational amenities, lakeside condominiums, and retail shops have disappeared; this section of Toronto's waterfront is primarily industrial.

Here you will find Redpath Sugars, named after John Redpath, who established Canada's first successful sugar refinery, in Montreal, in 1854. A century later, the company was the first industrial concern to locate on the City of Toronto waterfront as a direct result of the opening of the St. Lawrence Seaway. It has remained committed to the waterfront and continues to receive raw sugar by ship and to convert it into granulated and liquid forms before packaging and distributing products to customers in Canada and the United States. There is a fascinating, on-site museum that is well worth a visit. Open Monday to Friday from 10 a.m. to noon and 1 to 3 p.m. For more information, call Redpath at 416-366-3561.

TORONTO EAST

Given the anticipation that the newly opened St. Lawrence Seaway would bring with it a revitalized harbour, in 1959 the THC opened terminals 28 and 29 on the south side of Queen's Quay, to provide an inside storage area of 18,580 square metres (200,000 square feet). Today, these buildings sit vacant, testimonials to the changed uses of the Lake Ontario waterfront.

The Victory Soya Mills complex stands at the southeast corner of Front and Parliament streets. Established by legendary Canadian business tycoon E.P. Taylor during WW II, this unique facility processed soya beans from farms in eastern Canada and the United States into soya bean oil, meal, flour, and lecithin. As war raged in Europe and the Pacific, and in anticipation of ultimate success against the Axis powers, Taylor changed the name of his enterprise to Victory Soya Mills. In recent years, changing markets and an aging plant led to the decision to close the facility. The future of the mills is currently under discussion.

At this intersection of Front and Parliament streets, the Trail crosses Lake Shore Boulevard and continues along the north side of the road.

GOODERHAM & WORTS DISTILLERY

A short trip up the east side of Parliament Street to Mill Street, north of the Gardiner Expressway and Lake Shore Boulevard, brings you to the Gooderham and Worts Distillery which, until it closed in 1990, was Toronto's oldest industry. Established as a flour mill in 1832, and originally called Worts and Gooderham (the name was changed after Mr. Worts committed suicide in 1834), it soon became part of a more lucrative distilling and malting business.

G&W became the world's largest distilling operation and, in 1924, was absorbed into the Hiram Walker empire. In total the loop covers just 1 kilometre (0.6 mile).

INDUSTRIAL SOUTH

If you turn south off Lake Shore Boulevard onto Cherry Street and cross the Keating Channel, you enter what was once referred to as Ashbridge's Bay and is now the Port of Toronto. It is named for Sarah Ashbridge and her family, pioneer settlers who arrived from Pennsylvania in 1793 and eventually secured a total of 364 hectares (900 acres) of lakefront land east of the little town of York. Part of the holdings included property south of Queen Street between today's Greenwood and Coxwell avenues, as well as waterlots in what became known as Ashbridge's Bay.

In 1912, the THC proposed that the natural ponds and marshes of Ashbridge's Bay be filled, and that the Don River, which found its sluggish way into Toronto Harbour through the swampy bay, enter it through the Don Diversion Channel (now the Keating Channel).

In 1914, work began to convert the area into useable building lots and, within a decade, more than 200 hectares (500 acres) had been filled and serviced. In addition, the new ship channel, 120 metres (400 feet) wide and 2.1 kilometres (1.3 miles) long, the turning basin, and the Don Diversion Channel provided wharfage for dozens of lake freighters. Another 75 hectares (185 acres) of reclaimed land were used for industrial development and, by 1931, 41 new factories had located in the eastern harbour terminals district.

At Commissioners Street, the Trail crosses to the east side of Cherry Street and continues south. There, you will find the E.L. Cousins Docks (named for the THC's first chief engineer and general manager), where the tall silos of Essroc Canada, Great Lakes Cement Division, are located. On Cherry, just west of the Polson Street intersection, are the Canada Cement Lafarge silos.

SAURIOL OF THE DON

Born more than 90 years ago, Charles Sauriol has known the Don Valley since he was a child. In fact, his father came to Toronto to dredge the Don River. In those days, the valley was filled with the animals Ernest Thompson Seton described in his classic, *Wild Animals I Have Known*.

As a boy scout, Sauriol collected stories and photos of the descendants of pioneer families. A decade later, he began his lifelong work: writing books about the valley, and raising funds to rehabilitate what had been harmed and to protect what remained.

In 1950 he co-founded the Don Valley Conservation Association to protest emerging threats to the unspoiled woodland kingdom at Toronto's doorstep. Twice in ten years his property in the valley – painstakingly cared for – was expropriated to make room for the car lanes that would unalterably diminish the environment.

In 1957 Sauriol was appointed to the Metropolitan Toronto and Region Conservation Authority (MTRCA) and served for 14 years as a member of the executive committee and as chairman of the advisory board. In these roles, he continued to contribute to the preservation of the valley he always loved.

Beginning in 1968, he spent 21 years with the Nature Conservancy of Canada, first as co-administrator and projects director and, later, as executive director. In recognition of his unstinting commitment to the Don Valley he was given the Governor General's Award for Conservation, the 1991 Heritage Award, and the Order of Canada.

In 1989, the Charles Sauriol Conservation Reserve was dedicated in the East Don Valley; its land is to be preserved as a wilderness area in Toronto. It extends several kilometres along the Don Valley from the forks of the Don River to Lawrence Avenue.

A skilled advocate who once worked in the advertising business, Sauriol would go to any lengths to promote the concept of a Don Valley in which people and nature could co-exist. He once ran steam locomotive trips up the river's shores, and even restaged a trip Lieutenant-Governor John Graves Simcoe had made up the Don in 1793.

In addition to the legacy of his activism, Charles Sauriol has created a literary tradition of his own: a shelf of books about the Don Valley. They include his master work, *Remembering the Don*, a 30-year diary of his life in the valley. Since then, he has written *Tales of the Don*, *Green Footsteps*, A Beeman's Journey, and *Trails of the Don*. His latest book, *Pioneers of the Don*, will be published in 1995.

CHERRY BEACH

At the end of Cherry Street is the Eastern Gap, which joins Toronto Harbour to Lake Ontario. This is the point at which the Toronto Islands were once connected to the mainland.

The Trail leads directly into Cherry Beach (also called Clarke Beach); here, amid the heavily industrialized surroundings, is one of Toronto's cleanest, most pleasant sandy beaches. There is ample parking, a washroom (open only during the summer and not accessible to people in wheelchairs), a telephone booth, and barbecues.

From Cherry Beach, the Trail follows the 3-metre (10-foot) wide cycling, pedestrian, and in-line skating asphalt path that winds east through a wooded area along the waterfront. An on-road alternate route is to head north on Cherry Street for a short distance to Unwin Avenue and turn right. About half a kilometre (0.3 mile) along, watch for a rough road that heads south; it leads to a number of private and public sailing clubs as well as to a sailboarding (generally referred to as windsurfing) school. Even if you do not plan to take lessons, this is a great spot to watch the colourful sails and array of boats in the harbour.

The area's heavy industry was seriously damaged after WW I by a lack of tariff protection: companies that had once employed thousands of people went bankrupt after the war. Among them was British Forgings Limited, where more than three million shell casings had been manufactured in ten mammoth blast furnaces and the world's largest electric furnace.

Another victim was the Polson Iron Works Company, one of the city's busiest shipyards, established in 1883. Two Polson vessels still operate on Toronto Bay: Metro's restored 1910 ferry called the Trillium and the Royal Canadian Yacht Club's passenger ferry, Kwasind, which was launched in 1912.

The next stop in this tour of the industrial waterfront is the R.L. Hearn Generating Station, named for Richard Lancaster Hearn, a chairman of Ontario Hydro in the 1950s. It was erected by the public utility to help alleviate serious power shortages following the end of WW II. Originally coal-fired, it now has a soaring chimney, built in 1971, to better disperse stack gases. Although eventually converted to natural gas, the plant was mothballed when surplus electricity and the building's inefficiencies made it uneconomic.

The cycling and pedestrian Trail links up with Unwin Avenue just before the entrance to the Outer Harbour Marina. This 650-slip private marina is situated on a well-sheltered harbour of the Leslie Street Spit. Some of it is accessible to members of the general public who may want to make the 2-kilometre (1.2-mile) side trip into its grounds. For information, call 416-778-6245.

The Trail is aligned on Unwin Avenue for the short distance before it reaches Leslie Street. At the northwest corner of Leslie Street and Unwin Avenue is Teleport Toronto. Established in 1986, its 28 antennas link Telesat's television-station customers to myriad satellites. A satellite system pioneer, the company was created in 1969 and launched its first satellite four years later.

LESLIE STREET SPIT

At the south end of Leslie Street is the Leslie Street Spit, Toronto's accidental miracle. Originally a dump for old batteries and other by-products of modern life, it was created to a large extent by clean fill deposited from construction sites in the 1970s. Originally meant to be nothing more than a breakwater to protect the Outer Harbour, it took on a new role when the projected port expansion did not materialise and natural processes of regeneration took hold.

Today, the spit teems with wildlife, a place where scores of species of animals, plants, and birds can be found. To date, 297 species of birds have been sighted there; it is known to be a breeding ground for some 45 species, including black-crowned herons, double-crested cormorants, and common terns. The list of mammals that may be seen include red foxes, beavers, minks, muskrat, and even coyotes. But the Leslie Street Spit offers more: it is a perfect example of the tenacity of nature, of its ability to survive and adapt.

The spit is the site of the 27-hectare (67-acre) Tommy Thompson Park, named in honour of Metro's first parks commissioner. A blunt man, Thompson endeared himself to the public by having signs placed in Metro parks, urging visitors to "please walk on the grass".

The spit is closed to the general public Monday to Friday, because it is still used by the THC as a site for dumping construction materials. However, on weekends and holidays, it is accessible to those travelling on foot, bicycle, in-line skates, or in wheelchairs. While vehicles are not permitted, there is ample parking at the spit entrance. The round trip from the main entrance to the lighthouse covers 10 kilometres (6.2 miles).

Tommy Thompson Park is open to the public on weekends and holidays; for more information, call the Metro Toronto and Region Conservation Authority (MTRCA), which is responsible for interim management, at 416-661-6600.

The 3-metre (10-foot) wide asphalt Trail travels north on Leslie Street and east on Lake Shore Boulevard, passing Metro's sprawling main treatment plant; when it was established in 1913, it served a population of 350,000. But over the years, as the city grew, the plant was expanded and now processes the 800,000 cubic metres (28,250,000 cubic feet) of waste water generated daily by 1,250,000 people.

On the south side of Lake Shore Boulevard, at the foot of Coxwell Avenue, is the entrance to Ashbridge's Bay Park.

ASHBRIDGE'S BAY PARK

Located in Ashbridge's Bay Park is the Ashbridge's Bay Yacht Club; the club dates back to 1932 and moved into its present quarters in 1977. The park has public boat launches that are available on a first-come, first-served basis, as well as moorings for day use only. There is also a boardwalk along the shoreline, playground area, water fountains, and a seasonal washroom; the park is a popular spot for family picnics and windsurfing.

The Waterfront Trail follows the off-road, asphalt path through the park, parallel to the boardwalk; this route winds along the shoreline, to the eastern beach area, commonly referred to as the Beaches.

On the north side of Lake Shore Boulevard you will see the Greenwood Race Track, organized in 1875 as the privately owned Woodbine Riding and Driving Club. The oldest uninterrupted stakes race in North America, the Queen's Plate, was first run here in 1876, then annually at this site from 1883 to 1955. When the new Woodbine track was opened in Etobicoke in 1956, the race was moved there, and the old site was eventually renamed Greenwood. Now closed, its future is a matter of discussion among neighbours and in the City generally.

Just before it reaches the Eastern Beaches, the Trail passes the Donald D. Summerville Olympic Pool. Operated by the City of Toronto's Parks and Recreation Department, it was opened in June 1963 and named in honour of a young mayor who died suddenly while in office. The amenity is actually a trio of pools: one Olympic-sized; one a training pool; and one for deep diving. The latter has two one-metre (3.2-foot) spring boards, two three-metre (10-foot) diving boards and a diving tower with diving platforms that are five and ten metres (16 and 32 feet) in height.

EASTERN BEACHES

Continuing east, the Waterfront Trail enters the Eastern Beaches. Little more than a century ago this was mainly tree-covered countryside where, each summer, people could get away from the hustle, bustle, and heat of the big city.

Today, the Beaches is a popular destination, especially during the summer months when people flock to the area to soak up some sun, play a game of beach volleyball, or explore the eclectic shops, boutiques, and eateries that line Queen Street (just a block north of the lake). There are also public tennis courts, a baseball diamond, and many treed areas in which to relax. The boardwalk is reserved for pedestrians and people in wheelchairs, while the asphalt path can be enjoyed by both cyclists and in-line skaters. This is an area where speed should be kept to a minimum: many children and seniors use this area.

If you are arriving by car, be prepared to spend some time looking for a parking spot, especially during summer weekends; there is a small municipal lot on Lee Avenue, just south of Queen. Otherwise, parking is on Queen and the side streets. Because of the volume of traffic in the area, residents have been successful in getting the police to continually patrol the streets, tagging and towing illegally parked cars.

If you're walking in this area, you may want to look for the Beach Hebrew Institute at 109 Kenilworth Avenue, just south of Queen Street. The congregation, which is still active, was established in 1917 to serve vacationing Jewish families who would not ride to their Toronto synagogues on the Sabbath.

The first settler in what became known as the Beach (the name was pluralized later, with the development of individual beach areas such as Kew and Balmy) was Joseph Williams, a Londoner who immigrated here in 1853. The produce from his farm was labelled Kew Farms, an obvious reference to the much-loved Kew Gardens of his native city. In May 1879, Williams opened the Canadian Kew Gardens, an 8-hectare (20-acre) pleasure ground that fronts on Lake Ontario. In 1907, the City acquired Williams' property and, combining it with other adjacent lands, created the still-popular Kew Gardens. Williams' 1902 stone house, now the park-keeper's residence, stands near the foot of Lee Avenue.

As you travel east you will notice a red wooden structure on the beach. This is the Leuty Avenue Life Saving Station, which was built by the THC in 1920. It is one of only two stations of its type still in existence. To safeguard the structure, members of the community have been contributing to a restoration fund.

Farther east, adjacent to the boardwalk, is a Toronto Historical Board plaque describing Scarboro Beach Amusement Park. It was opened in 1907 on property that had previously been the site of a farm that grew produce for the unfortunates of the House of Providence, operated by the Sisters of St. Joseph. As a park, it quickly became a summer tradition, attracting thousands to its rides, games of chance, sporting spectacles, restaurants, and concerts. Torontonians saw their first air machine here – American aviator Charles Willard's Golden Flyer. It lifted off the sand without difficulty, but the pilot was forced to land in the lake when the cheering crowds filled the space available on the beach.

The boardwalk and cycling lane ends at Nurse Road, just west of Victoria Park Avenue; this marks the boundary between the cities of Toronto and Scarborough.

...the *shore is extremely bold and has the appearance of chalk cliffs. They appeared so well that we talked of building a summer residence there and calling it Scarborough.*

– Elizabeth Simcoe

◄.....

Scarborough

DANFORTH

MARKHAM

EGLINTON

KINGSTON ROAD

Bellamy Creek

South Marine Park

Sylvan Park

Bellamy Ravine

Cudia Park

Cathedral Bluffs Park

s Park

2 KM.

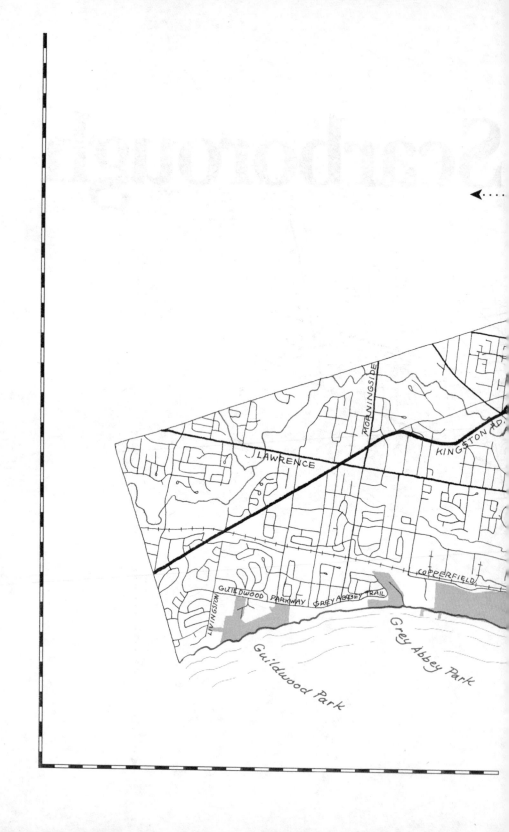

Scarborough

Rouge River

SHEPPARD

HIGHWAY 2

MEADOWVALE

401

PORT UNION

Rouge Beach Park

st Point Park

N

2 KM

HE MAGNIFICENT Scarborough Bluffs, among the most striking features of Lake Ontario's north shore, form most of Scarborough's waterfront. Created and continually evolving through the interplay of sand, water, and waves, they are remnants of the Lake Iroquois shoreline. The 90-metre (300-feet) high bluffs mark the place where old shore meets the more recent Lake Ontario. In fact, about 10,000 years ago, much of what is now waterfront was under water.

The bluffs sandy texture makes them vulnerable to erosion, which also threatens the sites atop them. As waves continually cut away at the foot of the bluffs (made of a fine-grained sediment, with a small amount of cobble and boulders), the eroded sandy material is dispersed along the shoreline, usually ending up at a beach. Historically, material from the Scarborough Bluffs was deposited at eastern beaches and Toronto Island beaches. Today, the combined effect of erosion control and the Leslie Spit, which thrusts into the water, has diminished the volume of sand reaching Toronto Island.

Erosion at the Scarborough Bluffs is less than 0.75 metre (2.5 feet) per year; some of the other Great Lakes shorelines erode more than 1.5 metres (5 feet) per year. More than half the shoreline in front of the bluffs has been artificially protected in some form against erosion. There are many parks and private properties along the top of the bluffs and, if the erosion process were allowed to continue unchecked, these would eventually become part of the lake. Intervening in the natural process slows or stops erosion, allowing the slopes to stabilize; but, as they gradually become vegetated, the striking sandy bluffs disappear.

The Scarborough shoreline isn't all bluffs, however: they taper off around East Point, a headland just west of Highland Creek. East of East Point, along the remainder of the Scarborough waterfront, the old Lake Iroquois shoreline runs inland, and is mainly cobble and boulder, with low bluffs and cobble beaches.

Highland Creek flows into the lake along this stretch, and at the eastern end of Scarborough, the Rouge River forms the boundary with Pickering.

PUBLIC TRANSIT

Local Transit
(416-393-4636)

VIA Train
(416-366-8411)

GO (416-869-3200)

•**Scarborough – Reeve Ave.** at St. Clair & Midland Ave. 3 km from Bluffers Park

• **Eglinton – Eglinton Ave.** at Bellamy Rd. 2.75 km from Sylvan Park

• **Guildwood – Kingston Rd.** at Celestre Drive 1.5 km from the Guild Inn

• **Rouge Hill – Lawrence Ave.** at Port Union Rd. just west of Rouge Beach Park

Scarborough is a city of extraordinary environmental diversity. But the sheer richness of the built and natural environment means there are different viewpoints on the future of the Scarborough waterfront. There is currently no Waterfront Trail route along the Scarborough shoreline; a number of shoreline management issues remain to be addressed before one can finally be put in place. These are currently under study and discussion. However, a description of the breathtaking Scarborough waterfront follows.

When the land that was to become the City of Scarborough was first surveyed by Augustus Jones in 1791, it was given the name Glasgow. Only two years later, when Lieutenant-Governor John Graves Simcoe and his wife, Elizabeth, arrived in Toronto, Elizabeth took one look at the bluffs and named them Scarborough, after the chalk cliffs of the Yorkshire town of that name. In establishing the connection with a site in Yorkshire, Simcoe was also honouring the Duke of York, who had recently defeated the French in battle.

Scarborough was incorporated as a township in 1850; in 1953, that township became part of Metropolitan Toronto. From the beginning it was the largest municipality (in area) within Metro. Re-named the Borough of Scarborough in 1967, it became a city in 1983.

Suburban development began in 1910 in the Birchcliff area, but it was only after World War II that the most dramatic residential and business growth occurred. With 23,000 people in 1945, the city had grown to more than 530,000 in 1995. It is now Canada's seventh largest city.

R.C. Harris Filtration Plant

The water purification plant at the foot of Victoria Park Avenue is named for Roland Caldwell Harris, one-time commissioner of works and city engineer for Toronto. We take the purity of our water for granted today, but it took decades to achieve. Associated with the filtration plant, is a 3-kilometre (1.8-mile) rock tunnel into the lake, a supply tunnel 20 metres (70 feet) below street level, that stretches across the city, and several reservoirs.

The first route cut through the Scarborough forests from west to east was Danforth Road, constructed in 1799 by Asa Danforth.

In 1801, William Cornell and Levi Annis cut out the Front (Cornwell) Road closer to the lake; it followed roughly today's Kingston Road. By 1817, the road was completed all the way to Kingston, replacing much of Asa Danforth's road and, for the first time, allowing suitable long-distance land transportation in Upper Canada. In 1817, a stage line was established between York and Kingston.

From the filtration plant you can view the Toronto skyline. The plant itself is worth a good look: a stunning building set against the blue waters of Lake Ontario, it was built in Art Deco style in the 1930s.

KINGSTON ROAD

Scarborough extends along the waterfront from Victoria Park Avenue to the Rouge River and the Pickering Town Line. Kingston Road (Highway 2), a major thoroughfare for nearly 200 years, is always within easy reach of the lakeshore. Access to the lake is gained by way of Kingston Road, where you will find all the amenities you need.

TORONTO HUNT CLUB

In 1895, the Toronto Hunt Club, already about 50 years old, purchased this property, which extends from Kingston Road to the lake. Hunting ceased to be its main activity in 1930, and since then it has been a private golf club.

ROSETTA MCCLAIN GARDENS

The formal gardens, originally planned and developed by Robert Watson McClain and his brother-in-law Joseph McDonald West, were donated to the City of Toronto in 1959 as parkland in memory of Robert's wife, Rosetta.

Today the 9-hectare (23-acre) park is operated by the Metro Parks and Property Department, which has developed it into a unique, fully accessible garden. There are braille signs, raised planters, textured paths, ramps, scent gardens and a rock fountain, arranged to allow people to touch the cascading water. Facilities include a paved parking lot, a drinking fountain, and a washroom accessible to people in wheelchairs; no bicycles are allowed.

SCARBOROUGH HEIGHTS PARK

In 1960, Scarborough transferred its land along the bluffs to the Metropolitan Toronto Region Conservation Authority (MTRCA). Like other waterfront parks in the city, Scarborough Heights Park is maintained by Metro Parks, under an agreement with the MTRCA.

It will be part of a strip of bluffs parkland that will include footpaths, picnic areas, and points of access to the lake.

There is a parking lot off Fishleigh Drive. There are no facilities and paths yet in the 10-hectare (25-acre) park; however, the Ontario Historical Society has installed a plaque about the bluffs history. (People should be particularly careful on the edge of the bluffs and should go up and down only on established pathways.)

CLIFFSIDE VILLAGE

Cliffside Village, which lies between Cliffside Drive and Midland Avenue, has several restaurants, gas stations, and most of the other facilities visitors need.

On the walls of several village buildings are murals depicting scenes from Scarborough's history. The pictures are part of a larger project: to paint murals along major roads and transit routes in Scarborough, highlighting its heritage, natural beauty, transportation history, and rural life. One of murals depicts Elizabeth Simcoe admiring the sandy cliffs from a boat off the bluffs. The plan is to have as many as 100 walls painted, in Scarborough and in other parts of Metro Toronto, over the next few years.

ST. AUGUSTINE'S SEMINARY

Built in 1913 as a school for training priests, and named for St. Augustine of Hippo, the seminary on the south side of Kingston Road is hard to miss. Its large, imposing dome makes it visible from great distances both on land and on the lake. In fact, cruising sailors use the dome as a signpost to guide them back to harbour.

BLUFFERS PARK

Bluffers Park is the best place for viewing the Scarborough Bluffs and is reached by way of Brimley Road. This is a ten-minute walk from Kingston Road, along a very steep drive and should be approached with care. From the base of Brimley Road you can see the odd-shaped pinnacles and buttresses created from the erosion of the cliffs.

This 15-kilometre-long (9-mile-long) park was developed in two
stages by the MTRCA, using a total of 2.6 million cubic metres
(3.4 million cubic yards) of lakefill. The first phase, completed in
1975, provided parking and walking areas. The second phase
created the launching and docking areas for boaters.

Bluffers Park's 42 hectares (105 acres) have a lot to
offer both general users and yachters. Four lots are available for
parking. There are picnic areas with tables and fire pits, fully accessible washrooms, drinking fountains, a water tap, public telephones,
footpaths, and scenic lookout points. A supervised beach with
change rooms is open in July and August and Bluffer's Restaurant
and Dogfish Bar is open year-round.

There is a public boat launch for boaters, as well as a
500-slip public marina and four yacht clubs.

CATHEDRAL BLUFFS PARK

The bluffs in this park, which rise more than 90 metres (300 feet)
above the lake, mark the highest point on Scarborough's lakeshore.
The 10-hectare (24-acre) park can be reached from Kingston Road
via Cathedral Bluffs Drive and Lyme Regis Crescent (a ten-minute
walk from Kingston Road). There is a playground maintained by the
City of Scarborough. From the park you have a great view of the
lake and the bluffs.

CUDIA PARK

Named for the Cudia family, long-time residents in the area, this
16-hectare (40-acre) park has no facilities yet, but provides a scenic
view of the bluffs and the ancient Lake Iroquois shoreline. It has an
unpaved parking lot, reached from Kingston Road via Pine Ridge
Road and Meadowcliffe Drive.

SYLVAN PARK

Once named the Cherry Orchard, it is called Sylvan Park because of
the area's wooded, rural character. The land was purchased in 1966
by Metropolitan Toronto and placed under MTRCA authority.
There are no facilities in the 10-hectare (25-acre) park; however
there is a scenic lookout from which the shipwrecked *Alexandria*

DORIS MCCARTHY

Life has a way of weaving seemingly random threads into whole cloth. Artist Doris McCarthy still remembers being 11 years old and canoeing along the lakeshore with her usually busy father. After paddling and bird-watching, they enjoyed a picnic one day below Scarborough Bluffs. A deep nearby ravine offered sanctuary to local wildlife while offshore lay the wreck of an old freighter, the *Alexandria*, a rusting hulk that can still be seen today.

As a young art teacher, McCarthy lived at home, but yearned for the freedom of her own studio. Eventually she found a small stucco cottage on 5 hectares (12 acres) of meadows and ravine – all tucked between two ravines on the Scarborough Bluffs and all blessedly inaccessible by road. Best of all, this was the bluff where, all those years ago, she and her father had enjoyed their picnic.

Today she remembers, "Mother called it 'that fool's paradise of yours.' I thought it was a good name and I called it Fool's Paradise". Now a world-renowned artist and winner of the Order of Canada and many other honours, she paints while at her cottage on Georgian Bay, enjoys travelling, and has visited the Arctic several times. But she is always happy to return to Fool's Paradise. There, she sees her friends, some of whom she has known since her school days; as a result, Fool's Paradise is full of people's comings and goings. Nonetheless, 65 years after graduating from the Ontario College of Art in 1930, she still spends the time alone needed for her work.

After years of fruitlessly trying to battle the ravages of shoreline erosion, she deeded 4 hectares (10 acres) of her land to the MTRCA. Its regeneration program ensures that her home isn't about to tumble down the cliffs and means that visitors will be able to enjoy well into the future the land she has deeded to the MTRCA.

Now 85 years old and surveying her full, active life, she still insists that, "There are still so many things I'd love to do. But now, time is the only thing I'm short of. I'm jealous of time and I'm not prepared to do anything that isn't part of my focus".

The first of two volumes of McCarthy's autobiography, *A Fool in Paradise*, is available through the publisher, McFarlane Walter and Ross; phone: 416-924-7595. For information on her art, call Wynick-Tuck gallery located at 80 Spadina Road; 416-364-8716.

can be observed. Entry points: via Gates Gully off Ravine Drive (with very limited on-road parking) and from the west end of Sylvan Avenue. You gain access to Sylvan Avenue by turning south off Kingston Road onto Bethune Boulevard, then right onto Catalina Drive.

GUILDWOOD PARK/GUILD INN

The original building, erected in 1914 by General Harold Bickford, was known as Ranelagh Park.

In 1932, Spencer and Rosa Clark purchased the estate, and despite the Great Depression, established the Guild of All Arts, a rent-free colony for more than 100 artists and artisans. For the next ten years, they worked in a number of media including sculpture, weaving, painting, woodworking, and ceramics. To accommodate an increasing flow of visitors, the Clarks added dining facilities and guest rooms.

These artistic pursuits were interrupted during World War II, when the Guild was turned over to the government for war use. For a time, it was the naval base HMCS Bytown II, where the first WRENS (Women's Royal Navy Service) were trained; it then served as a specialized military hospital known as Scarborough Hall.

The Guild returned to use as an art colony and country inn in 1947, when it was given back to the Clarks. Spencer Clark added to the grounds architectural artifacts salvaged from old Toronto buildings that were being demolished.

The Clarks had added about 200 hectares (500 acres) to the property, but as taxes rose in the 1950s, they were forced to sell much of it to developers. This land became the residential community of Guildwood Village.

Although the Clarks sold the Guild in 1978, they left their stamp on it. Today, visitors will still find a country inn in a sylvan setting. The inn has 95 guest rooms, tennis courts, a swimming pool, fitness and games room, and a fine restaurant. The 36 hectares (90 acres) of forest, gardens, lawns, and woodland trails are maintained by Metro Parks. The Guild, operated by a board of management formed by the Province and the City of Scarborough, oversees the Spencer Clark Collection of Historic Architecture and other cultural properties. There are several artists in residence, one of whom has a studio in an old log cabin. For information, call 416-261-3331

There is a path along the top of the bluffs, a stairway that leads down to the shore, and another path along the lakefront. At this point, Kingston Road veers north, away from the lake. Consider following Lawrence Avenue East or Coronation Drive as you continue east.

EAST POINT PARK

Just east of the Frank J. Horgan Filtration Plant (take Lawrence Avenue East to Manse Road; go south, then turn east on Copperfield Road), Metro Parks has constructed four newly opened playing fields. Parking is available.

Some people will assume that the parkland east of the playing fields is overgrown and pass by it quickly. It is, however, unique in this area, combining old field growth with bluff habitat. In addition, there are a number of prairie wildflower and grass species, many of them categorized as local and rare; for example, the spiked blazing star, which generally grows only in extreme southwest Ontario. This is also a good place to find bottle and fringed gentian and nodding ladies' tresses. Because of the open fields of asters and goldenrod, it is also a major migratory stopover for monarch butterflies.

Side Trip
COLONEL DANFORTH PARK

At the end of Copperfield Road, follow Beach Grove Drive north to Lawrence Avenue East. At this point you may decide to follow a 3-metre (10-foot) asphalt trail that takes you to Colonel Danforth Park. Alternatively, you may continue east on Lawrence to the Rouge Park.

This park is named for Asa Danforth (who was never a colonel) and is situated in the deep, heavily wooded valley of Highland Creek. There are picnic tables with barbecues, as well as washrooms that are open in summer. Parking is available

from the entrance off Kingston Road. A paved trail follows the creek for 5.5 kilometres (3 miles), from Colonel Danforth Park to Morningside Park. The valley is well known for its spectacular fall colours.

Following this trail will take you past Scarborough College, set amid 120 hectares (300 acres) of forest and ravine on a hill overlooking the valley. ■

ROUGE PARK

With its 4,700 hectares (11,600 acres), the Rouge Park is the largest park in an urban area in North America. It begins at Lake Ontario, east of Port Union Road, and currently extends north to Steeles Avenue. Its woodlands, valleys, meadows, and the relatively pristine waters of the Rouge River account for the diversity of wildlife – at least 27 mammals, 123 birds, 55 fish, 19 reptiles and amphibians, and 762 plant species. In this park conservation and renewal are a priority and development is minimal. It is, after all, a national ecological treasure.

Rouge Beach Park, at the mouth of the Rouge River, has two distinct areas. On the north side of the CN tracks is a marsh that is home for such breeding populations as the rare least bittern, Virginia rail, and blue-gray gnat-catcher. Wetlands are important to the park as a stopover point for migrating waterfowl. The area has an unpaved parking lot, a public boat launch, and a pedestrian bridge (where Cliff swallows nest) that crosses the river.

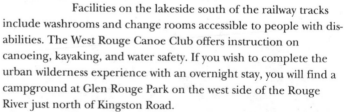

Facilities on the lakeside south of the railway tracks include washrooms and change rooms accessible to people with disabilities. The West Rouge Canoe Club offers instruction on canoeing, kayaking, and water safety. If you wish to complete the urban wilderness experience with an overnight stay, you will find a campground at Glen Rouge Park on the west side of the Rouge River just north of Kingston Road.

The southern part of Rouge Park already resembles old-growth forest with its groves of hemlock, white pine, and red and white oak, some more than 150 years old. Pastures have been colonized by white birch, trembling ash, and green ash. The steady increase of mature trees in the lower Rouge Valley provides nesting cavities for owls, woodpeckers, flying squirrels, and one of the most spectacular of all Ontario birds, the pileated woodpecker, which has vanished from heavily deforested parts of southwestern Ontario. The diversity of this forest results not only from the natural renewal process, but also from protection and reforestation programs provided by the park.

Located within the Rouge Park is Ganestigiagon, Canada's only traditional Seneca village site.

This ancient community is illustrated in a 1674 map by the French explorer Jolliet, so is the adjacent Rouge Trail, which connected the forks of the Rouge with Lake Simcoe, Georgian Bay, and the upper Great Lakes. This route was once an important connection between New France and Huronia.

Ganestigiagon was used as an important base for the Seneca to control the supply of furs for trade with the Europeans. The sandy soil and mild climate provide a good base for agriculture and the river provided an important food source of fish.

A co-operative venture including the province, the federal government, municipalities such as Scarborough, Markham, and Metro Toronto, and citizens' organizations including Save the Rouge Valley System Inc. manages Rouge Park.

The decision to knit together Rouge Park and adjacent public lands is a tribute to the success of Toronto's environmental and native movements, which are bringing about an ever-enlarging green corridor stretching from Lake Ontario to the Oak Ridges Moraine.

The goal of a recently approved plan for managing Rouge Park is to increase wildlife habitat by naturalizing the farmlands, abandoned fields, and hydro corridors that interrupt the forest cover. Some 970 hectares (2,400 acres) or 15 percent of the Rouge Park that is now farmland is zoned as a restoration area. Among the returning species are the cooper's hawk, the Carolina wren, orchid oriole, and northern mockingbird.

Over time, the park will be extended along the corridors of several Rouge tributary streams to their headwaters in the Oak Ridges Moraine. Revegetation, which lowers water temperature in these stream valleys, will be crucial to reintroducing Atlantic salmon, which vanished after the deforestation of the 19th century.

For more information on access points to the Rouge Park, telephone 416-28-ROUGE (287-6843).

The Waterfront Trail resumes once you cross the Rouge River and enter the town of Pickering, where you can enjoy such natural areas as Petticoat Creek, Frenchman's Bay, and Duffins Creek.

Pickering *is a place of contrasts, a historic community that is a home to nuclear technology, country estates, hamlets, and expanses of natural open spaces*

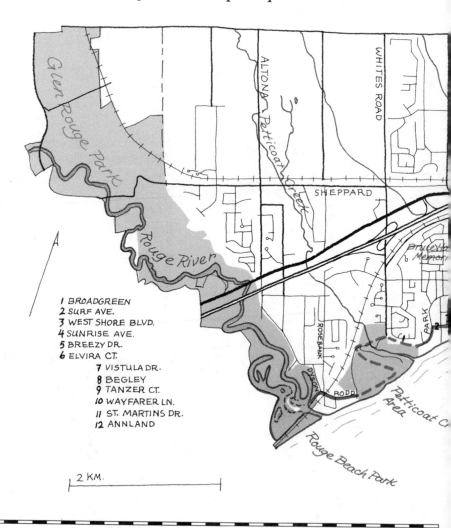

1 BROADGREEN
2 SURF AVE.
3 WEST SHORE BLVD.
4 SUNRISE AVE.
5 BREEZY DR.
6 ELVIRA CT.
7 VISTULA DR.
8 BEGLEY
9 TANZER CT.
10 WAYFARER LN.
11 ST. MARTINS DR.
12 ANNLAND

2 KM.

Pickering

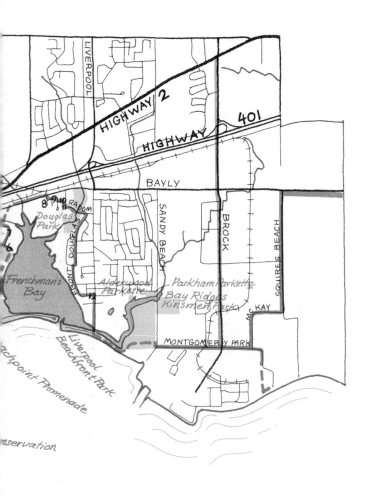

ICKERING IS A PLACE of contrasts, a historic community that is a home to nuclear technology. But the town also includes country estates, hamlets, and charming rural villages, rich farmland areas, and expanses of parkland and natural open spaces. The Pickering Nuclear Generating Station and the Duffins Creek Water Pollution Control Plant are, of necessity, on the waterfront and have become virtual built-form landmarks there, visible over enormous distances along Lake Ontario.

Pickering, a town of almost 75,000 people, borders the eastern reaches of Metropolitan Toronto; the present town, which was established in 1975, encompasses 15 urban and many rural areas.

In 1791, Pickering Township was surveyed by Augustus Jones; when the first land grants were made under Lieutenant-Governor Colonel John Graves Simcoe, it was named Edinburgh. By the time the original settlers arrived about 1800, however, the name of the township had been changed to Pickering, probably after the town by the same name in Yorkshire, England.

Pickering Township's population increased rapidly in the first half of the 19th century, as the products of its grist, saw, and woollen mills, its breweries and tanneries, were exported from its fine natural harbour. However, as lumber supplies became depleted and American import duties made it unprofitable to export grain, the population declined steadily.

Toward the end of the century, Pickering was discovered by vacationers from Toronto and cottage communities grew along the lake, swelling the number of inhabitants every summer. Eventually, the cottages were winterized and the number of residents stabilized. Since the 1960s, however, many new subdivisions have been built and the flow of traffic has been reversed: every weekday morning, hundreds of Pickering residents travel by rail and car to offices in downtown Toronto.

The Waterfront Trail in Pickering starts at the mouth of the Rouge River and stretches to the mouth of Duffins Creek.

PUBLIC TRANSIT

Local Transit
(905-683-4111)

GO (416-869-3200)

Pickering – Bayly St. at Liverpool & Hwy–401, 2 km from waterfront (Nuclear Generating Stn.)

There is evidence at both sites that human beings lived here long before European settlement began: archaeological material from Duffins Creek dates back 4,000 years. In more relatively recent times, the mouth of the Rouge was the beginning of a major native portage between Lake Ontario and the Holland River, giving access to Lake Huron.

In the mid-17th century the Five Nations Iroquois drove the Hurons out of the area and established a number of villages along the north shore of Lake Ontario. One of these, Ganatsekiagon, established by the Senecas, was located on the east bank of the Rouge.

Many early French traders and explorers came to this village, including Jean Peré and Adrien Jolliet (brother of the more famous Louis Jolliet), who stopped here in the summer of 1669 on their way to Lake Superior in search of copper.

The only remaining suggestion of the French presence is in some place names: the Rouge River refers to its red clay banks, while Petticoat Creek was originally Petite Côté ("little side") Creek, probably derived from the fact that its east bank is quite high, while its west bank is almost flat near its mouth.

Leaving Scarborough's Rouge Beach Park, you begin the Pickering portion of the Waterfront Trail by crossing the pedestrian bridge over the Rouge River, climbing the escarpment stairs to Dyson Road, and entering the Regional Municipality of Durham. It is suitable only for walking and, if you're strong, cycling. Bikes can be carried over the bridge, but there are many stairs up the escarpment, and cyclists may prefer to start from the Pickering side of the Rouge River.

You will find only limited parking on the Pickering side, but ample parking on the Scarborough side at Rouge Beach Park at the Lawrence Avenue East entrance, past Rouge Hills Drive.

Follow Dyson Road to Rodd Avenue (you have to go over a level rail crossing at the junction of Rodd Avenue and Rosebank Road) and turn right. This area of Pickering is known as Rosebank.

ROSEBANK

Rosebank was one of several cottage communities established in Pickering Township in the early part of this century. In fact, it was so popular as a summer resort that it eventually had its own train station, which served seven passenger trains as well as Picnic Specials. From 1916, Rosebank also boasted its own post office; today, the older cottages of that time are mixed with some very modern homes.

The town has an interesting physical heritage, left by the glacial age. Most significant is the Oak Ridges Moraine, which was formed by the convergence of two ice lobes that deposited glacial till between them. The moraine marks Pickering Township's northern boundary.

The area between the Oak Ridges Moraine and Lake Ontario is a till plain. Running west to east across it, the shoreline of the ancient Lake Iroquois can readily be discerned. Dispersed throughout the plain are long ridges or oval-shaped hills, known as drumlins, formed by glacial drift. The summer colony at Rosebank was built around one such drumlin and a dozen others are scattered throughout the present town.

Follow Rodd Avenue to the end, taking care when crossing over the railway tracks; there you will find a pedestrian entrance to Petticoat Creek Conservation Area.

There is no parking allowed in the turn-around just outside the conservation area, and only limited parking on Rodd Avenue. There is parking, however, just outside the main entrance to the conservation area, off White's Road, and, of course, ample parking is available inside the park, but, to get to it, you must enter from White's Road.

PETTICOAT CREEK CONSERVATION AREA

The Trail follows the top of the bluffs to a point overlooking the mouth of Petticoat Creek. Just west of the stairs that lead down to the creek, the Trail turns left and along the top of the bluff, where, after a short distance, it is paved. Follow the paved road as it winds around to the park entrance (it curves left, then sharply right,

crosses the creek, then ascends the embankment on the other side).
Just after the entrance toll booth, the Trail turns off to the right,
then right again almost immediately. It descends to the creek, follows it to its mouth, and ascends the bluff again, before exiting the
park onto Park Crescent. The last part of the Trail through the conservation area can be very muddy in early spring, making it difficult
to ascend or descend.

Petticoat Creek Conservation Area is managed by the
MTRCA. It is a 72-hectare (178-acre) park created in 1976 from
grown-over farmland on which there are remnants of a Carolinian
hardwood forest. You will find woods of hemlock, white pine, white
cedar, sugar maple, and black cherry. Along the lakefront, the bluffs
rise 10 metres (33 feet) above the waterline.

The park contains abundant picnic facilities and can
accommodate large groups. There are washrooms, which are
disabled-accessible, walking trails, and a refreshment booth. But the
main feature is a large, 0.6-hectare (1.5-acre) swimming pool with
the capacity to handle 3,000 people. Bikes can be used in the
Petticoat Creek Conservation Area's paved roads and paths, but are
discouraged on the dirt paths.

The main entrance is from the south end of White's
Road (which connects with Highway 401). The park opens in mid-
May, weekends only, is open seven days a week from 10:00 a.m. to
dusk, and closes in October. Entrance fees: $2.50 for adults; $1.25
for children. The pool is open from about mid-June to Labour Day,
from 10 a.m. to 7:30 p.m. Pool fees: $1.75 on weekends; $1.25 on
weekdays. The Trail, however, is open year-round.

For up-to-date information and group rates, contact
the MTRCA at 5 Shoreham Drive, Downsview, Ontario M3N 1S4;
you can reach them by phone 416-661-6600, or by fax at 661-6898.

The land on which the conservation area sits was once
owned by William Moore, a lawyer and local MP, and was known as
Moorelands. The road leading into the park on the north side was
named Moore Road until the 1970s, when it became part of White's
Road. The Moore name is preserved at Moore's Point, which overlooks the Creek mouth and where you can still find parts of the
foundation of the old Moore house.

The Rouge and Petticoat Creek valleys include remnants of the Carolinian (or southern deciduous) forest. The western end of Frenchman's Bay marks the northern limit (and, in Ontario, the eastern limit) of the Carolinian forest. East and north of it is the Great Lakes-St. Lawrence Forest Region, a mix of conifers and hardwoods. At the boundary of these two forest regions, Pickering accommodates species of both, making it interestingly diverse.

You will find nearby convenience stores at: White's Road and Oklahoma (which also has a gas station); 677 Marksbury Road, just north of Park Crescent; and West Shore Boulevard and Bayly Street.

Follow Park Crescent to Surf Avenue and turn east. At West Shore Boulevard the Trail heads north; however, turning south on West Shore Boulevard and then east just before the lake will bring you onto Beachpoint Promenade.

FAIRPORT BEACH COMMUNITY/ BEACHPOINT PROMENADE

What is now MTRCA land was once a thriving summer resort complete with its own summer post office. Originally called Dunbarton Shores, the name was later changed to Fairport Beach. A few cottages, winterized for year-round living, still remain. The West Rouge Canoe Club (416-281-8620) maintains a seasonal facility (with portable washrooms) on the spit of land that juts out between the bay and the lake; the spit is a favourite launching area for windsurfing. There is a marsh on the bay side of the spit – a good place to look for such birds as rails, marsh wrens, and swamp sparrows.

The Waterfront Trail goes north on West Shore Boulevard to Sunrise Avenue. Turn east and follow it to Breezy Drive. Go north at Breezy Drive and then right into Bruce Handscomb Memorial Park.

BRUCE HANDSCOMBE MEMORIAL PARK

This park offers an excellent view of Frenchman's Bay. It has paved pathways and, at the north end, a playground. It is named for a local resident whose interests included the preservation of open space and parkland, and the development of minor sports in the West Shore area.

Bruce Handscombe Park has recently been adopted by the children and staff of Frenchman's Bay Public School, who are participating in a Town-wide program dedicated to preserving Pickering's parkland. They will co-operate with the Town in maintaining the park as a place to be enjoyed by West Shore families and by visitors.

FRENCHMAN'S BAY

Some residents of Pickering still remember when ice was cut from the bay each winter. The Lake Simcoe Ice and Fuel Company sawed huge blocks of ice, sometimes almost one metre (three feet) thick, which were hauled by horse-drawn sleigh to the ice houses, packed with sawdust as insulation, and stored for use, especially during the warmer months. Much of the ice was shipped to Toronto, where, in the summer days before popsicles, small children clambered on ice wagons seeking little chips.

Frenchman's Bay is the largest natural bay along the north shore of Lake Ontario between Hamilton and Trenton. Its waters are protected from Lake Ontario by two relatively stable sand spits that stretch out from the shore, like long arms, leaving only a narrow channel for boats. Material dredged from this channel was used in the construction of the Bloor Street Viaduct in downtown Toronto, 1918.

Frenchman's Bay has two marshes: one to the north of the bay, Frenchman's Bay Marsh, and the other on the eastern side of the bay. The larger eastern marsh is called Hydro Marsh and is discussed later in this chapter.

Frenchman's Bay is one of the most significant natural sites in the Greater Toronto Bioregion. It is a highly valued ecological community with provincially rare plants, regionally rare breeding birds, and important fish habitat, and is an important stopover for migrating waterfowl and shorebirds. One hundred and twenty-six bird species (34 of them breeding) and 44 fish species (18 spawning) have been recorded in the marsh at the north end of the bay. In late summer and fall look for hundreds, sometimes thousands, of shorebirds in the mudflats at the north end of the bay.

The Ministry of Natural Resources has designated the marsh a Class 2 Provincially Significant Wetland, and MTRCA has identified it as an Environmentally Significant Area (ESA).

After European settlement began, Frenchman's Bay became increasingly important as a port through which ship masts, pine logs, and squared timber were exported. A wharf was built at the north end of the bay, and dredging, begun as early as 1843, cleared a channel big enough to admit larger ships from Lake Ontario. It is said that, in 1845 alone, 20 sawmills operating in the township shipped one million metres (1,093,600 yards) of lumber through Frenchman's Bay. Small wonder that by mid-century more than half of Pickering Township was cleared of its once abundant trees.

When the Grand Trunk Railway (later CN) was opened through Pickering in 1856, use of the bay declined sharply. However, the provincial government poured money into upgrading the facilities: a new wharf replaced the old one, a lighthouse was built, a new channel was dredged, and a 50,000-bushel barley elevator was constructed. Once again, the port bustled, but this time barley was the chief export. Wagons would line the road to Liverpool Road, waiting to unload cargoes of barley destined for U.S. breweries. But the flourishing trade – and the port – declined when the Americans placed a duty on imported barley, which closed the market.

Frenchman's Bay Today

In the 20th century the bay became a centre for recreation, first for summer cottagers, now for year-round residents; sailors, canoers, and windsurfers will find that all the equipment they need can be rented from operators on the bay. Most marinas have docking spaces reserved for visitors. You can fish from shore or charter a fishing boat to take you out on the lake. There are a number of favourite sunbathing areas beside the bay and lake. In winter, there is skating and even ice boating.

Residents on the east side of Frenchman's Bay sponsor an annual Frenchman's Bay festival each June. Events include live entertainment, activities for children, historical exhibits, nature walks, boat rides, and a popular street dance in which more than 3,000 people participate. For details and exact dates, phone the Pickering Culture and Recreation Department at 905-420-4620.

The Trail leads out of the park into Elvira Court; follow Elvira a short distance to Vistula Drive and turn right. Just after the road curves left, the Trail turns off to the right, cutting across to

THE FRENCH MEN OF FRENCHMAN'S BAY

Frenchman's Bay was probably named for François de Salignac de Fenelon, a Sulpician missionary who spent the winter of 1669-70 with the Seneca of Ganatsekiagon. It was an extremely harsh winter, forcing the natives to scatter into the surrounding forests to hunt for food. Fenelon, who probably intended to establish a mission school in the aboriginal village, had to go with them. He survived on the few squirrels and other small animals he could find, and at times was reportedly reduced to eating the fungi that grew at the base of the trees. In the spring he retreated to Quinte, discouraged and in broken health. Fenelon's sojourn at Frenchman's Bay is notable for two reasons: he was the first European resident in the Toronto area, and he established the first school in the region.

In contrast to the famine faced by Abbé Fenelon, the Marquis Jacques René de Brisay Denonville, governor of New France, who stopped at Ganatsekiagon in 1687 as he was returning from burning Iroquois villages on the south shore of the lake, feasted on some of the 200 deer killed for his party by natives sent ahead to hunt on the north shore. One writer remarked: "[This was] probably the largest party ever held in Pickering."

Bayly Street at the West Shore Community Centre. The centre is a town-owned facility that presents regularly scheduled events. Parking is available in a lot that overlooks Frenchman's Bay Marsh.

From the north end of Frenchman's Bay, you can see pylons out in the marsh, probably all that remains of the original wharf built in the 1850s. Over the years, other structures graced the bay: several wharves, grain elevators and, on the east side, some ice houses, as well as a lighthouse on the east spit. All are now gone.

The Trail heads east along Bayly Street. After a short distance there is a large tunnel cutaway on the left side, in the embankment beneath the railway tracks. This tunnel, which seems to lead nowhere, is the Dunbarton Culvert, sometimes called the "hole in the wall".

DUNBARTON CULVERT

At one time, Bayly Street (then Baseline Road) stopped here and turned north into the tunnel (built about 1900), then west on Kingston Road to the Village of Dunbarton. When a second set of railway tracks was added, the road north was closed.

Dunbarton was named for its first settler, William Dunbar, a wheelwright from Fifeshire in Scotland who was largely responsible for building the docks in Frenchman's Bay in the 1850s.

If you need a break or supplies, you will find a shopping mall just past St. Martins Drive; there are other shops and services (260 of them) at the Pickering Town Centre, north of Highway 401 on Liverpool Road. The Pickering Civic Complex, Central Library, and Recreation Complex are just east of the mall.

In the same area, you will find the Old Liverpool House at the corner of Liverpool Road and Highway 2 (Kingston Road). Now a restaurant for fine dining, in its long history it has served as a hotel, a general store, a rooming house, and a post office. When it was opened in 1878, one of its early guests was the prime minister himself, Sir John A. Macdonald.

To continue on the Trail, turn right off Bayly at St. Martins Drive, then left on Radom Street, which passes over Douglas Creek Ravine. Pine Creek is one of the streams that feeds Frenchman's Bay; at one time it had a run of water sufficient to support a mill. While it is not easy to see, the ravine holds the remnants of an old dam; furthermore, it is a good place to find migrating warblers in the early spring.

Turn right on Douglas Avenue, which passes by Douglas Park, a small community park with a playground. To reach Massey's restaurant, a favourite of local boaters, or the Liverpool South Mall (at Krosno and Liverpool), turn left at Old Orchard Avenue. The Trail, however, continues to the end of Douglas, turns west (right) on Browning Avenue, then immediately south again (left) on Front Road. Front Road leads through the old centre of Fairport Village, past a number of old cottages, as well as the private Port Pickering Marina.

RUM-RUNNING AT FRENCHMAN'S BAY
in the 1920s

It was not common knowledge even at the time, but, in the prohibition years in Ontario, Frenchman's Bay was a port-of-entry for many a cargo of bootlegged booze. The liquor was brought into the bay by boat, transferred to motor cars, and taken into Toronto. Apparently, the rum-runners had powerful engines in their boats and could outrun any coast guard vessels. At least two stories of rum-running in the bay have been handed down over the years.

As reported by the *Pickering News* of June 1, 1923, the provincial police got wind of a shipment of whiskey en route from Belleville and probably to be unloaded at Fairport. The police department sent only two men to intercept the smugglers. The officers waited a long time and, at last, the boat appeared and the smugglers began unloading their cargo into five cars.

The officers stayed put until the cars were loaded, and they then headed into town along a sideroad leading to the Dunbarton school, before attempting an arrest. When the officers began to overtake the smugglers, one of the drivers manoeuvred his vehicle onto the Grand Trunk Railway tracks and escaped. Another car tried to follow, but blew a tire, and its occupants, as well as those in the other three cars, were caught.

Seven men were arrested and 118 cases of whiskey, later valued at $8,000, were confiscated. Brought before the court in Whitby, the seven pleaded not guilty and were released on $1,000 bail each. The Pickering News reported that one of them had more than $1,700 on his person but, at a time when crimes were carried out less ferociously than now, none carried a gun.

A number of area residents still remember "Black Jack", the very young skipper of the *Hattie C*, a small runabout of about six metres (20 feet), which often visited the sheltered waters of Frenchman's Bay. Jack's cargo was usually bound in burlap sacks, and was not discussed, but the content of the sacks was obviously in bottles.

Black Jack's story, however, has an unhappy ending. One night, when he landed at Ashbridge's Bay in Toronto, he found the police waiting in hiding for him. He ignored their shouted demands that he stop, and his attempts to make a run for it were met with a shower of bullets, during which Jack was shot and killed.

FAIRPORT VILLAGE

Development of Frenchman's Bay began on its east side, which became the economic centre of Pickering Township when the bay was a shipping port. The village itself, as shown on the *Ontario County Atlas* in 1877, was a very small area around Front Road and Commerce Street, and apparently never expanded beyond these limits.

In the first half of the 20th century, Fairport Village and its environs became a cottage community, most of whose residents knew the east shore simply as Frenchman's Bay. To them, Fairport referred to the beach community on the west side.

At the corner of Commerce and Front is a small building that used to serve as a post office and store; all that remains is the old post office sign, still in the window. A summer post office opened in 1921.

BAY RIDGES

The larger community on the east shore of the bay is now known as Bay Ridges, the first subdivision built in Pickering in the boom that followed WW II. The development was begun in the early 1960s on what was then farmland. Many of the landowners and/or their descendants still live in the area.

Turn left on Annland Street and right (south) at Liverpool Road to the lake. You will pass the East Shore Marina, Swan's Marina, Coolwater Farms Ltd., a french fry outlet, and a pub, before reaching Beachfront Park.

COOLWATER FARMS LTD.

This innovative company uses heated water discharged from the Pickering Generating Station to raise rainbow trout. Established in 1986, Coolwater produces about 454,500 kilograms (one million pounds) of rainbow trout each year for the wholesale market. The facility is not open to the public.

BEACHFRONT PARK/HYDRO MARSH

There is limited parking at the foot of Liverpool Road. The park has a pebbly beach and a playground; there is unsupervised swimming, but the water is tested regularly for quality. Check that the water is safe before you go.

Ducks, geese, and swans may be found year-round in the pond north of the spit. In the spring, summer, and early fall, black-crowned night herons roost in the alder thickets of the marsh. Both black and common terns and American coot breed there in the summer and it has an abundance of other wildlife as well. Like the marsh at the head of Frenchman's Bay, this is an important stopover for migrating waterfowl and shore birds.

The Trail crosses the sand spit that is Beachfront Park, but there is access here only for walking. Cyclists will probably have to walk their bicycles over the sand.

ALEX ROBERTSON COMMUNITY PARK

Named for a long-time member of the town council, this beautifully landscaped park is on Ontario Hydro property, but is maintained for public use by the Town of Pickering. Its trails are unpaved, but along them you may see a variety of wildlife, including red fox, snapping turtles, and both breeding and migrating birds.

BAY RIDGES KINSMEN PARK

Just east of Alex Robertson Park, across Sandy Beach Road, is Bay Ridges Kinsmen Park. It has a playground, tennis courts, and several ball fields and soccer pitches, with lights for night games. This is where the Town of Pickering holds its annual Canada Day celebrations. The program, which now attracts 25,000 participants, includes games and activities for children, displays and demonstrations, an evening of entertainment, and a giant fireworks display as a grand finale. It is an event the entire family will enjoy, and is held every Canada Day from noon to 11 p.m.

The Trail cuts across the south end of Alex Robertson Community Park, along the fence line of the Pickering Nuclear

Generating Station to Montgomery Park Road at Sandy Beach
Road. Head east along Montgomery Park Road, past the generating station.

ONTARIO HYDRO PICKERING NUCLEAR
GENERATING STATION

Pickering Nuclear Generating Station, one of the largest in the
world, was begun in 1965; the first two of its present eight units (in
the distinctive domed buildings that house the reactors) began producing electricity in 1971. The station now generates about 20
percent of Ontario Hydro's annual load, or about twice the total of
all water-driven generating stations on the Canadian side of the
Niagara River.

The Pickering station has an information centre that
is open to the public, free of charge, Monday through Friday, 9 a.m.
to 4 p.m. (Times are subject to change.) Inside, visitors walk
through a life-sized cutaway model of a CANDU nuclear reactor,
and see exhibits and films that explain how the reactors generate
electricity. The centre also has information for students to use in
school projects. The entrance to the information centre is off
Montgomery Park Road (follow the signs). Tours are offered, but
must be arranged in advance. For information or to arrange a tour,
contact the Pickering Energy Information Centre, P.O. Box 160,
Pickering, Ontario L1V 2R5; 905-839-0465.

The generating station sits on 270 hectares (667
acres) of land of which about 40 hectares (99 acres) are taken up by
Alex Robertson Community Park and Bay Ridges Kinsmen Park.

Continue east past Brock Road to the end of
Montgomery Park Road (the road turns right toward the lake at the
Duffins Creek Water Pollution Control Plant).

Side Trip
NORTH ON BROCK ROAD TO POST MANOR

Brock Road was the earliest north-south road in Pickering
Township, and probably followed an old native trail. It
opened in 1808-1809, connecting Quaker settlements in

Pickering, Uxbridge, and Whitchurch. The area south of Bayly Street, both west and east of Brock Road, is now industrial.

A short drive (about 6 kilometres or 3.7 miles) on Brock Road to Highway 2 (Kingston Road) brings you to one of the township's older structures, Post Manor, which was built in 1841 by Jordon Post but now is a real estate office. Post owned a sawmill at Duffins Creek near Brock Road and probably had Pickering's largest lumber operation. The house is of fieldstone, in the Classical or Greek Revival style. To rejoin the Waterfront Trail backtrack south on Brock Road and go east on Montgomery Park Road. ▪

On the south side of Montgomery Park Road just east of Brock Road, you will see a huge mound of earth. Originally a drumlin, the hill rose even higher when landfill, removed in the building of the generating station, was added to it.

DUFFINS CREEK WATER POLLUTION CONTROL PLANT

If you value Pickering's rivers and lakefront, you will admire the work at this facility. Municipalities no longer simply discharge the effluent from water pollution control plants into the nearest river. Duffins Creek Water Pollution Control Plant is a state-of-the-art facility for treating sewage, the most visible part of a system that services the towns of Newmarket, Aurora, Richmond Hill, and Markham; the City of Vaughan in York Region; and the towns of Pickering and Ajax in the Region of Durham.

The plant was designed to be expanded in several stages. The initial phase, completed in 1981, could handle 182,000 cubic metres (40 million gallons) of sewage per day, while the present capacity is half as great again. Ultimately, the fully expanded and operational plant will be able to treat twice that amount each day.

While the facility is not generally open to the public, it occasionally has an open house in connection with Public Works Week in the early fall. For information about such events, or to learn more about the operation of the water pollution control plant (a brochure is available), phone the Works Department of the

Regional Municipality of Durham at 905-668-7721 or fax them at 905-668-2051.

It is expected that, if current plans are implemented, the Trail will cut across the water pollution control plant property from Montgomery Park Road and connect to Ingrid Road; along Ingrid to Conmara Avenue; and along Conmara to the Ajax line at the mouth of Duffins Creek. In the future, the creek may be crossed by a bridge to the Ajax Waterfront Trail.

However, until the bridge is built, you will have to detour around Duffins Creek by following Montgomery Park to Mckay Road (exercise care as Mckay is a busy road), turning north on Squires Beach Road and travelling east on Bayly Street West.

SQUIRES BEACH/DUFFINS CREEK

Along Ingrid and Conmara you will see what is left of what once was a thriving summer cottage community; those that survive have long been winterized and all the residents are tenants, the property now being owned by the Province. The names Ingrid, Sandra, and Susan recall three daughters of Gustave Plitz, a farmer who owned the land in the 1940s and 1950s.

Simcoe Point

The point of land that overlooks the mouth of Duffins Creek is known as Simcoe Point. Here, in 1912, John Henry Greenlaw built Simcoe House as a summer resort. Unfortunately, the property had to be sold when he died shortly after the resort opened. However, the new owners made it a popular destination and for a quarter-century or more, it attracted visitors from all over Ontario. During the Depression, the resort fell on hard times and declined rapidly. The end came in the 1950s, when the building was destroyed by fire.

At that spot you will now find the Simcoe Point Pioneer Cemetery. It contains a plaque summarizing the area's history and lists some of the people buried there.

In earlier times, Duffins Creek teemed with salmon, so many that the French called it Rivière au Saumon. Early settlers built numerous mills and dams along the creek, thus preventing the

SAILING IN HAMILTON HARBOUR, *Hamilton*   Lisa Ohata

SAND SCULPTURE, HARBOURFRONT PARK, *Hamilton*   Lisa Ohata

St. Luke's Church, *Burlington*   Irene Rota

Gairloch Gardens, *Oakville*   Town of Oakville

BRONTE CREEK PARK, *Oakville*   Sheila Creighton

CORONATION PARK, *Oakville*   Town of Oakville

ERCHLESS ESTATE, *Oakville*   Sheila Creighton

BRADLEY MUSEUM, *Mississauga*   City of Mississauga

ADAMSON ESTATE, *Mississauga*   Landplan Collaborative

ETOBICOKE WATERFRONT PARK

Carlo Bonanni

LAKESHORE COMMUNITY FESTIVAL, *Etobicoke*

Don Bell

LION MONUMENT, *Toronto*

Darcy Baker

SKYLINE, *Toronto*

MTCVA

QUEEN'S QUAY, *Toronto*

MTCVA

MARTIN GOODMAN TRAIL, *Toronto*

Greg Rich

ONTARIO PLACE, *Toronto*   Ontario Place Corporation

TURTLE UNDER ICE, *Toronto Islands*   Rick/Simon

LEUTY AVENUE LIFE SAVING STATION, EASTERN BEACHES, *Toronto*   Barry Linetsky

MARINA SUNSET, ASHBRIDGES BAY, *Toronto*   Dr. J. D. Murray

MONARCH BUTTERFLY, LESLIE STREET SPIT, *Toronto*   Seniors for Nature

SCARBOROUGH BLUFFS, *Scarborough*   Helen Juhola

GUILD INN, *Scarborough*   Irene Rota

FISHING THE ROUGE RIVER, *Scarborough*   Patricia Brooks

SHORELINE, *Pickering*   Ian Deslauriers

MOUTH OF DUFFINS CREEK, *Ajax*   Suzanne Barrett

DUFFINS CREEK THICKET, ROTARY PARK, *Ajax*

Andrew Farncombe

LYNDE SHORES WETLAND, *Whitby*

Irene Rota

LYNDE SHORES BOARDWALK, *Whitby*

Region of Durham Planning

ROBINSON HOUSE, SYDENHAM MUSEUM, *Oshawa*　　　　　　　　Irene Rota

LAKEVIEW PARK, *Oshawa*　　　　　　　　Ed Ufniak

EAST BEACH, *Clarington*   Donald Piper

FISHING IN THE FOG, *Clarington*   Dr. J. D. Murray

St. Mary's Cement, *Clarington*   **Donald Piper**

Waterfall, *Port Hope*   **Don McLean**

CANADIAN FIRE FIGHTER'S MUSEUM, *Port Hope*   Don McLean

GANARASKA RIVER, *Port Hope*   Randy Brown

VICTORIA PARK, *Cobourg*   Ted Amsden

VICTORIA HALL, *Cobourg*   Irene Rota

Victoria Beach, *Cobourg*   Ted Amsden

Public Boat Launch, *Haldimand*   Lisa Ohata

NAWAUTIN NATURE SANCTUARY, *Haldimand*   Barry Linetsky

APPLE BLOSSOMS, *Colborne*   Northumberland County Tourist Bureau

APPLE HARVEST, *Brighton*   Northumberland County Tourist Bureau

PRESQU'ILE LIGHTHOUSE, *Brighton*   Northumberland County Tourist Bureau

PRESQU'ILE PROVINCIAL PARK, *Brighton*   Don Bell

TRENT RIVER FROM JACK LANGE MEMORIAL WALKWAY, *Trenton*   Don Bell

salmon from swimming upstream to spawn, which led to their inevitable decline.

The name Duffin, which was attached to the Creek as early as 1791, comes from an Irish trader who lived in the area of what is now Pickering Village. Although a shadowy figure about whom little is known, he was reputed to have been a "genial Irishman" who opened his home to passing travellers. One of them, however, repaid his hospitality by murdering him.

Apart from the unfortunate Duffin, the earliest European settlers of Pickering Township were fur trader and native interpreter William Peak and his wife Margaret, who came to the mouth of Duffins Creek about 1800. They cleared the land on the west side of the creek; John Greenlaw, of Simcoe House, was married to their granddaughter.

By 1808, the population of Pickering had increased to 180 people. A year or two later the first considerable influx of settlers occurred when Timothy Rogers, a native of Vermont, brought a number of Quaker families. Rogers also built the first grist mill on Duffins Creek, and probably the first sawmill.

Here, where aboriginal tribes roamed some 4,000 years ago, and where Pickering's European settlers first put down roots, the Pickering section of the Waterfront Trail ends.

Side Trips
PICKERING MUSEUM

The Pickering Museum Village in the village of Greenwood is a re-creation of the life of settlers in the region more than a century ago. It includes restored buildings, pioneer demonstrations, and hands-on creative programs and events. In addition, there are a number of annual special events: Steam-up Days, Teddy Bears' Picnic, a Festival of Early Canadian Music and Folk Art, and History in Action.

To reach the museum, take Brock Road north to Brougham; turn right on Highway 7 and follow it to Greenwood. The museum is open in July and August from Wednesday to Sunday, 11 a.m. to 5 p.m. In June and September, it opens on weekends and holidays only, for the same hours. For further information, phone 905-683-8401 or 905-420-4620. ■

SEATON HIKING TRAIL

The Seaton Hiking Trail is a 10-kilometre (6-mile) track that winds its way through the beautiful West Duffins Creek Valley, north from Rossland Road to Green River. Divided into three sections, the trail offers choices for the prospective hiker.

The section from Rossland Road (at Camp Pidaca, west of Brock Road) to Clarkes Hollow is a fairly easy walk and provides a good opportunity to see a variety of wildlife. The trail from Clarkes Hollow (west from Brock Road on Taunton Road, then left on White's Road and first left again) to Whitevale offers more of a wilderness habitat. Whitevale Village has recently gained heritage status and has some beautiful heritage homes to enjoy. From Whitevale (west from Brock Road on the 5th Concession Road), this heritage trail goes north past old millworks, ponds, and lowland woods to Green River on Highway 7. ■

POSSIBLE FUTURE TRAIL CONNECTIONS

Among the trails being planned are those that would go north from the Waterfront Trail to follow the valley of the Rouge River in the newly created Rouge Park. Because of the ecological sensitivity of the Rouge Marsh near the lake, a route will probably be needed on residential streets to connect with the valley north of the marsh. In addition, the Town of Pickering and the conservation authority, MTRCA, hope to create a trail along Petticoat Creek from the Waterfront Trail to the Altona Forest. ⇒

ICE VOLCANOES

The sea is always restless. Even when the surface seems calm, there are currents in its depths, and in the bleakest winter, there is the unremitting flurry of life. Clusters of thick shards stack themselves into bizarrely shaped ice floes, while caves are carved beneath. If conditions are right, all this combines to create an ice volcano.

These are conical peaks of shore ice that resemble the land-bound variety. Fully developed, they are topped by a crater, and a central vent, with steeply sloping sides and a height of as much as 7 metres (23 feet). But rather than spouting lava, these volcanoes spew lake water as large waves surge beneath, shooting spray up the vents. This water eruption freezes almost instantly as it lands on the exterior, and each wave builds the cone a little higher.

If the volcano is to grow, it needs below-freezing temperatures and a steady supply of water. But, as the edge of the shore ice moves beyond the cone, it is more difficult for waves to reach the peak. Eventually, old volcanoes become dormant, and new ones start to form on the lake side. Under ideal circumstances, the cones form ranges, each row of peaks parallel to the shoreline.

Ice volcanoes can form anywhere thick shore ice develops. However, it can be dangerous to venture from the shoreline to inspect the forms up close since there may be invisible fissures in the ice. Ice volcanoes should be observed from land, using binoculars or a camera with a telephoto lens.

Unobstructed *beauty and graceful simplicity, giving the sense of a waterfront that is oceans away from the Big City*

◄······

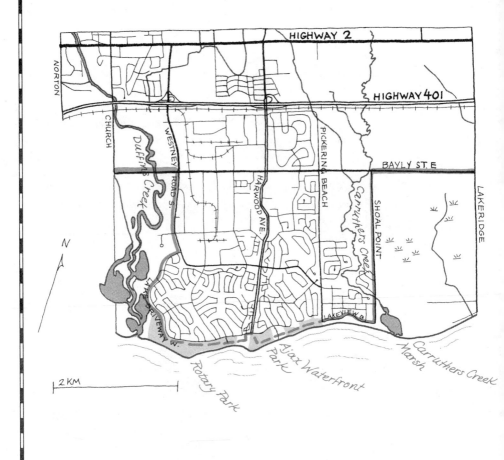

Ajax

HERE ARE TIMES when progress is the ability to leave things alone, a definition that certainly applies to the Ajax waterfront. Although just a short reach from Toronto, it unfolds in unobstructed beauty and graceful simplicity, giving the sense of a waterfront that is oceans away from the Big City.

The Town of Ajax is named for a historical WW II fight, the Battle of the River Plate: in December 1939, a fleet of British warships, HMS *Ajax* prominent among them, engaged and defeated the Nazi pocket battleship *Graf Spee*, in what was then a rare victory.

The area that became Ajax was made up of farms resting comfortably on Lake Ontario's shores. With the advent of war, it became necessary to find a suitable location for a shell filling factory that could supply Canadian troops – ideally, one a short distance from Toronto but far enough away to ensure the fewest casualties if the plant became an enemy target. The quiet landscape, only 37 kilometres (23 miles) east, was about to change forever as munitions manufactured in Ajax became the area's newest and most urgently needed crop.

When the war ended, some 3,000 veterans took advantage of education credits and enrolled in University of Toronto courses being offered in Ajax. In 1949, when that program closed, Canada's Central Mortgage and Housing Corporation announced that Ajax would become the country's first fully planned industrial/residential community. The following year Ajax was incorporated as an "improvement district"; it became a town five years later and part of the Municipality of Durham in 1974, when Ontario established the system of regional government. By the late 1980s, as a prime location for light industry, Ajax experienced the third-fastest growth of any community in Canada.

The town's waterfront is a gem of unspoiled beauty. Host to more than 4 kilometres (2.5 miles) of the Waterfront Trail stretching along the municipality's western coastline, it remains one of the most picturesque lakefronts in southern Ontario. The 60,000 people who live in Ajax are delighted to keep it that way.

PUBLIC TRANSIT

Local Transit
(905-427-5710)

GO (416-869-3200)
• Ajax – Westney Rd. at Fairall St. 5 km from waterfront

The main street leading to the waterfront's edge is Harwood Avenue, which can be reached from Highway 401; the street, flanked on either side with mature trees, was named after Admiral Sir Henry Harwood (1888-1950), who commanded the HMS Ajax. The 4-kilometre (2.5-mile) drive south leads directly to Lake Driveway, the southernmost road running parallel to the shore.

Those who are following the route from Pickering will enter the Waterfront Trail along the interim route that travels east on Bayly Street West to Westney Road. Turning south on Westney will take you to Lake Driveway West; this road leads directly to Duffins Creek.

DUFFINS CREEK AND WETLAND

There are plans that will see the construction of a pedestrian bridge across Duffins Creek near its mouth. This will allow Trail users to follow the path from Pickering through the thicket, remaining close to the waterfront and avoid the lengthy on-road detour. This is a beautiful area for a picnic or just for enjoying natural surroundings and should not be missed.

Until recently, little attention was paid to wetlands and their environmental importance; now, however, these areas of marsh are understood to be vital to sustaining the natural ecosystem. Home to various species of fish and wildlife, they control water quality, absorb floodwaters, help stabilize shorelines, and, because they are essential habitat, are life supports for species of wildlife.

It is estimated that, in the past two centuries, Ontario has lost at least 70 percent of its wetlands and that, each year, Southern Ontario loses one to two percent of what remains. For this reason alone, Duffins Creek remains a significant part of the surrounding landscape, and a treat for visitors to the Waterfront Trail.

Officially classified as a Class 3 Provincially Significant Wetland (see page 5 for information about classification of wetlands), it exists under the jurisdiction of the Metropolitan Toronto and Region Conservation Authority (MTRCA), which has a mandate to protect and manage natural resources in the region's watershed. The MTRCA works toward the protection and restoration of healthy wetlands. For more information on Duffins Creek or the MTRCA, please contact the MTRCA Communications Department at 416-661-6600.

The creek has its own natural character many kinds of fish, including spottail shiner, trout, white sucker, carp, and bass, spawn here, and such waterfowl as the common loon and Canada goose use it as a breeding ground. The area has long been considered a fishing paradise in a setting that makes its urban location easy to forget. Local bird populations include white-throated sparrows, rock doves, yellow-rumped warblers, and blue jays.

The small sandy beach at the mouth of the creek is easily accessible and provides views of the CN Tower to the west and the Ajax bluffs to the east. At the creek's mouth is very sandy natural beach, which is experiencing some westward shift. The area is classified as a 'dynamic beach' with sand expected to shift back and forth within a small expanse, resulting in a contantly changing beach. Steps to protect the shoreline are not considered necessary because the degree of drift at the mouth does not endanger any nearby property, and is not expected to do so in the foreseeable future.

Side Trip

DUFFINS CREEK

Canoeists can take a 4-kilometre (2.5-mile) excursion up the creek and around its various inlets. There is a public boat launch and parking area nearby, just off Lake Driveway. The Town discourages the use of jet skis and other motorized transport on the creek, which means that the water is quiet for canoeists. ■

If you are walking the Trail, you will find that the east side of the Creek leads to a 3-metre (10-foot) wide asphalt path that winds its way through a thicket area and directly into Rotary Park, the westernmost waterfront parkland in Ajax.

ROTARY PARK

Rotary Park sits on what was first a farmstead and then a campground; today, it lines the western portion of the Trail in Ajax with
a blend of woodsy natural environment and recreational facilities.
This makes it one of the most popular spots along the Ajax
waterfront; there is parking off Lake Driveway, in the same lot used
for gaining access to the boat launch at Duffins Creek.

Through most of the park, the Waterfront Trail is
3 metres (10 feet) wide and asphalt-covered, making it perfect for
bikers, joggers, strollers, in-line skaters, and people in wheelchairs.
The woodlands and orchard that border the western end of the
marsh make it easy to forget the city. Framed by thick shrub growth,
the area offers a mixture of wild and naturalized roses, honeysuckle,
raspberries, and dogwood and is ideal for viewing the marsh's reedy
riverbeds and open waters.

Some of the area's largest trees grow here, including
red oaks and maples; they are important to the park and, in an
effort to maintain and enhance their growth, park authorities
recently co-ordinated a regeneration program through which
schoolchildren, members of service clubs, and volunteers planted
more than six thousand trees donated by Trees Canada.

Continuing east, the Trail is aligned along the southeast shores of the marsh, the park's main recreational area; there is
an adventure playground with swings and climbers, a picnic area,
and a pavilion housing wheelchair-accessible washroom facilities
and a snack bar. Against a background of willow trees and silver
maples, a nearby water inlet marks a meeting place for waterfowl.

Running parallel to Lake Ontario, the Trail stretches
east along the bluffs, which slope outward toward the lake to
provide an exceptional, unobstructed view of this magnificent body
of water. The area is exposed and offers a sense of infinite space.
with the few benches simply adding to the enjoyment.

The bluffs at this point are not very high, making
access to the beach possible at a number of points. The beach,
which is mainly a large sandbar descending into the mouth of
Duffins Creek, is one of the most extensive along the Ajax
Waterfront Trail.

In winter, the Trail is not cleared and becomes ideal for cross-country skiing, snowshoeing or hiking. In September, it is possible to enjoy the thousands of monarch butterflies on their annual migration south. (See page 291 for more information on this phenomenon.)

Rotary Park's diversity seems, at first, to include a neglected area; this is, in fact, a "naturalized" portion of the park and grows without interference. This area began with preliminary plantings of indigenous trees and other plants; once those take hold the land will be left to flourish without human intervention or prettifying. The result is a regenerated landscape reflecting the region's natural flora and fauna.

EVENTS

A popular place in summer, the park is the site of events and activities from May to October: for example, in mid-July, the Toronto Kite Fliers Club holds the annual On the Edge Sport Kite Championships, featuring competitions, demonstrations, and free lessons. Contact Pina Sicari at 416-747-9106 for dates and other information.

The Town of Ajax hosts a series of events, including a two-week Gone Fish'n' instructional/environmental program for youngsters aged six and older. Music in the Park, which is presented every other Sunday from June to August, features local bands performing everything from jazz to country to rock and roll. The music gets under way at 1 p.m. and continues until 4 p.m. The festivities also include a barbecue and a snack bar.

There is also Bug Mania, an entomology program for children between the ages of five and eight. It is held each Monday evening between 6 and 7:30 p.m. in May and on the first Saturday afternoon in June, from 10 a.m. to noon.

Home Week, which has been held every year since 1970, kicks off on the Sunday before Father's Day and winds up on the evening of Father's Day. Throughout the town, there are activities for the whole family, including a barbecue, parade, pancake breakfast, concerts, and the Mayor's Derby horse race.

It is capped off with a fireworks display, held in Rotary Park on the final evening.

One of the most popular festivities, of course, is Canada Day, when celebrations begin at noon and last until 4 p.m. Highlights include live music, a barbecue, and children's activities. For more information about these and other events, contact the Ajax Parks and Recreation Department at 905-427-8811.

LION'S POINT

As you continue east along the Waterfront Trail, you reach Lion's Point, which rises more than 20 metres (65 feet) from the rocky coast – a spectacular area that is the highest elevation on the Ajax waterfront. Originally named after the Sparks family, which owned the land, it was designated Lion's Point in the late 1980s; the move marked appreciation of the local Lions Club which, over the years, has supported tree planting and other community programs.

But it is not height alone that makes the point so striking, it is also shape. With its maximum reach along the bluffs, it rolls gently back to flatten out near Lake Driveway. The unusual formation makes it stand out from the surrounding landscape; it is a popular viewing area, even offering glimpses of Toronto's distant shore, framed by its famous skyline.

About 0.5 kilometres (0.3 mile) east, the Trail turns north, away from the water; it is necessary to follow the route to Lake Driveway in order to skirt a privately owned parcel of land. At the Driveway, the Trail passes the Duffin Bay neighbourhood. A modern residential area, its pastel homes are enviably located just a stone's throw from lakeshore, parkland, and woodland. Here, the Trail heads south, back to the water, and continues east through Ajax Waterfront Park.

AJAX WATERFRONT PARK

Like Rotary Park, this 27-hectare (66-acre) landmark was originally farmland. Located at the southern end of Harwood Avenue, it has been beautifully transformed in the twenty years since it came under MTRCA stewardship. Bordered on the north by

Lake Driveway, it is between 100 and 275 metres (330 and 900 feet) wide, generally in rolling greenspace.

The Trail running along the top of the bluffs through this park is also asphalt-covered and is excellent for walking, jogging, biking, and skating, and for people in wheelchairs. Take your time: there are exquisite lake views from here. Over an open field to the northeast is the Durham Region Water Filtration Station; it is scheduled for expansion and will supply water to parts of Pickering and Whitby, in addition to serving Ajax.

The sandy bluffs are no higher than 5 metres (16 feet) and provide easy access to the beach. Unfortunately, the sandy escarpment is vulnerable to erosion and deterioration, primarily because of the ceaseless action of the lake and of weather, but also as a result of human traffic. Therefore, extreme care and environmental sensitivity are a must here.

People interested in flora will enjoy the nearby locust grove that lines the view to the east. Past the locust trees, the Trail continues east along The Hill, a favourite local toboggan run; it then covers relatively flat ground and is easy to traverse.

The view from this point on the bluffs is a less aesthetic sight, but a fascinating environmental lesson: in the mid-1960s, concrete sewer pipes were dumped into the lake. This irresponsible act inadvertently created something of a breakwater in front of the cliffs, permitting vegetation to take hold; in turn, the vegetation helps buffer the shoreline from abrasion although the intersting geological feature (bluffs) is thereby destroyed. The effectiveness of this unplanned shield can be seen by comparing the spot with the more eroded sections to its immediate east and west.

The Trail's walkways lead to residential areas that flank The Hill, as well as to a parking lot. Because it is easy to gain access to the water, this is a favourite spot for neighbouring children and teenagers. It is also close to an open area at the foot of McClarnan Road which, before Waterfront Park was fully developed, was the only maintained section of parkland. Once the site of local pick-up games of football, baseball, and soccer, as well as of frisbee throwing and kite flying, it is still used occasionally for those activities.

The Trail continues east along the asphalt path to Pickering Beach Road, where the park ends. If you have walked the path through Rotary Park and along this stretch of the Trail, you have covered some 4 kilometres (2.5 miles) of the waterfront. The Trail continues east along Lakeview Boulevard for about 1 kilometre (0.6 mile). The boulevard is a two-lane road with no shoulder but, because of the rural nature of the area and the general absence of heavy traffic, it is usually safe for pedestrians, although somewhat awkward for people in wheelchairs.

PICKERING BEACH

Known as Pickering Beach, this portion of the Trail offers pleasing scenery. Many of the original cottage-style homes built after the war still dot the landscape, providing examples of the architecture prevalent in the years when housing for veterans and new families was a vital public issue. The soft, rural undertones are a reminder of life before skyscrapers and before highways (either paved or electronic). Aside from the architecture, the area is known for its abundance of mature silver maples, ash, and willows, their crowns weaving an almost impenetrable leafy arch overhead and unforget-table scenery for visitors.

In order to increase areas of public access, and to pro-tect the shoreline's diversity and natural habitat, MTRCA has purchased all but a few of the lakefront lots. Flanked by Lakeview Boulevard and the residential community to the north, and with points of easy, sloping access to the beach to the south, this is an almost continuous area of public open-air parkland and shoreline. Moreover, Paradise lies within.

Once the site of a school, then a fire hall, and finally a shop, Paradise Park is in the middle of the setting; it houses two asphalt tennis courts, a baseball diamond, and a kids' playground. There is a small portion of land to the west that is still undeveloped but is earmarked for park purposes. Until then, some original structures remain, including the small grey, red-trimmed brick building that was the town's original fire station but now serves as a storage facility.

If you detour from the Trail to visit the shore, note the railway ties standing upright on the beach; they are one of several methods used by local landowners as protection against erosion from the lake. Another strategy was to place concrete blocks on the beach in an effort to fortify the land against wind and waves. However, these methods are not effective in the long run. For more information on how to integrate cost-effective shoreline treatment with fish habitat enhancement, see the *Lake Ontario Greenway Strategy*.

Following Lakeview Boulevard east brings you to Shoal Point Road, where you may catch a glimpse of a llama or goats on the property straight ahead. This is privately owned land, not accessible to the public.

At this point, the Trail goes north and, is aligned on-road. However, there is an enjoyable mix of residential, farming, and wooded scenery along either side. At Bayly Street East, the route travels east along the gravel shoulder of what is a very busy road, making it necessary for visitors to use extreme caution. With vehicles roaring by at 80 kph (50 mph), this section should be travelled only by car or on a bicycle with wide tires (and an experienced rider). In the future, the Trail will go north only a short distance on Shoal Point Road before turning south through the wooded area along Carruthers Creek Marsh and east into the Municipality of Whitby.

Side Trip

CARRUTHERS CREEK MARSH

While today's Trail uses the interim route of Shoal Point and Bayly roads, you can enjoy an excursion into the Carruthers Creek Marsh area; although it has no formal paths, it has numerous informal ones at its northern and eastern rims, created by generations of nature lovers. This is a Class 3 Provincially Significant Wetland, accessible only to hikers or walkers and well worth a gentle visit. Filled with sedges and rushes, its expanse of open water nurtures various species of ducks, birds, and fish that come to feed. ■

Cleaning Up Our Own Backyard

According to Ajax resident Errol Sarpkaya, "We have eliminated 80 percent of Ontario's wetlands. Without wetlands, we don't have pure water. Without water, there is no life. Period."

For more than two decades, as an explorer and underwater naturalist, Sarpkaya has observed the decline of our natural resources. His concern with healthy biodiversity prompted him to become involved in Project Aware, a worldwide organization that promotes environmental education for preserving and protecting the aquatic environment, now and in future.

"Our wetlands are equivalent to rainforests because they purify the water", he points out. "Everything is connected. If we foul our water, it filters through the fish and wildlife chain and into the human food chain. We need to spend our money on regenerating that efficient natural process. Once it's in place, it's free."

Through Project Aware, and his own organization, Aquatic World Awareness, Sarpkaya is doing his part to inform and educate people. An optimist, he is the process of having his program on the aquatic environment approved by the Durham Board of Education for use in its schools. "Essentially", he says, "the focus will be on the waterfront, wetlands, creeks, rivers, and streams."

The goal is to interest young people in the issue and use their ideas and energy to bring about change. In 1994, for instance, Sarpkaya and teams of young people removed 30 garbage bags of foam and plastic from just one 200-metre-square (650-foot-square) area of Duffins Creek. The collection also included 400 cans and 200 bottles, abandoned fishing lines which are dangerous to birds, and enough oil to render one million litres (220,000 gallons) of water unfit for human consumption.

Mr. Sarpkaya's message is to the point: "We need to rebuild existing Ontario parkland and wetlands to the point where they are ecologically self-sustaining. We might not be able to save the world, but we can have an impact on our own small corner of it."

The farm on the southeast corner of Shoal Point and Bayly is owned and operated by the Layter family. The large farmhouse and surrounding grounds were once part of the munitions factory that gave birth to the town: the structure originally served as the barracks for Canadian service personnel working at the military operation. Now the Layters' home, it has been in the family since the 1950s, when they emigrated from Ukraine.

Today, Mrs. Layter and two daughters operate the 45-hectare (110-acre) farm, where they keep cattle and harvest 4 hectares (10 acres) of raspberries. These are sold across Ontario; however, in July and August, the Layters sell directly from their farmhouse, making a visit well worthwhile.

Bayly Street East is not only busy, it is primarily commercial, with few places to stop. After crossing Lakeridge Road, Bayly becomes Victoria Street, the starting point of a trip to Whitby.

Cranberry *Marsh offers one of the best spots for watching raptors – majestic birds of prey*

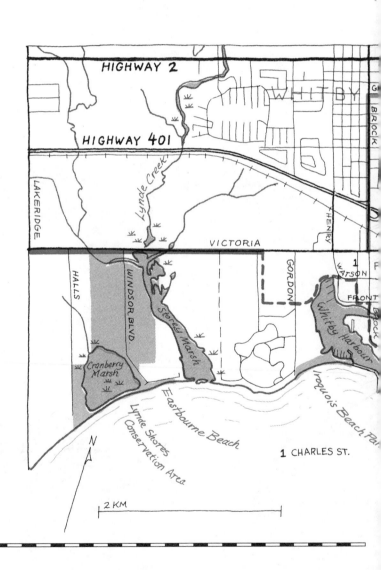

HIGHWAY 2

WHITBY

HIGHWAY 401

Lynde Creek

LAKERIDGE

HENRY

VICTORIA

HALLS

WINDSOR BLVD.

Starkey Marsh

GORDON

WATSON

1

FRONT

Whitby Harbour

Cranberry Marsh

Iroquois Beach Park

Eastbourne Beach

Lynde Shores Conservation Area

N

1 CHARLES ST.

2 KM

Whitby

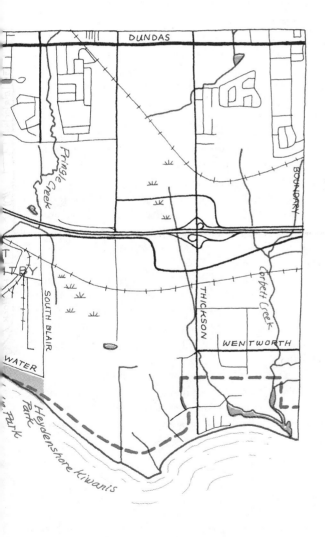

PUBLIC TRANSIT

Local Transit
(905-668-3544)

GO (905-579-4224)
• Whitby – Brock St. at
Hwy. 401, 1.5 km from
Whitby Harbour

HE FIRST SETTLERS in what is now the Town of Whitby – most were Late Loyalists – arrived from the United States in the 1790s and early 1800s, making their homes near the bay and along Kingston Road. (Now Dundas Street in Whitby, it was once part of the old Highway 2.)

By the early 1830s, Whitby's natural harbour, Windsor Bay, was an active port and the community was thriving. In 1848, a plank road (now Highway 12) was built to Port Perry so that farmers could transport their grain from the area north of the village to the harbour. Seven years later, Whitby was officially incorporated as a town and the boundaries set then remained unchanged until 1968, when the town amalgamated with the Township of Whitby; it now accounts for more than 7 kilometres (4.3 miles) of waterfront between Ajax and Oshawa.

Today, Whitby is home to approximately 70,000 people, and is well served by Highway 401 and the GO Transit commuter system. People who live and work in Whitby have all the benefits of proximity to Metropolitan Toronto while still maintaining the advantages of a small community.

Generally, Whitby's historically and architecturally significant buildings are located in the town centre, in and around Dundas and Brock streets. Many of Whitby's early buildings are still intact, these can be seen on informal walking or cycling tours, and are part of this portion of the Waterfront Trail.

A continuous public trail along Whitby's waterfront and access to the lakeshore would have been impossible without the cooperation of Whitby's industries, which own lands that front on Lake Ontario. Both DuPont Canada and Co-Steel LASCO allow public access to approximately 26 hectares (65 acres) of lakefront to be used for the Trail.

Community groups, such as the Kiwanis Club and the Thickson's Woods Heritage Foundation, also helped make the Waterfront Trail a reality. As the Trail developed, other community organizations, including the Whitby Rotary Sunrise Club, have become involved in it.

In Whitby, the Trail is on asphalt and boardwalks, both wheelchair-accessible, and extends east from Gordon Street to the Oshawa boundary, a distance of approximately 5.7 kilometres (3.5 miles). There are plans to extend the Trail west of Gordon Street, across the Whitby Mental Health Centre's waterfront, along the east side of Lynde Creek and through the Lynde Shores Conservation Area.

Until then, the Waterfront Trail follows Victoria Street east from Lakeridge Road, which is the Ajax/Whitby Municipal boundary. Because there are no sidewalks on Victoria and the street is well travelled, users may prefer to see it by bicycle. It is expected that, in time, the Trail will follow along the waterfront from Ajax and go around Cranberry Marsh. Today, however, this interim route places users about 2.0 kilometres (1.2 miles) north of Lake Ontario.

LYNDE SHORES CONSERVATION AREA

The Central Lake Ontario Conservation Authority (CLOCA) owns 156 hectares (385 acres) of land on Lake Ontario and along Lynde Creek. Known as the Lynde Shores Conservation Area, it includes portions of the Lynde Creek and Cranberry marshes, both of which provide natural habitat for marsh birds and many other forms of wildlife. If you arrive by car, park in the main lot off Victoria Street, approximately a half-kilometre (0.3 mile) east of Halls Road South. There are also two pedestrians – only entrances into the conservation area off Halls Road South.

CLOCA has built several viewing platforms around Cranberry Marsh, as well as a boardwalk that extends into the Lynde Creek Marsh. Here, but not in the more fragile ecosystem of Cranberry Marsh, there is fishing and canoeing, as well as winter ice skating.

The Conservation Authority provides picnicking areas and tables near the parking area, just off Victoria Street. There are also nearby restroom facilities. Visitors should note that the Lynde Shores Conservation Area is garbage-free; anything brought in must be taken out when they depart. For more information about the area and the marshes, call 905-579-0411.

RAPTOR WATCH AT CRANBERRY MARSH

Cranberry Marsh offers one of the best spots for watching raptors – the majestic birds of prey that migrate along the Lake Ontario shoreline in September and October, having left summer breeding grounds in Quebec and the Kawartha Lakes area to winter in the mid-United States. Sixteen species have been reported; two, the osprey and broad-winged hawk, travel as far south as Central and South America by way of the Gulf of Mexico and Vera Cruz, Mexico.

Organized raptor watches and counts began in eastern North America in the 1960s, after populations of peregrine falcons and bald eagles dropped significantly; the DDT found in their eggs resulted in shells so thin that birds sitting on them caused them to break and birth rates dropped to very low levels. Because hawks are at the high end of the animal food chain, this seemed to indicate that human reproduction would also be at risk; since DDTs were banned in the 1970s, hawk migration has been closely monitored throughout North America, Europe, and the Middle East.

Situated about 100 metres (330 feet) above the shore of Lake Ontario, Cranberry Marsh has a 3-by-3-metre (10-by-10-foot) wooden platform with an unobstructed view of the eastern sky, the direction from which the birds migrate and, therefore, an excellent place for viewing hawks. The best time of day is between 9 a.m. and 3 p.m.; during these hours there are air updrafts or thermals that permit the bird to soar using less energy. In fall, a northwesterly wind of at least 7 kph (4 mph) will bring them closer to the lake and the viewing platform.

Golden eagles usually fly in pairs, often just above the treetops, with the male in the lead, followed by the female a few minutes later. But goldens are the rarest of eagles: in October 1990, the one-day high was ten, with only two seen in a single day in October 1994. Therefore, their numbers are being monitored closely.

The Cranberry Marsh hawk count is conducted by John Barker and the Greater Toronto Region Raptor Watch. Data collected from these annual counts are deposited with the Hawk Migration Association of North America and used in achieving a better understanding of birds of prey and their role in the environment. For more information, contact John Barker at 416-291-1598 between 5 and 9 p.m.

Continue east along Victoria Street. Just before Gordon Street, the Waterfront Trail turns south onto an asphalt path on the Whitby General Hospital grounds. It then heads east to Gordon Street. Eventually, it will extend south to Lake Ontario along the east side of Lynde Creek. Until then, the lands remain in private ownership, and trespassing is prohibited.

WHITBY MENTAL HEALTH CENTRE

The Whitby Mental Health Centre is at the south end of Gordon Street. Built between 1913 and 1916 as the Ontario Hospital for the Insane, it was a garden community of approximately thirty cottages. But by the time it opened in 1917, Canada was at war and it was pressed into service as a convalescent hospital for wounded soldiers returning from Europe.

A year after the war ended, however, the hospital was returned to its original purposes; between 1918 and 1925, the facilities were enlarged; in time, the name changed to the Whitby Mental Health Centre. In 1994, the centre celebrated its 75th anniversary, and construction began on a modern new facility that will include a museum to take visitors through the history of mental health care in Ontario. More than 15 hectares (38 acres) of waterfront have been left as open space across the new centre's waterfront.

Nearly 1 kilometre (0.6 mile) of the Waterfront Trail will cross the lakefront between Gordon Street and Lynde Creek. The future of lands surplus to the hospital and the open parkland is under discussion. These lands could incorporate a research and development centre for health and life sciences, and the preservation of the garden village setting as well as the hospital's old theatre and recreation hall, Building 28. Building 28 also contains a canteen and a bowling alley; it looks very much today as it did in the military hospital days, and has potential as a small waterfront theatre.

The Trail continues east off Gordon Street, to the town's public boat launch and around the north end of Whitby's harbour, to Watson Street, and the Port Whitby Marina. There is open space with picnic tables, soccer fields, and a small parking lot just off Watson Street, near the marina.

IROQUOIS PARK AND RECREATION COMPLEX

Iroquois Park is a Town-owned recreational facility with an indoor swimming pool, soccer and baseball field, and two ice rinks. Located at the northwest corner of Victoria and Henry streets, it offers ample parking and restroom facilities that are available during the arena's normal hours of operation. Public swimming is also available; for more information, call 905-668-7765.

WHITBY STATION GALLERY

At the northeast corner of Victoria and Henry streets, you may be surprised to see a train station in a field. Originally constructed in 1903 as the Whitby Junction Station for the Grand Trunk Railway, the building was moved to its present location at 1453 Henry Street in 1970. Today, it houses the Whitby Arts Station Gallery, a public facility that presents a variety of exhibits, workshops, and classes. In 1974, a 1923 boxcar was added to the station and refurbished to contain a printmaking studio. For more information about the Whitby Station Gallery, call 905-668-4185.

In 1918, a railway spur line was constructed between Whitby Junction and the military hospital, in order to move patients, visitors, and supplies more easily.

The spur-line train was operated by J.J. Lynde, whose ancestors were among the first pioneer families in the Whitby area. Lynde House, built by Jabez Lynde in about 1814, is thought to be Whitby's oldest home, and is now a museum prominently displayed at Cullen Gardens. (For more information, see page 191.)

WHITBY HARBOUR (FORMERLY WINDSOR BAY)

Whitby's harbour had an active port where grain from nearby farms was shipped, beginning in 1833. Lumber – including white pines so large they were used as ships' masts by the Royal Navy – was also shipped from the harbour, on the Whitby, Port Perry, and Lindsay Railway.

By the 1840s, piers had been installed at what was then still called Windsor Bay, in order to fit it for more extensive trade. In 1857, a lighthouse – 4.3 metres (14 feet) at its base and towering 12 metres (40 feet) – was built, replacing the much smaller original that dated from 1844. It was said that the light from the newer lighthouse, which was dismantled in 1958, could be seen from as far away as 24 kilometres (15 miles).

With the birth of the Grand Trunk Railway in 1856, the harbour shipping business gradually declined.

Port Whitby Marina

Boaters will enjoy approaching the town from the publicly operated Port Whitby Marina; if you are arriving from the United States, you can make a phone declaration from the marina by calling Canada Customs at 1-800-387-1510. As well, the marina (905-668-1900 or VHF Channel 68) and the nearby Whitby Yacht Club have transient docking but require advance notice; the yacht club's telephone number is 905-668-1391.

Fishers interested in one-day Lake Ontario charters should contact the marina or the Port Whitby Sport Fishing Association at 416-431-1330.

The area of the marina, which is also residential, is known as Port Whitby; in 1867, it had a population of 617, about 25 percent of Whitby's total. Today, its 1,155 people account for only 1.7 percent of the population.

The remaining historically significant buildings in the Port Whitby area are worth a small side trip.

Side Trip
Port Whitby

Cross to the east side of Brock Street and walk along Front Street to Dufferin Street and continue north. At 1751 Dufferin Street, you will find the Richard Goldring House. A Lake Ontario sailor, Goldring moved, probably from Mimico, to Whitby in 1893. He retired from sailing in 1911, when he purchased the general store at the southwest corner of Brock and

Victoria streets. The store and post office were operated by members of the Goldring family until 1967, when the building was torn down. The house was occupied by two of Richard's daughters until 1990 and remains in private hands.

The John Watson House at 1733 Dufferin Street is designated under the Ontario Heritage Act. It stands on land John Watson bought in 1856 and on which he built his home, probably the following year. On the death of his business partner, Mr. Watson took over James Rowe and Company, the area's largest grain-shipping business; the two had also been partners in the unfinished Lake Scugog and Huron Road Company, formed to build a road from Lake Huron to Port Whitby.

Watson was also actively involved in politics and was one of the most vigorous campaigners for the separation of Ontario County from York County in 1854. When that campaign succeeded and the Town of Whitby was incorporated, Mr. Watson became councillor for the South Ward (Port Whitby) and, eventually, the town's deputy reeve. John Watson died at his home in 1879, aged 73.

Continue walking north along Dufferin until you reach Victoria Street; you will find St. John's Anglican Church and cemetery on the north side of Victoria Street. This is Whitby's oldest church, opened in July 1846.

The owner of much of the land in the Township of Whitby was John Scadding, who had been John Graves Simcoe's property manager and who, when Simcoe was appointed first lieutenant-governor of Upper Canada, moved to the colony with him. Appreciative of Scadding's loyalty, Simcoe gave him 404 hectares (1000 acres) on the natural harbour in Whitby.

John Scadding died in 1824, when a tree fell on him; in 1848, his sons Charles and Henry (the latter having become the first rector of Toronto's Holy Trinity Church) donated 0.4 hectares (1 acre) of land at the corner of Victoria and Brock streets to the Anglican Church. The stone used to build the church is limestone from the Kingston area, cut into blocks by prisoners at the Kingston Penitentiary for use as ballast in grain ships.

Many prominent families in the Port Whitby area, including the Goldrings and the Watsons, were members of St. John's and are buried in its cemetery. ■

Continuing south on Brock Street brings you back to the Waterfront Trail, which goes east along Front Street, around the Sea Cadet building, to Windsor Bay Park, a passive amenity with picnic tables and barbecues.

Pringle Creek, which runs through the park, offers access to the east wharf and Lake Park. The original wooden pier was built in the mid-1800s, and the wharf around 1914. The present concrete wharf was constructed during the 1950s by the federal government and is now used as a small craft harbour.

LAKE PARK

Lake Park is directly east of the pier; Whitby's Sunrise Rotary Club has committed itself to constructing a gazebo as part of the Waterfront Trail, to enhance public use and enjoyment of the park.

OLD WATER WORKS

The Old Water Works building is a wonderful structure, built in 1904 as Whitby's first pumping system; originally coal-powered, the pumps ran on coal brought by the Grand Trunk Railway on a spur built beside the water works for that purpose. A portion of that old rail track still exists but, by the 1960s, power was being supplied by electricity.

A new regional pumping facility was built in 1959, and when it expanded in 1978, the old water works ceased operation. Whitby Works is one of the few original pumphouses of its vintage remaining on Lake Ontario but, unfortunately, its future is uncertain. When there was public bathing nearby, the Public Utilities Commission permitted people to use the pumphouse as a change room; in 1940, fear of war-time sabotage forced it to close the pumphouse to the public.

Immediately east of the newer regional water pumping station, the Trail enters Heydenshore Kiwanis Park.

HEYDENSHORE KIWANIS PARK

The area that is now Heydenshore Kiwanis Park was a popular summer resort in 1900, with cottages lining the Lake Ontario shoreline. They remained there until 1965, when most were purchased and torn down by the Town in order to create this lakefront park.

During the early 1900s, Heydenshore Park was the site of the Methodist Deaconess Fresh Air Home, which offered opportunities for children in Toronto orphanages to spend summers in the country.

Heydenshore Kiwanis is a beautiful park with access to Whitby's largest public beach area and facilities that include picnic areas, barbecues, a picnic shelter, and a playground; the Kiwanis Club is working with the Town to continue making improvements.

The Heydenshore Pavilion on the grounds is a perfect venue for celebrations, meetings, and seminars; there is ample parking. For more information, contact Whitby's Parks and Recreation Department at 905-668-5803.

As it goes east, the Trail moves onto higher ground and is separated from the shoreline and beach by bluffs. At this point, turn around for a spectacular view of Lake Ontario and the Toronto skyline.

DuPONT CANADA INC. AND CO-STEEL LASCO

The Trail continues east, south of Whitby's established industrial area. Whitby's largest employers, DuPont Canada Inc., and Co-Steel LASCO, have leased approximately 26 hectares (65 acres) of land to the Town for recreational purposes. As the result of their co-operation, the Trail crosses vacant lakeside land. The DuPont property was originally called Pinder's Point, after a pioneer family that had settled there.

The Trail leaves DuPont and aligns on lands owned by steel manufacturer Co-Steel LASCO. You are now approximately 10 to 15 metres (33 to 50 feet) above the lake, and should keep well back from the edge of the bluffs.

You will notice a very large berm to the north of the Trail; it is built from left-over materials from the recycled old cars the company uses in its products and is a monument to corporate concern for the environment. Some days you can hear the large shredder on the north side of the berm, and, as the berm continues to grow, it will act as a noise and landscaped barrier to the steel mill and shredding operations.

The Co-Steel LASCO site and lands to its east as far as Oshawa, were used for military purposes during WW II. Although there was a grass air strip on the Co-Steel LASCO lands in 1941, little was written about it.

Now used as LASCO's main office, Ringwood House was built in 1876 by Barnabas Gibson, a railway contractor who had arrived in Whitby from England in 1854. Gibson built the Queen and King Street railway bridges in Toronto, and was also contracted to construct the second Union Station in Toronto.

Ringwood House is an exuberant mix of styles: the high chimneys, centre door, and contrasting window sides popular in the Regency period; the decorative cresting grill along the full length of the roof, much favoured in the Second Empire; and Gothic Revival's decorative woodwork and gingerbread detail.

From LASCO, the Trail crosses approximately 6.5 hectares (16 acres) of open space owned by the town and moves north of the shore and of homes that are part of the Thickson's Point Community. It continues north along Thickson Road and then east along the old access road to the Corbett Creek Water Pollution Control Plant. The road is on the northern limit of Thickson's Woods, which are owned and protected by the Thickson's Woods Heritage Foundation.

THICKSON'S WOODS

Thickson's Woods is a 7-hectare (17-acre) forest containing some of the most magnificent white pines left in Southern Ontario. With the adjacent Corbett Creek Marsh, a lovely little wetland, the ancient pines form a green oasis in an increasingly developed landscape, offering food and shelter to weary birds migrating north to their nesting ground. Botanists have identified more than 360 species of vascular plants in this pocket of remnant wilderness.

The Thickson's Woods Heritage Foundation was formed in 1983, when the owner of the woods, unable to obtain a building permit, sold the timber rights for the big trees. A handful of local citizens, appalled by the destruction that resulted, incorporated as a non-profit charitable organization, and purchased the property. The Thickson's Woods Heritage Foundation, supported by hundreds of people who value nature, raised $150,000 in five years to pay off the mortgage.

The group is committed to protecting native flora and fauna in the area and to working in partnership with the Town of Whitby to help naturalize and reforest areas near the Trail, providing valuable habitat for wildlife and enjoyment of nature for humans. For further information phone 905-725-2116.

CORBETT CREEK WATER POLLUTION CONTROL PLANT

A portion of the Trail is routed around the plant's lands. The Corbett Creek Water Pollution Control Plant, which is being expanded, is operated by the Regional Municipality of Durham and treats sanitary sewage from the Town of Whitby and City of Oshawa. The facility provides "biological secondary treatment" and operates under a Certificate of Approval issued by the Ontario Ministry of Environment and Energy. This certificate governs the quality of effluent which is ultimately discharged into Lake Ontario through an effluent sewer extending approximately 600 metres (2,000 feet) offshore.

The Trail then bridges Corbett Creek and, at the marshy section, is on an elevated catwalk retrofitted to accommodate pedestrian traffic. The walkway enables people to watch the marsh inhabitants, such as great blue herons, ducks, and swamp sparrows.

Because the Trail narrows at the catwalk, cyclists should dismount and walk their bikes across the catwalk. Alternatively, they can travel north to Wentworth Street, east to Boundary Road, and south to join the Trail again at the lakeshore.

Once the Trail crosses Corbett Creek, it travels south to an elevated boardwalk overlooking the Lower Corbett Creek wetland, a large and active marsh clearly visible from the Trail.

INTREPID PARK

At this point, the Trail opens into the town-owned Intrepid Park, named after Sir William Stephenson, "the man called Intrepid". Between 1941 and 1946, this site was used by the British Security Coordination as a communications centre and it also served as a training camp for WW II spies. "Camp X", as it was known, was constructed and operated by Stephenson and staffed by Canadians. There, more than 500 agents, many of whom were later parachuted into occupied Europe, were trained. Many never returned.

Ian Fleming, famous for the creation of the best known spy, James Bond, was a trainee at Camp X. In his book, *A Man Called Intrepid,* author William Stevenson describes 007's creator:

Ian Fleming, creator of the James Bond intrigues, was an aide to the chief of British Naval Intelligence. He worked closely with Intrepid and received much of his training at BSC's secret establishment outside Toronto, in Canada. Many of the techniques and devices later portrayed in his fiction were derived, according to Fleming, from Intrepid's operations.

Photographing Camp X was forbidden, and the whole area was fenced off by barbed wire. However, before the buildings were removed in about 1964, photographs were taken; they can be seen at the Robert McLaughlin Gallery, 72 Queen Street, Oshawa; call 905-576-3000.

The Town of Whitby constructed a cairn at the north end of Intrepid Park, in honour of the men and women who worked at Camp X. The memorial was unveiled in 1984, in a ceremony attended by surviving agents from the camp, along with representatives from all levels of government.

The Trail then reaches the town of Whitby's eastern boundary, and joins the sidewalk leading into the city of Oshawa.

From Thickson Road to the Oshawa boundary, this portion of the Trail covers some 1.3 kilometres (0.8 mile).

Side Trips
DOWNTOWN WHITBY

On Brock Street, only 2 kilometres (1.2 miles) north of Victoria Street, is Whitby's historic business centre. Development of this area began in 1836, when Whitby's founder, Peter Perry, arrived; it was known as Perry's Corners. At the site of the present Canadian Imperial Bank of Commerce, he built the Red Store, which stood for thirty years, before it was demolished to make room for the Lowes and Powell store.

Because of confusion with the City of Windsor, Perry's Corners and Windsor Bay (as the port area was known) took the name Whitby in 1847, after the seaside town in Yorkshire, England. In 1852, Whitby was designated as the seat of the County of Ontario, which had been split from the County of York.

As the new county seat, Whitby needed a court house, jail, and meeting place for a county council. A design competition was held for the court house and won by a Toronto architectural firm, Cumberland and Storm, which was also responsible for buildings at the University of Toronto and for the centre portion of Osgoode Hall.

The building's three-storey centre block had a domed roof, with one-storey wings on either side. In 1910, more space was needed, and a second storey was added to both wings. The County Court House was in active use until 1964, when the courts were moved to the new building on Rossland Road at Garden Street. In 1967, the Ontario County Court House was renamed the Centennial Building and altered: a theatre occupies the former courtroom, and there is a dinner and dance hall in the old county council chambers.

A local troupe performs there and the building now houses Whitby's archives. The Centennial Building is at 416 Centre Street South, two blocks west of Brock between Ontario and Gilbert streets. For more information, or to arrange a tour, call 905-668-5803.

You may also want to see Trafalgar Castle, 401 Reynolds Street, four blocks east of Brock at the head of Gilbert Street. The castle, begun in 1859 and three years in construction, was designed by Joseph Sheard for Nelson Gilbert Reynolds, the sheriff of Ontario County, who found it too expensive to maintain. In 1874, he sold his home to the Methodist Church to establish the Ontario Ladies' College, which has operated there ever since. It is a private school; neither the grounds nor the building are open to the public.

Whitby's downtown has more than four hundred shops and services that serve residents and visitors: Pearson Lanes, at Brock and Mary Street West, has shops, an English-style pub, and Pearson's Fine Dining. For more information about these and other restaurants, shops, and hotels in Whitby, contact Whitby Information Centre at 905-668-0552, or stop by at 900 Brock Street South (at Burns Street, north of Highway 401). ∎

CULLEN GARDENS AND MINIATURE VILLAGE

Cullen Gardens and Miniature Village is west of Lynde Creek at 300 Taunton Road West in Whitby, just west of Brock Street. The miniature village offers a wonderful tour of 150 historical Ontario buildings, constructed to one-twelfth their original scale, and displayed among the flowers for which the firm is famous. Since the miniature village opened in 1980, the tiny structures have delighted millions of visitors.

Cullen Gardens produces a number of seasonal festivals and entertainments throughout the year. Its restaurant overlooks the miniature village and valleyland below. When the company relocated Lynde House, reputed to be Whitby's oldest home, to the Taunton Road site, it refurbished the building as a museum with animated figures that depict life in early rural Ontario. For more information, contact Cullen Gardens at 905-668-6606 or 1-800-461-1821 in Ontario and Quebec.

In the foreseeable future, access to Cullen Gardens will be available along a municipal greenway system beside Lynde Creek, where the Town owns a continuous ribbon of land between Highway 401 and a point about 1 kilometre (0.6 mile) south of Cullen Gardens. ■

FAMILY KARTWAY

Not far from Cullen Gardens you will find Family Kartway, the world's largest go-kart track. Located on Baldwin Street (Highway 12), just north of Taunton Road, it is an amusement park for the entire family: those not interested in go-karting may enjoy the 18-hole miniature golf course, hardball and softball batting cages, bumper cars, bumper boats in a 24-metre (80-foot) pool, or the kiddyland. The facility also has a water slide that features a drop of more than three storeys. For more information, contact Family Kartway at 905-655-3384. ■

LAKERIDGE ROAD: SIDE TRIP FOR A CYCLIST

Lakeridge Road extends north from Lake Ontario over the Oak Ridges Moraine, all the way to the east shore of Lake Simcoe and the community of Beaverton, some 74 kilometres (46 miles) distant by road. Only cycling enthusiasts who enjoy both a challenge and the countryside should take Lakeridge Road; north of Victoria Street, it is a well-travelled, two-lane road, with posted speed limits of as much as 80 kph (50 mph), and requires skilled and careful cycling.

If Beaverton seems too far away, there are many stops on Lakeridge Road: some 21 kilometres (13 miles) north of Victoria Street there is one of Durham Region's major ski areas, in the Oak Ridges Moraine. Ski Lakeridge, Skyloft Ski Club, and Dagmar Ski Resort are close to each other, just north of the Whitby boundary.

But, just south of the ski area, at Towline and Lakeridge roads, is a wonderful little spot, Hy Hope Farm, where you can stop for refreshments, freshly baked goods, and seasonal vegetables. It's the perfect turn-around, so you can leave, refreshed, and either head higher into the hills or coast back down to the Waterfront Trail.

This part of the Oak Ridges Moraine is one of the highest points of land in southern Ontario: from it, you get a breathtaking view all the way to Lake Ontario.

For those who are cycling but don't want to take too long a journey, the Heber Down Conservation Area is the perfect destination, a 10-kilometre (6.2-mile) journey from Victoria Street. Follow Lakeridge north to Taunton Road, which is slightly more than 6 kilometres (3.7 miles) away, and take it to the entrance at Coronation Road. ■

HEBER DOWN CONSERVATION AREA

Like the Lynde Shores Conservation Area further south, the Heber Down Conservation Area is operated by the Central Lake Ontario Conservation Authority. It offers fifty campsites, service buildings with washrooms and showers, as well as laundry facilities. The nature trails at Heber Down can be explored throughout the seasons, and there is cross-country skiing and sleigh riding in winter. For more information, contact the conservation authority at 905-579-0411. ■

Now that you have completed one or more of the side trips, retrace the route back to the the municipal boundary, to take the Waterfront Trail into Oshawa. ≋

Swallows *nest in the banks and the sandy beach stretches on...*

Oshawa

HARMONY

Harmony Creek

COLONEL SAM

Second Marsh

General Motors

Oshawa Harbour

Trail Access

N

McLaughlin Bay Wildlife Reserve

1 MUSKOKA AVENUE
2 BIRCHCLIFFE AVENUE
3 KLUANE AVENUE

SHAWA HAD ONLY three stores, two hotels, and a few houses when it was founded in 1842. That year, Edward Skae, owner of a general store at the southeast corner of what is now King and Simcoe streets, applied to call the hamlet Skae's Corners. He was told there were too many places named Corners; if he wanted a post office, the community would need a new name.

There was great debate about the name at Monro's Tavern, where community meetings were held. Everyone claimed to have the perfect name, but emerging favourite was Sydenham, which was what the growing settlement around the harbour at the mouth of the Oshawa Creek was called. However, Moody Farewell, a fur trader, asked one of the native people who accompanied him what they called the area. "Oshawa", he said, which means the place where a trail crosses a stream or the canoe is carried from one lake to another.

From its beginning as Skae's Corners, the village of Oshawa grew slowly. The library, which started as a reading room, was not established until 22 years after the naming controversy had been settled. However, the community's future as an automotive manufacturing centre was cast as early as 1877, when Robert McLaughlin moved his carriage works to Oshawa to gain access to the railway. Just two years later, Oshawa – rutted, muddy, with bumpy roads, plank sidewalks, and only recently installed oil street lamps – became a town.

From about 1915, when the automobile industry began to develop, Oshawa grew quickly. By 1921, it boasted paved streets and water distribution. Moreover, the Oshawa Railway ran through the nearby village of Cedardale to Port Sydenham. Most of the docks and Lakeview Park (a gift from Robert's son, Robert Samuel McLaughlin, and General Motors) were owned by the City of Oshawa.

In 1923, Oshawa annexed the village of Cedardale and continued to expand, to become the 25th community in Canada to become a city. In 1994, Oshawa had a population of 132,000.

PUBLIC TRANSIT

Local Transit
(905-579-2471)

VIA Train
(1-800-361-2135)

GO (905-579-4224)
• Oshawa – Thornton Rd.
at Bloor St. 1.25 from
the Lakefront West Park

According to Statistics Canada, it was the fastest growing metropolitan area in Canada between 1986 and 1991.

The Waterfront Trail enters Oshawa at the corner where Boundary Road becomes Phillip Murray Avenue. This is a wide road with a sidewalk on its southern length, making it suitable for walkers or cyclists.

LAKEFRONT WEST PARK

Lakefront West Park, located beside Intrepid Park (see page 189) and behind the Canadian Auto Workers Union Hall, contains eight baseball diamonds, a snack bar, and washrooms that are accessible to people in wheelchairs, and open when the ball diamonds are in use. The telephone, picnic benches, junior play equipment, and parking are available year-round. The main entrance to Lakefront West Park is opposite Skae Drive.

If you walk south from the parking lot to the lake, you will find a grass path along the top of the bluffs. The walk there is beautiful and well worth the time.

On the west side of the property, beside the drainage swale, you can make your way down the bluffs to the sand and pebble beach below. Exercise caution, as there are no stairs or formal paths. Approximately 1.5 kilometres (1 mile) east you will find access back to the top of the bluffs. Swallows nest in the banks and the sandy beach stretches on.

GENERAL MOTORS OSHAWA AUTOPLEX

East of Lakefront West Park and heading north on Stevenson Road, a left turn takes you to General Motors Oshawa Autoplex. Except in the summer months, tours are conducted from Monday to Friday at 8:45 a.m. and 11:45 a.m. (children under 12, cameras, and camcorders are not permitted). For tour information, phone 905-644-5777.

To follow the Waterfront Trail from Lakefront West Park, take Phillip Murray Avenue to Park Road, then travel south to Stone Street and go east on Stone Street to the Pumphouse Marsh.

REVEREND DR. R.H. THORNTON

Thornton Road is named in honour of the Reverend Dr. R.H. Thornton, a brilliant scholar and Presbyterian minister who came to the area in 1833. He was the only Presbyterian clergyman between Port Hope and Toronto. The land in the area was Crown land, known locally as Queen's Brush, at a time when there were no real roads, only paths through bush.

Dr. Thornton travelled by horseback or on foot from church to church, establishing many congregations in the area, and it is said he never missed a service.

The church he served in 1837, built inside the front gate of Union Cemetery, is still standing. He worked to improve schools in the area, edited the *Instructional Reader*, and was District Superintendent of Education for East Whitby Township from 1853 to 1861. In that year, he was appointed secretary of the Board of Public Instruction, the county organization responsible for education.

When Thornton died in 1875, as a sign of respect and affection for this remarkable man, all the stores in the village closed and all the blinds were drawn while funeral services were conducted. A 5-metre (15-foot) stone cairn in his memory stands at the southwest corner of Kendalwood Road and Highway 2, where the first Presbyterian services were conducted by Dr. Thornton.

Park Road south of Phillip Murray Avenue and Stone Street have sidewalks suitable for walking and people in wheelchairs. It is about 3 kilometres (1.8 miles) from Lakefront West Park to the Pumphouse Marsh, which can be entered from Stone Street, east of the Pumphouse Marsh sign.

The private homes on Stone Street that back onto Lake Ontario are exceptions to most Oshawa lakefront property, which has been preserved for public use. The reason so much of it is in public hands can be found in the city's development pattern. The community first developed around Skae's Corners and Highway 2. When Highway 401 was built, after the Second World

War, more development took place in the north, and it became easier to preserve waterfront properties for public use.

PUMPHOUSE MARSH WILDLIFE RESERVE

This 0.8-kilometre (0.5-mile) section of the Waterfront Trail, which is wheelchair accessible, leads to three observation platforms. They provide an excellent view of the marsh and the many birds attracted to the area, while protecting delicate vegetation along the marsh edge. Birders have reported sightings of 195 species including pied-billed grebe, common moorhen, wood duck, and blue-winged teal. The Waterfront Trail continues south on Ritson Road.

Side Trip
OSHAWA CREEK

Heading north on Ritson Road will bring you to the Oshawa Creek Trail which winds its way through 6.8 kilometres (4 miles) of the Oshawa Creek valley. Along the way you will pass the Harbour View Plaza. Entry to the Oshawa Creek Trail is one block north of the plaza, at the intersection of Ritson Road and Valley Drive. This is one of the prettiest valleys in southern Ontario, an urban wilderness well worth visiting. The path is paved and has few road crossings, making it suitable for cyclists, in-line skaters and people in wheelchairs.

As you follow the creek north past Wentworth Street, you will reach the site of the former Robson Lang Tannery, one of early Oshawa's major industries. Its offices are now used by the Central Lake Ontario Conservation Authority (CLOCA).

The Oshawa Creek Trail continues under CN tracks, Bloor Street, and Highway 401 as far as Mill Street. At that point, you will find the site of one of Ontario's first hydroelectric generating stations, built in 1887. The Trail continues north west of downtown, to Adelaide Avenue where the Oshawa Creek Trail ends. North of Adelaide Avenue and west of Simcoe Street is Parkwood, the home of the founder of General Motors in Canada, the late Colonel Sam McLaughlin. ■

R.S. McLaughlin

In 1915, Robert Samuel McLaughlin bought Prospect Park where he built Parkwood. The stately 55-room home, with its indoor swimming pool and bowling alley, was designed by Darling and Pearson, the architects who designed the Provincial Parliament buildings. The grounds, landscaped by the husband-and-wife team of Dunington-Grubb, founders of Sheridan Nurseries, are an excellent example of landscape architecture of this period.

Colonel Sam, as he was called, was one of this century's early international titans of industry. Interested, from youth, in his father's carriage business, he worked for a time in New York. In 1892, he joined his father and brother George in a partnership, the McLaughlin Carriage Works. Fire destroyed the plant in 1899, but the McLaughlins remained in Oshawa, thus securing its role as one of Canada's major auto manufacturing centres.

In 1908, the company was making car bodies for Buick and, later, for Chevrolet. In 1918, it was incorporated as General Motors of Canada (though the McLaughlin name plate remained for many years). McLaughlin retired from active involvement in 1942, but remained as chair of the board until 1967. In 1972, full of years and honours, he died in the city he had helped shape.

In addition to Parkwood, his many generous contributions include an addition to the Oshawa Library, Lakeview Park, a bandshell, Camp Samac (a Boy Scout/Girl Guide camp), medical facilities, and the planetarium that bears his name, next to the Royal Ontario Museum in Toronto.

There are tours of Parkwood and its grounds, but you should book by calling ahead: 905-433-4311. And, of course, the McLaughlins loom large at the Canadian Automotive Museum, also on 99 Simcoe Street South; to arrange a tour there, call 905-576-1222.

Continuing east from Pumphouse Marsh and Ritson Road, the Waterfront Trail goes through Lakewoods Park and approaches the pioneer cemetery at the intersection of Muskoka, Birchcliffe, and Kluane avenues.

Originally on the east side of Oshawa Harbour, the cemetery was relocated when plans were made to expand the harbour. Port Oshawa Pioneer Cemetery includes the burial plots of some of Oshawa's founding families. Captain Benjamin Wilson, a Loyalist who settled Port Sydenham in 1790, was laid to rest here in 1821, when he died at 89. There are Robinsons and Henrys as well. The beauty and serenity of the location is mirrored in the words on the plaque: "The choice of this new site ensures that the waves of Lake Ontario will continue to sound a requiem to the early settlers and their progeny here interred." If you wish to visit, contact the Sydenham Museum.

Just south of the cemetery, Bonnie Brae Point offers a panoramic view of the Oshawa waterfront. You can see Darlington Nuclear Generating Station to the east.

LAKEVIEW PARK

Lakeview Park is Oshawa's major waterfront park. From Bonnie Brae Point, the Waterfront Trail enters Lakeview Park via an asphalt path that heads northeast along Kluane Avenue before it skirts the western edge of Lakeview Park and passes through the centre of the park along the north side of Lakeview Park Avenue.

On the south side of Lakeview Park Avenue you will see a brass sculpture of a young woman within a fountain. At its foot is a carved stone reminder that Lakeview Park was donated to Oshawa by General Motors of Canada in July 1920. Beside it, a plaque pays tribute to the Honourable Gordon Conant (1885-1953) who was mayor of Oshawa in 1916, Ontario's twelfth premier, and a Master of the Supreme Court of Ontario.

Six generations of the Conant family have been closely associated with Oshawa's development. Roger Conant settled on the east side of Oshawa Creek in 1792 and used profits from trade in furs and salmon to invest in land. His son, Daniel, built Whitby's

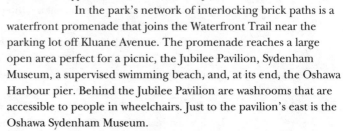
deep water harbour, while Thomas Conant wrote such outstanding histories as *Upper Canada Sketches* and *Life in Canada*.

In the park's network of interlocking brick paths is a waterfront promenade that joins the Waterfront Trail near the parking lot off Kluane Avenue. The promenade reaches a large open area perfect for a picnic, the Jubilee Pavilion, Sydenham Museum, a supervised swimming beach, and, at its end, the Oshawa Harbour pier. Behind the Jubilee Pavilion are washrooms that are accessible to people in wheelchairs. Just to the pavilion's east is the Oshawa Sydenham Museum.

Sydenham Museum: The Three Houses

The Sydenham Museum comprises Henry House, Robinson House, and Guy House. The trio are an excellent starting point for exploring Oshawa's history. Each is on its original site, near what used to be Port Sydenham, now Oshawa Harbour.

Henry House

Henry House was constructed in 1849 by Harbourmaster Joseph Wood, using limestone that had been ballast in ships from the Kingston area. However, when Wood died of cholera, Thomas Henry and his family moved in. Both Thomas and Lurenda Henry were deeply involved in community life, Thomas as a circuit preacher and Lurenda as an herbalist. Over time, the Henrys needed to enlarge their home and a second storey of wood was added. As a result of the odd combination – a limestone base with a wooden top, reminiscent of a corked jug – the building was sometimes referred to as "the jug house".

The home's interior is especially inviting, giving visitors a glimpse of the way the Henrys would have lived in 1870; note the Steinway piano, hair wreaths, period furniture, rope bed, and beautiful stoves.

Outside, the large herb garden and perennial gardens also add to the Victorian flavour of the museum. Such kitchen herbs as parsley and rosemary grow there, as do medicinal and colouring herbs including horehound and lady's bedstraw.

Robinson House

To the north is Robinson House, with its interesting gabled roof. Home of the Robinson family, it was built about 1846. Today, the rooms display various aspects of life in early Oshawa: One room is dedicated to the history of the Robinson family, while others have exhibits showing life in the small community.

Of particular interest is the Howard McLeod site exhibit, centred around native artifacts from 1450 that were unearthed in an archaeological dig on McLeod's property between 1967 and 1970. The life of the Iroquoians of the area can be glimpsed through models, photographs, and the artifacts themselves.

In the music room, you will find a 200-year-old melodeon (a small reed organ), a Williams piano made in Oshawa, a harmonica tester, a gramophone, a dulcimer, and a bassoon belonging to John Ritson. A turn-of-the-century schoolroom has been recreated in the house, complete with picture of Queen Victoria, slates, and a dunce cap.

The house has other exhibits, which change every few months.

Guy House

Guy House, a typical 1835 frame farm dwelling, is the museum's administration centre, as well as the home of Oshawa's archives. At the gift shop, visitors can browse through folk art, historical reference books, and pioneer toys, and enjoy refreshing iced tea or lemonade.

The three houses are open year-round. In spring and summer the herb gardens are a major attraction while, in fall, you can see hundreds of monarch butterflies clinging to tree branches.

The museum is open for tours every day from 1 p.m. to 5 p.m. between mid-May and Thanksgiving; the rest of the year, it is open Sunday to Friday from 1 p.m. to 5 p.m. For further information or to book a tour, call 905-436-7624.

In front of Guy House is a plaque honouring Captain Benjamin Wilson. From here, you can look out over the sandy beach, where there is a volleyball court, supervised swimming area, and fishing pier.

Canada Day celebrations at Lakeview Park include entertainment and fireworks. Parking in the park is prohibited that day. For more information, call 905-725-7351.

Make your way to Lakeview Park Avenue and continue east following the tree-lined Waterfront Trail to Simcoe Street South. As you head north on Simcoe Street you will once again cross Oshawa Creek. Here is another access point to the Oshawa Creek Trail.

Simcoe Street, the city's main north-south street, originally linked Skae's Corners to the busy Sydenham Harbour. In 1895, the Oshawa electric railway ran up Simcoe from Port Sydenham to the Grand Trunk (now the CN) station and then further north to Prospect Park, now called Parkwood. People travelled from Toronto by rail or steamship and took the electric railway north to Prospect Park for the day.

Simcoe is a wide street with only moderate traffic. You can take it north to Harbour Road, which is quiet, with no sidewalks, but generous boulevards. By following Harbour Road east, you will reach the Port Oshawa Marina, which accommodates vessels from around the world. It has 250 slips, eight charter fishing boats, and facilities for people who live year-round on their boats.

Continue east from the marina on Harbour Road and cross Farewell Street. Harbour ends at Farewell but the Second Marsh portion of the Waterfront Trail proceeds directly opposite, and turns gently north.

This path will lead you to a steel pedestrian bridge that goes over Harmony Creek. At this point, there is a fork in the Trail. You must choose whether to keep going north to Colonel Sam Drive or enjoy a 1-kilometre (0.6-mile) walk through a wooded wetland. (Eventually, this route, too, leads to Colonel Sam Drive.)

Alternatively, turn north on Farewell and right onto Colonel Sam Drive, which is wide and beautifully landscaped with flowering bushes and plants. On the north side of the road is an observation platform overlooking part of Second Marsh at Harmony Creek.

SECOND MARSH

Second Marsh is a Class 2 Provincially Significant Wetland (see page 5 for wetland classification) that covers some 120 hectares (300 acres). It provides an important stopover for more than 250 species of migratory birds. Such fish as rainbow trout and coho salmon spawn in the streams that feed the marsh.

Second Marsh is being rehabilitated: habitat islands are being built, and nesting boxes are being set to encourage breeding. Removing log jams has improved water circulation by restoring the original outlet to the lake. By the time the work is completed, there will be new observation towers, interpretive signs and rest room facilities. An interpretive centre is also planned.

For more information about the marsh, write to Friends of Second Marsh, 206 King Street East, P.O. Box 26066 RPO, King Street, Oshawa, Ontario L1H 8R4 or phone 905-725-7351, extension 304.

Keep going east along Colonel Sam Drive to General Motors of Canada Corporate Headquarters. There are trails into the McLaughlin Bay Wildlife Reserve from the GM parking lots; signs point the way.

McLAUGHLIN BAY WILDLIFE RESERVE

McLaughlin Bay Wildlife Reserve covers more than 40 hectares (100 acres) within a 84-hectare (208-acre) parcel of land owned and operated by General Motors of Canada Limited. The reserve lies between the Second Marsh on the west and Darlington Provincial Park on the east. The reserve consists of open rolling meadows, beachfront, and an interesting drumlin from which there are panoramic views of Second Marsh and the waterfront.

In the late 1980s, when General Motors was planning its new corporate headquarters, it invited representatives of the Second Marsh Defence Association (now the Friends of Second Marsh) to discuss environmental concerns such as migratory birds flying into windows, storm water management, and other matters.

From these discussions grew the idea of a wooded buffer between Second Marsh and the office complex. When

Saving a Marsh

One of the people who love Second Marsh is Jim Richards, naturalist, photographer, and co-author of *Birds of the Oshawa-Lake Scugog Region*. As a child, he played near First Marsh, which was eventually filled and dredged out of existence to create Oshawa Harbour. Thirty years ago, it seemed that Second Marsh would suffer the same fate. But thanks to Jim Richards and others like him, it did not.

In 1964, the Oshawa Harbour Commission began negotiations with the City to acquire Second Marsh as part of its plan to expand the harbour. The Oshawa Naturalists Club (now the Durham Region Field Naturalists), the Oshawa and District Sportsman's Club, and other groups strongly opposed the view, expressed by one city councillor, that the Second Marsh was an "insignificant swamp". Nonetheless, the site was sold in 1970, for one dollar.

A dyke constructed in 1974 to block the marsh outlet caused extensive damage. Emerging vegetation died off, there was increased sedimentation, and a new outlet was formed. A year later, 11 groups, determined to save the wetland, formed the Second Marsh Defence Association. From the beginning, Jim Richards, who is now the manager of the McLaughlin Bay Wildlife Reserve, played a leading role.

In the early 1980s, independent studies by the Canadian Wildlife Service of Environment Canada underlined the importance of the marsh. Other research suggested that it would be no costlier to expand the harbour into the lake than into Second Marsh. A marsh preservation agreement was reached in 1984, but it was not until 1992 that a steering committee, composed of representatives from the City of Oshawa and eight other interested parties, was able to complete a marsh management plan. In the new spirit of co-operation, the Defence Association was renamed Friends of Second Marsh.

Among the remedial measures already under way are realignment of the creek flow to its previous channel and outlet, removal of upstream logjams, and reduction in sedimentation. Habitat improvements will involve vegetation plantings, carp control, and creation of habitat islands and nesting structures. In addition, an interpretive trail system with viewing towers is planned, along with an education and interpretive centre. A $1.3 million grant from Environment Canada under the Great Lakes Clean-up Fund is being combined with local sources of funding to undertake this work.

construction of the complex began in 1990, the creation of numerous habitat islands and wildlife corridors were integrated into the project.

There are almost 5 kilometres (3 miles) of groomed trails and, beginning in 1995, a program to establish native wild-flowers and ferns will begin. While some trails are hard surfaced and allow access for people in wheelchairs, most are either grass paths or woodchip walkways.

The result is a tribute to the determination of the Friends of Second Marsh and to a multi-national corporation with a strong sense of local citizenship.

For more information about Oshawa, call Information Oshawa at 905-434-4636. Now, proceed to the end of Colonel Sam Drive and follow the gravel road east to Darlington Provincial Park and the municipality of Clarington.

…**quiet** *setting, lovely sight lines, and the richness and variety of its surrounding flora and fauna*

◄······

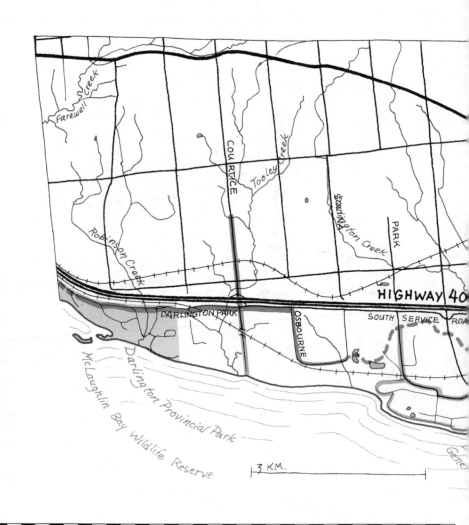

Clarington

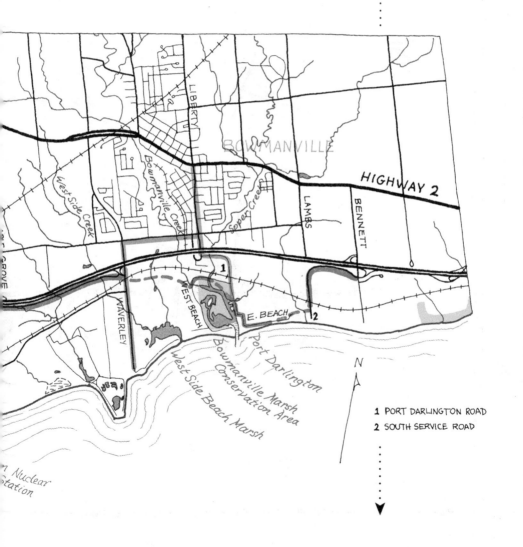

BOWMANVILLE

HIGHWAY 2

LIBERTY

LAMBS

BENNETT

West Side Creek

Bowmanville Creek

Soper Creek

WAVERLEY

WEST BEACH

E. BEACH

Port Darlington

Bowmanville Marsh
Conservation Area

West Side Beach Marsh

Nuclear
Station

1

2

N

1 PORT DARLINGTON ROAD
2 SOUTH SERVICE ROAD

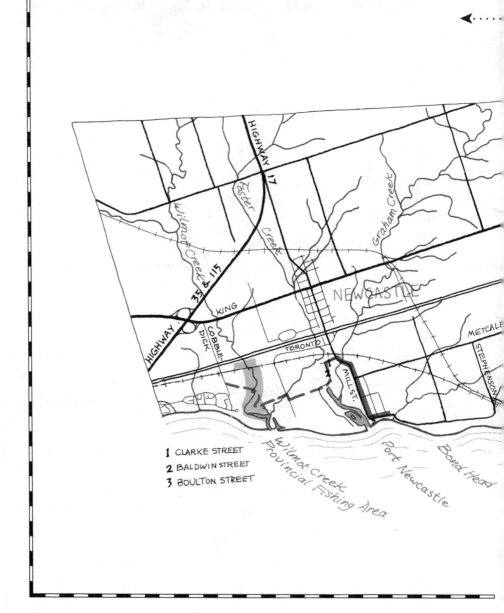

1 CLARKE STREET
2 BALDWIN STREET
3 BOULTON STREET

Clarington

HIGHWAY 2

HIGHWAY 401

NEWTONVILLE

PORT
GRANBY

LAKESHORE

ond Head Bluffs

Bouchette
Point

N

3 KM

OU HAVE ENTERED this section of the
Waterfront Trail in the Municipality of
Clarington from Colonel Sam Drive, once
known as the Ghost Road. Before the area was
developed, the road had been constructed over
a marsh. As the marsh gasses rose at night,
especially in shimmering moonlight, there seemed to be a ghostly
presence – thus the name.

DARLINGTON PROVINCIAL PARK

The Trail follows the Ghost Road to Darlington Park Road, the
park's main east-west route. (Darlington was the township, now
renamed, in which the park's western section is located.) From this
western boundary, access to the park is on foot and by
bicycle only; people in vehicles must use the main entrance at
the eastern end.

        Darlington Provincial Park also has its own network of
roads where pedestrians and cyclists can enjoy diverse scenic walks,
from hilltop climbs to shore and beach explorations. There is a designated route for pedestrians that follows the lakeshore, while
cyclists should stay on the roads; both routes are signed.

        There is a lookout at the park's centre, well worth
seeking, where you can look across the McLaughlin Bay Wildlife
Reserve to the west. The reserve's wetland and meadow, and the
park's woodlands are habitat for many species of wildlife, including
the provincially endangered peregrine falcon. A careful walk in the
park will also reveal a pioneer log cabin and an ancient cemetery,
relics of the first settlement in 1794.

        Family and group camping are available in the park
from the second Friday in May until Thanksgiving Monday, with a
total of three hundred campsites. Among the amenities that visitors
will find are a convenience store and canoe rentals.

SOUTH COURTICE

When you leave Darlington Park, the Trail continues east along
Darlington Park Road for 2 kilometres (1.2 miles) to Courtice
(pronounced Curtis) Road; here, you can stop for refreshments at

the service centre. A short jog in the road as you cross Courtice
leads into the South Service Road, where the Trail continues east.
However, you may prefer to pause and make some of the short side
trips and loops that are part of the Trail adventure.

Side Trip
EBENEZER UNITED CHURCH

About 1.5 kilometres (1 mile) north on Courtice Road,
you will find Ebenezer United Church; it was once the
foremost congregation of the Bay of Quinte Conference of Bible
Christians, an offshoot of Methodism whose various branches
came together in 1884 and were among the groups that coa-
lesced to become the United Church of Canada more than forty
years later.

After your visit to Ebenezer, return to the corner of
Darlington Park and Courtice roads, and continue south for a little more than 1 kilometre (0.6 mile); here you will find a narrow
winding road that takes you to the lakeshore. The land on either
side is private and, while not fenced, it is closed to the public.
However, the reward for a trip to the southern end of Courtice
Road is a picturesque beach. Although pebbly rather than sandy,
it has interesting plant life, and a view of places where agricultural
land meets Lake Ontario. ■

To continue along the Trail, return to South Service
Road and go east; however, you may run into some heavy traffic if
you are travelling in mid-week. On Wednesdays there is a large, well-
attended auto auction; while it is open only to licensed dealers, the
traffic is heavy from Tuesday evening on, as auto transport vehicles
come and go. There are as many as five lines being auctioned at one
time, each organized according to cars' ages, types, and conditions.

Once at the intersection of Osbourne Road, turn
south from the Service Road and follow a 2.4-kilometre (1.5-mile)
excursion through wild rose country. While the abundance of wild
roses growing along the roadsides are lovely, beware: they are
wickedly prickly! With its narrow roads, planted fields, and with lake

views devoid of wires, neon, and the other paraphernalia of modern life, this area holds a sense of time past.

The other-worldliness of the trip is enhanced as you go along the east-west road at the south end, where you will find a lovely old Victorian farmhouse. Home of John C. Trull, the son of an original settler named John W. Trull, it is an instant lesson in how deeply pioneers understood the environment, how they chose a housing site for its quiet setting, lovely sight lines, and the richness and variety of its surrounding flora and fauna. There are mountain ash trees, choke cherries, beach peas, clover, asters (and, less happily, a particularly virulent patch of poison ivy). Groundhogs and chipmunks scurry self-importantly through the grass and around the bushes while, in the trees, songbirds audition for each other – keeping a wary eye out for owls and a variety of hawks. Bring your bird books!

If you are travelling by car you should follow Solina Road north to get back to the South Service Road. Along the way, watch for the large house on the east side; the date stone in the front gable of this Queen Anne structure bears the inscription "Maplecliff 1894".

DARLINGTON NUCLEAR GENERATING STATION

A right-hand turn at the South Service Road puts you unequivocally back in the 20th century: the Darlington Nuclear Generating Plant can be seen a short distance to the east. Cyclists and those on foot do not have to travel back up to the Service Road to gain entry to the grounds of the generating station: the Trail follows a path at the south end of Solina onto these lands.

This marks the beginning of a 3.8-kilometre (2.3-mile) segment of off-road Trail that makes its way east before ultimately bringing you back onto the South Service Road at Maple Grove Road. These grounds are not accessible for people in wheelchairs or for those using in-line skates.

The large number of deer that make their home in the park were found occasionally wandering away from these safe confines; as a result a series of "deer-proof" gates have been constructed. Although they may look as if they are designed to keep pedestrians out, they are actually to keep the deer in, so please close the gates securely behind you.

To get to the generating station entrance by car, follow the South Service Road east from Solina Road for about 0.8 kilometres (0.5 mile) to Park Road. Clear markings make it easy to find Hydro's information centre: go south to the lights and the bridge; turn right and follow the winding road to the centre. (You are actually travelling on what used to be the face of bluffs that overlooked the lake). There is ample parking and a baseball diamond, as well as a small area of manicured grounds where you can stretch your legs.

The glass wall of the information centre looks south out over the generating station and the lake, and on a clear day one can see the skyline of Toronto to the west. Straight ahead you may even be able to see smokestacks in Rochester, New York.

There are knowledgeable guides to explain nuclear power in general and the station in particular, as well as displays of interest to adults and children. If you haven't yet been on Hydro's walking trail, guides can also explain how to enter it from this point. A co-operative project of Hydro and the Municipality of Clarington, these trails were completed by Ontario Hydro employees working as volunteers. Views from this high ground are spectacular and you may see some of the deer that wander the bordering woods. There are points along the way that are ideal for watching the many breeding bird species that live in the marshy areas of the property.

To get back on the Trail, return to South Service Road, and continue east for about 1.6 kilometres (1 mile), which brings you to Waverley Road in Bowmanville. There is a service centre at this intersection.

There is also the opportunity for a "loop" – whether you are travelling on foot or by bike – by heading south toward the lake on Waverley Road. If you are a birdwatcher, photographer, or artist, you will enjoy the trip, which is more than 1 kilometre (0.6 mile) alongside through the West Side Creek Marsh, which provides habitat for many kinds of breeding and migrant wildlife. No matter what time of year, you're likely to find some species in residence: mallards, teal, wood or black ducks; Canada geese; even trumpeter swans. In addition to a camera, binoculars or sketch pad, you'll need waterproof boots for a visit to this Class 2 Provincially Significant Wetland.

The marsh is on land licensed by St. Mary's Cement Company, which mines the nearby limestone and produces cement sold to customers around the Great Lakes.

Go back up toward South Service Road and Waverley, watching for the sign that indicates where the Trail leaves Waverley to continue east. If you are travelling by car, you leave the designated alignment for the Trail at this point, as it heads off-road to follow the Hydro right-of-way. If you are on foot or in-line skates, or travelling by bicycle, stay on the asphalt path, which is on the north side of the marshlands with their interesting lake vistas. Vehicles can continue north on Waverley to Highway 2, then travel east to Liberty Street; this brings you into the Town of Bowmanville.

Along the Hydro right-of-way, you will notice the Brookdale Kingsway Nursery, founded near the turn of the century by businessman and philanthropist John H.H. Jury. His house, which is now a museum depicting life in the first third of this century, is located in the Town of Bowmanville.

For a short distance, the Trail connects with West Beach Road, before briefly making its way into the northern section of the Bowmanville Marsh Conservation Area and then meeting Port Darlington Road. (See Old Port Darlington [page 218] for information on the continuation of the Trail at this point).

The conservation area is operated by the Central Lake Ontario Conservation Authority (CLOCA) and features a public boat-launch ramp and ample room for picnicking.

Side Trips
BOWMANVILLE

This is another of the loops that add enjoyment to the Trail experience. It covers quite a bit of territory so, unless you are an avid hiker or cyclist, you may want to go by car.

A good place to start is at the Tourist and General Information Centre, located at Liberty Street and Highway 401, next to the Flying Dutchman Hotel. There you will find details on all local attractions, including the Bowmanville Zoo and Jungle Cat World. You can reach the centre by going north on Waverley Road from the South Service Road; cross the bridge that spans Highway 401 to the stoplights; you are at Baseline Road. Turn right and drive about 0.8 kilometre (0.5 mile) to Liberty Street; turn right again. The Tourist and General Information Centre is the first driveway on your right.

From September to May, the centre is closed on the weekends and open during the week from 8:30 a.m. to 4:30 p.m. From May 1 to June 30 it is open Saturday and Sunday from 9 a.m. to 5 p.m. and during the week from 8:30 a.m. to 8 p.m. Beginning on July 1, it is open during the week from 8 a.m. to 4 p.m. and on Saturday and Sunday from 10 a.m. to 6 p.m. It can also be reached by phone at 905-623-0733. Once you have the information you want, follow Liberty Street for 2.5 kilometres (1.5 miles) north into the commercial area of the Town of Bowmanville.

Bowmanville's main street has retained much of the flavour of its past and even the old town hall remains, although with a modern addition. Proud local merchants promote the community and its surroundings: there is a Strawberry Festival in June where you can sink your teeth into what are arguably the best strawberry shortcakes you will find anywhere, and an Apple Festival in October with plenty of apple pies, cider, and apple fritters. The traditional Santa Claus Parade takes place on the third Saturday in November, as it has since 1961. Downtown is closed to through traffic for these events and the streets become an entertainment centre.

Bowmanville has many restaurants, shopping (including exclusive boutiques and antique shops), as well as a modern mall at the east end of the town, and a shopping complex in the old Vanstone Mill, which is at the west end. The museum in the Jury home also houses one of Canada's finest doll collections and draws visitors from across North America.

People who appreciate the architecture of the 1800s will enjoy Bowmanville: the area has more than 300 heritage buildings, several of which have been officially designated under the Ontario Heritage Act. Many are within easy walking distance of the commercial main street, and make for an interesting tour. For more information, contact the Bowmanville Local Architectural Conservancy Advisory Committee (LACAC) at 905-623-3379 or the Bowmanville Museum at 905-623-2734. ■

BOWMANVILLE ZOO

Located at 340 King Street East, and opened in 1919, the Bowmanville Zoo (a member of the Canadian Association of Zoological Parks and Aquariums [CAZPA]) is Canada's oldest. Situated on 19 park-like hectares (47 acres), the zoo is open seven days a week, year-round except for the month of April. It has four hundred animals, including elephants, lions, tigers, camels, and zebras. Except on extremely wet days when the unpaved back half of the zoo is difficult to traverse, its paths and amenities are wheelchair-accessible. Parking is free. For further information, call 905-623-5655. ■

OLD PORT DARLINGTON

This part of the Trail will be of special interest to those who like boats and boating. To reach it from the Bowmanville Marsh Conservation Area, turn right onto Port Darlington Road. (Or, if you are coming from Bowmanville, follow Liberty Street south to Lake Road. Turn east onto Lake Road, which leads you to Port Darlington Road and back onto the Trail.)

  Follow Port Darlington Road south to the marina: the slips house many different kinds of boats and the variety of spars and masts reflecting off the water provide a photographer's paradise. Those interested in fishing or simply in cruising the lake can hire a boat at the Port Darlington Marina. There you will also find a restaurant with a screened balcony, providing an ideal setting for a meal.

The evening view of the boat lights twinkling on the water, combined with the soft lake breezes, make this an ideal place to end a day on the Trail; fortunately, the marina offers comfortable, reasonably priced accommodations for those who decide to stay overnight.

Once known as Port Darlington, this area was separate from Bowmanville, of which it is now a part. It was among Lake Ontario's busiest ports, shipping millions of tonnes of grain, lumber, and other products annually. While one wharf housed a grain elevator and was used for industrial shipping, the other welcomed the passenger steam ships that called daily. In fact, the port was so busy that produce-laden wagons had to wait their turn at the docks, in a line that snaked to the point on Liberty Street where the Tourist and General Information Centre now stands.

Here, too, are the remnants of the once-stately Victorian summer cottages that recall the area's history as a popular vacation spot; this was also very popular with campers, who pitched their tents wherever they could find a spot. (There were often so many tents the community was nicknamed "Cotton Town".)

The Municipality of Clarington recently purchased the Harbour Master's House, located on Port Darlington Road; it is marked with a plaque, but is not yet open to the public. The Clarington Museum and the Port Darlington Community Association hope that, in time, it will be home to artifacts and displays depicting the community's early history.

An eastward turn onto East Beach Road makes it easy to understand why this was a good area in the 1880s and '90s for people thinking of building a cottage: the view is breathtaking. But there was even more: in the words of one prominent scientist of the time, "There is no place like the high north shore of Lake Ontario for health giving pure air..."

Across the channel, you can see West Beach Road; before it was built, supplies were brought to it by a hand-operated ferry that crossed the creek mouth from East Beach. Both the East and the West Beach once boasted dance halls; dancers and revellers at the West Beach had to use the ferry to cross. Now a deeper creek mouth allows boats to travel up to the marina.

Today there is windsurfing through the channel and out onto the lake, as well as swimming in good weather, and a sandy beach for family fun.

The ideal way to travel along East Beach Road is by foot or bicycle, so that you can stop frequently to enjoy the view. Only the first 0.5 kilometre (0.3 mile) of East Beach is paved, making this portion of the Trail unsuitable for people in wheelchairs. Continuing along East Beach takes you to Lambs Road, where the Trail heads north. Lambs Road turns into South Service Road as it bends east before it reaches Bennett Road. A few kilometres to the east, the Trail picks up again at Cobbledick Road. To get there, follow Bennett Road north as far as Highway 2.

At Highway 2, take the Trail east; note that, on the north side, east of Cobbledick Road, you will find the site of the historically and economically important Ontario Fish Hatchery. While it may seem like a novel idea today, the hatchery, begun by Samuel Wilmot (a naturalist and conservationist) in 1867, was so successful that Wilmot played a major role in establishing twelve more hatcheries across the Dominion of Canada.

Although the ponds and hatchery are gone, the brick farmhouse in which Wilmot began his experiments still stands. To see the plaque that commemorates the site, follow the path by taking Rudell Road north off of Highway 2, then west on Given Road.

Cyclists and hikers will want to take Cobbledick Road to its south end, for this is where the Trail begins to wind its way through the Wilmot Creek Marsh valley.

WILMOT CREEK MARSH

Most of the lands along the lakefront between Bennett and Cobbledick roads belong to the Wilmot Creek Retirement Village. These are private lands and not accessible to the public. The south end of Cobbledick Road is in the northeast corner of the retirement village.

From this point, the Trail involves a moderately strenuous hike along the footpath, across one side of the marsh valley, across the creek by pedestrian bridge, and back up the other side of the valley. Although bicycling is permitted, the valley's winding, steeply inclined path makes it rather difficult.

The marsh, which is home to many species of breeding birds, and, in some areas, a habitat for fish species, has been designated a Class 2 Provincially Significant Wetland (see page 5 for explanation of wetland classification). Surveys are underway to identify the precise number of animal and plant species that depend on the marsh for survival.

At the marsh exit, the Trail skirts a woodlot before connecting with Toronto Street; it's worth stopping and enjoying the spectacular view of Lake Ontario, particularly from the seating area located at the foot of Toronto Street. This was also the site of the Robert Baldwin home until it was torn down in 1988.

The Baldwin home was an important link to a distinguished attorney general, co-premier and councillor of Upper Canada, Robert Baldwin, grandson of one of the original settlers, also named Robert Baldwin. Baldwin and his father, William Warren Baldwin, were joined in their devotion to the core principle and goal of the colony's early Reformers: Responsible Government. (In the Canadian political system, this phrase has a specific meaning: government that is responsible to the people – i.e., dependent on maintaining a majority of votes in a duly elected parliamentary body.)

It was over this issue, in fact, that Baldwin crossed swords with Sir Francis Bond Head, governor of Upper Canada (see page 223). His resignation from the legislative council, in response to Bond Head's high-handedness, played a major role in the constitutional and political events leading to the 1837 Rebellion in Upper Canada. (Nor would it be the last time Baldwin resigned from office rather than compromise on Responsible Government.) Morose and withdrawn for much of his life, his role in our country's early history was not fully appreciated for many years. More recently, however, Robert Baldwin has been recognized as "the popularizer of responsible government and one of the first, if not the first, proponents of a bicultural nation".

The Trail continues east of Toronto Street on an unopened road allowance across the front of the Water Treatment Plant. It is along this off-road path that the Trail is aligned to connect with Baldwin Street. Follow Baldwin north to Clarke Street and make a right hand turn to Mill Street.

A short side trip north leads to the Village of Newcastle, which is the last stop for shops or amenities for about the next 28 kilometres (17.4 miles).

VILLAGE OF NEWCASTLE

The farm machinery empire that grew to be Massey Ferguson started here in Newcastle. With it began the remarkable public career of a family whose members would include Canada's first native-born governor general (Vincent), a radical right-wing actor (Raymond), and the force behind the creation of Massey Hall (Hart). Masseys were also connected with good works (the Fred Victor Mission in downtown Toronto) and with a certain, very grand level of society. Or, in those most famous lines of Canadian doggerel, penned by editor B.K. Sandwell:

Let the Old World, where rank's yet vital,

Part those who have and have not title.

Toronto has no social classes –

Only the Masseys and the masses.

A walk or drive through the older section of town, where well-kept Victorian and Georgian mansions still stand, makes it clear that the Masseys were not Newcastle's only wealthy inhabitants.

The informative volunteers at the Memorial Library in the Newcastle Village Community Hall, the large red brick building at the corner of Highway 2 and Mill Street in the heart of the village, are members of the Newcastle and District Historical Society. They open the society's room Tuesday mornings from 9 to 11:30 a.m. and are eager to tell you all about the area. They are very proud of the fact that the community hall was a gift to the Village of Newcastle from Chester Massey, father of Vincent and Raymond.

If someone in the Village of Newcastle tells you there are lions and tigers in the hills to the north, they're referring to Jungle Cat World. Just 11 kilometres (7 miles) north of Newcastle, it has a variety of animals, including bears, deer, wolves, and monkeys; possibly the greatest attractions are the thirty or so large exotic cats, including lions, Siberian tigers, leopards, and cougars.

Located in the Village of Orono, the zoo is on the
southeast corner of Highway 35 and Taunton Road and is open
every day from April to September and on weekends only in March,
October, and November. For more information, call 905-983-5016.

Following Mill Street south puts you back on the Trail
and leads to Port Newcastle and the residential area of Bond Head.
At the foot of Mill Street you will find the Bond Head Parkette,
which is adjacent to a private marina. Although the marina is not
open to the public, Trail users can lunch at The Brig, which is on
the west side of the mouth of Graham Creek. From that vantage
point, you can see the marshlands that line the creek where it empties into the lake and is rich in wildlife. When you've rested long
enough, walk along the pier to the lighthouse and enjoy the view
along the shore.

BOND HEAD

The name Bond Head is given to the small community on the
eastern boundary of Newcastle; at the southern end of Mill Street
turn left at Boulton Street. It was once a busy port and – like the
identically named village some 90 kilometres (56 miles) north of
Toronto – was named for Sir Francis Bond Head. The bluffs to the
west provided shelter from the prevailing winds and the deep basin
made it an excellent ship anchorage.

The decision to name anything after Francis Bond
Head is baffling. Even for a time when heads of government tended
to be autocratic and authoritarian, he was of a rare order. He had
come here, apparently in sympathy with the Reformers of the day,
but he interfered in an election, acted spitefully against the
Reformers, and stripped Upper Canada of troops when they were
badly needed.

While, in fairness, he cannot be held responsible for
the 1837 Rebellion, Bond Head contributed substantially to the
problems underlying it; he was recalled to England early in 1838
and was not appointed again to public office, although he lived
almost another forty years.

LAKESHORE ROAD

Boulton Street ends at Lakeshore Road and so, too, does the
Waterfront Trail. The next 13 kilometres (8 miles) follow Lakeshore
Road to the municipal border with Hope Township. Because this is
a narrow road with no sidewalks or shoulders, the local council is
reviewing this section to determine its suitability for people travelling by bike, in-line skates, or on foot. Although it is a popular route
for cyclists, cars are the recommended mode of transportation
along this section. There are no amenities –no food, fuel or rest
stops – on this stretch until you reach the Town of Port Hope, more
than 25 kilometres (15 miles) east. As it winds along the shore and
spectacular 30-metre (100-foot) bluff the road does, however, provide some of Clarington's most riveting scenery.

Approximately 0.8 kilometre (0.5 mile) along the
road, you will find a small parkette (it is easy to miss because it's on
a curve), which is also accessible from the beach near Bond Head
Parkette. The stones along the beach, with their many small fossil
treasures, have long delighted amateur archaeologists of all ages;
much of the rock is black shale, which makes perfect 'skippers' for
those who enjoy shying them along the water's placid surface. Even
before there was a parkette here, the spot was a popular picnic area,
where generations of local residents and visitors spent idle and no
doubt memorable afternoons.

At the 7-kilometre (4.3-mile) point along this portion
of the Trail, Lakeshore Road turns sharply northward over an old
wooden bridge (use it cautiously because, just over the bridge, there
is a double set of railway tracks on which Via Rail trains speed by).
The crossing has good safety mechanisms and signals that must be
obeyed at all times.

Lakeshore Road then makes a sharp right to continue
eastward; there you will find the Bond Head Bluffs Area of Natural
Science Interests (ANSI).

There are ANSI sites all along the bluffs of the
Clarington section of the Waterfront Trail – places where interesting and sometimes rare plants thrive as the result of local
mini-ecosystems. These are private lands and the bluffs and

FOSSILS

Especially in the hard days of winter, it is hard to believe but true: 450 million years ago, the north shore of Lake Ontario was inundated by a shallow tropical sea; in the time known as the Ordovician Period lime and clay sediments were deposited around it; these sediments formed, respectively, today's limestone and shale rocks. While there would also have been primitive fish and some plants, the only remaining evidence of the period are fossils, the ancient organisms preserved in what is now rock. Most are casts and molds, showing only an animal's hard parts: a snail fossil, for example, gives no indication of an internal organs or soft body. Nonetheless, the fossils often retain amazing details of the surface markings of the original shell.

Among the most common fossils are two extinct groups, trilobites and graptolites, as well as modern versions of five still-extant groups found in oceans: brachiopods, ancestors of today's lamp shells; crinoids (which evolved to become sea-lilies); cephalopods (predecessors to squids; corals; and snails. Sowbug-like animals, trilobites had segmented bodies divided into three lobes; graptolites were tiny colonial creatures. Their fossils are found in shale and look like long, narrow pencil markings, as much as several centimetres in length.

Brachiopods are similar to clams, but can be distinguished from them by the two halves of each shell, each different from the other. Crinoid fossils resemble miniature doughnuts that fit together to form a plant-like stem; the main body was cup-shaped and had tentacles, but fossil evidence is rare. Cephalopods were squids with long pointed shells; the largest predators of the deeps, these monsters reached five metres (16 feet) in length. Early corals and snails were similar to their modern descendants.

For further information, *Geology and Fossils of the Craigleith Area*, available from the Ontario Ministry of Natural Resources, and *Fossils: A Guide to Prehistoric Life; Golden Nature Guide Series*, available in bookstores.

gullies here are very unstable and present a hazard. Caution is recommended and visitors, no matter how experienced or well equipped, are urged not to attempt to climb the erosion-weakened bluffs. Because of the sensitive and delicate nature of ANSI sites, step with extreme caution in order to avoid treading on what may well be rare plants. No flowers or plants in these areas may be picked.

When you have travelled 10 kilometres (6.2 miles) along Lakeshore Road, you reach Port Granby, site of a controversial low-level radioactive waste site. What was once a bustling port community (it even had its own hotel) is now gone and the only access to the beach is via municipal road allowances; unless you have a vehicle equipped for driving on difficult terrain, walking and cycling are recommended in this area.

The route continues east along Lakeshore Road for another 3 kilometres (1.8 miles), then leaves Clarington and enters Hope Township, where you will find such delightful lakeshore communities as Port Britain.

DRUMLINS OF NORTHUMBERLAND

About 13,000 years ago, large sheets of ice across southern Ontario were scraping, scouring and altering the land. In addition to creating the Oak Ridges Moraine and the Pine Ridge Moraine, glaciation dramatically changed the Northumberland landscape into one with many little hills, or drumlins.

Drumlins are tear-shaped hills composed of glacial till – sand, silt, and clay with bedrock fragments eroded by the ice – left after the glaciers retreated. They appear in groups that usually form a distinctive pattern. About 4,000 of them have been counted north of Lake Ontario, most north of the Oak Ridges Moraine. However, many lie along the shore, and on the floor of Lake Ontario.

Most of the drumlins found in the Greater Toronto Bioregion can be seen between Clarington and Trenton, when travelling along Highway 2. The long, narrow part of these drumlins point northward in the direction of movement of the glacier (the Ontario ice lobe) that formed them. The steeper end faces the direction from which the ice came.

Some drumlins between Cobourg and Colborne reach a height of 45 metres (147 feet). Their hilltops add to the distinctive character of the region and provide opportunities to see out over the lake as well as to the north, east and west for great distances.

To *the north, the ground rises*
dramatically up the old
Lake Iroquois beaches and is
dissected by heavily forested ravines ◄·····

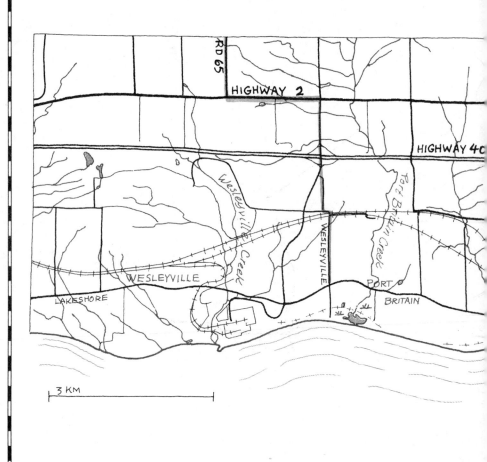

Hope
TOWNSHIP
& Port Hope

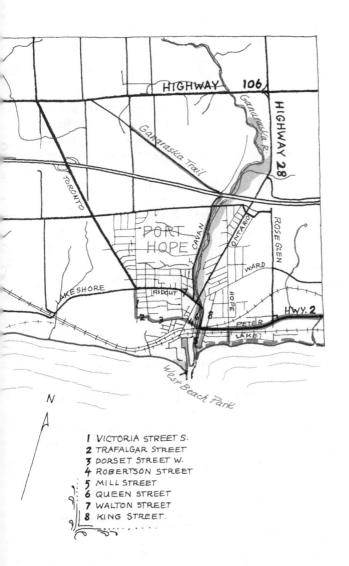

N

1 VICTORIA STREET S.
2 TRAFALGAR STREET
3 DORSET STREET W.
4 ROBERTSON STREET
5 MILL STREET
6 QUEEN STREET
7 WALTON STREET
8 KING STREET.

N 1792, Governor John Graves Simcoe issued a proclamation dividing part of Upper Canada into townships. This one is named for Colonel Henry Hope, who was Governor of Canada in 1787.

By 1803, 277 people lived in Hope Township, making it the second-most populous one in the counties. A report on the town meeting held in 1822 at the Wellington Inn is the first record of local government.

Resolutions were passed regarding the definition of a lawful fence and the kinds of livestock permitted to run at large. It was agreed that, in general, horned cattle would be allowed to roam. The ear-marks – a slit, a round hole, and various other symbols – were used for identifying the cattle and are still preserved, along with owners' names, in the Township records.

Hope Township, about 95 kilometres (60 miles) east of Toronto, is mainly agricultural. At this time, the Waterfront Trail does not have an alignment through the township. However, two main east-west routes crossing the municipality lead to examples of the natural and built environment that should not be missed. Both roads will also guide you to Port Hope, where the Trail continues.

PUBLIC TRANSIT

Local Transit
DJ Travel Services
905-885-4544

VIA Train
1-800-361-2135

HIGHWAY 2 ROUTE

Highway 2, roughly parallel to and north of Highway 401, provides a straight, smooth route through a number of the township's hamlets as it makes its way to the town of Port Hope. It also provides access to such wonderful areas as Garden Hill and Richardson's Lookout.

LAKESHORE ROAD ROUTE

South of Highway 2 and Highway 401, Lakeshore Road bends to the east and offers remarkable views of the lake. This windy, rural road is popular because it provides scenic views of the surrounding landscape.

Although the avid hiker will probably appreciate the terrain as it winds across Hope Township's southern tip, with its old farms and compelling vistas. Caution is required in traversing the varied topography of this well travelled road that lacks sidewalks.

Going along the historic Lakeshore Road, whether by car or bicycle, is an unforgettable experience, especially at sunset. Many people think this is among the most spectacular stretches of Lake Ontario's north shore.

Like Highway 2, Lakeshore Road goes all the way through Hope Township to its eastern boundary, Port Hope, from there you pick up the route for the Waterfront Trail.

WESLEYVILLE

According to the late historian Harold Reeve, the Township is covered with deposits from the most recent Ice Age; these rest on Palaeozoic limestone. The limestone dips at a low angle without folding or faulting, making this the only place in Hope Township where it can be seen. (See Harold Reeve: *A History of Hope Township*; 1967, Cobourg Sentinel Star.)

On the north side of Lakeshore Road, approximately 2 kilometres (1.2 miles) east of the township line, is a small brick schoolhouse built in 1899. Just a stone's throw east, also on the north side, is the tiny Wesleyville Church. These two structures are among the last reminders of the small settlement that served local farmers. Named after John Wesley, who in the 1740s founded the Methodist Society, it is located between the tiny ports of Port Granby and New Britain.

Situated on gently rolling ground on both sides of Wesleyville Creek, the village stretched east and west along Lakeshore Road. To the north, the ground rises dramatically up the old Lake Iroquois beaches and is dissected by heavily forested ravines up to Highway 401. Around the springs, aboriginal settlements abounded, from the camps of caribou hunters 9,000 years ago to early agricultural villages about a thousand years ago.

The landscape is now dominated by the Wesleyville Generating Complex, a huge coal-fired thermal electric plant that has never been in operation. A reminder of the technological world, it stands in contrast to the surrounding farms. The complex is now the site of firefighter training and storage facilities. Several thousand hectares of surrounding land were assembled for the plant development.

Neglect, demolition, and the ravages of time have taken their toll on this pretty rural settlement. However, several interesting structures remain, to tell the story of a small, determined group of transplanted Methodists, some of them Loyalists who had come in the early 19th century to domesticate the wilderness along Lake Ontario's shores.

At the northeast corner of the generating plant property is Wesleyville Road. It can take you north on an interesting trip to the hamlet of Garden Hill. Follow Wesleyville Road over Highway 401 to Highway 2 where Wesleyville Road ends. Turn west for a short distance to County Road 65 and continue north to County Road 9. You are in Elizabethville at this intersection. Turn east on County Road 9 which brings you to the entrance of Richardson's Lookout.

RICHARDSON'S LOOKOUT

On top of Dean's Hill is Richardson's Lookout, offering a panoramic view of the Ganaraska Forest and Lake Ontario from the wooden lookout tower. Parking is available.

GARDEN HILL

Dorothy's House Museum is located in Garden Hill and is reached by travelling further east on County Road 9. Originally a pioneer worker's cottage built in the 1860s, it is furnished with artifacts of that era. Dorothy's House is open from May to October or by appointment. Contact Marjorie Kenton, president of the East Durham Historical Society, at 905-885-6805.

East of Dorothy's House Museum, is the Garden Hill Conservation Area. Or you may choose to continue east on Lakeshore Road, which will bring you to Port Britain.

GARDEN HILL CONSERVATION AREA

The conservation area consists of 21 hectares (52 acres) of parkland and picnic area set in the Ganaraska Forest. Garden Hill pond attracts a wide variety of birds and is also popular with anglers. Washroom facilities are accessible to people in wheelchairs. For more information call 905-885-8173.

PORT BRITAIN

Port Britain is 95 kilometres (60 miles) north of Rochester and an hour's drive from Toronto and from the Haliburton-Kawarthas. Its century-old homes and brooks with their single-lane bridges create a very pleasant sense of having stepped back in time. There was once a sawmill, distillery, grist mill, tannery, blacksmith's and cooper's shops, hotel, and carding mill. As you cross a narrow bridge, you will see Sora Brook, one of Port Britain's original homes. To your immediate right is Port Britain Road, which leads to lakefront homes.

The best examples of the township's architectural heritage can be found on its county roads. One of the most impressive is Batterwood Estate, home of Vincent Massey, Canada's first Canadian-born Governor General, located at Canton, in the northeast corner of the township.

There is little access to the lake from this area, but it is seldom out of sight. Parts of the shoreline, generally untouched by industry, are virtually the same as they were a century ago.

There are sweeping views as you go along Lakeshore Road, past Haskill Road. The route meanders north through a set of railway viaducts (replete with graffiti), past Little Road, to Port Hope.

PORT HOPE

As you leave Hope Township, you enter one of Ontario's most beautiful towns, historic Port Hope. Lovingly restored and maintained, it has a population of 12,500 – people who are determined to preserve its fine architecture and small-town way of life. The town is also a member of the Green Communities Initiative, which promotes the greening of Ontario by encouraging members to increase energy and water efficiency, reduce waste, and prevent pollution.

Originally a native village called Cochingomink, by the 18th century it had become a busy fur-trading post known as Smith's Creek (for Peter Smith, one of the traders). Later, its citizens chose to name it in honour of Henry Hope.

In accordance with an agreement with Hope Township, in 1782 the colonial government began to recruit settlers. Two United Empire Loyalists, Elias Smith and Captain Jonathan Walton, were given extensive land grants in exchange for a commitment to settle 40 families.

FROM DREAM TO REALITY:
People Make a Difference

In her book, *Cargoes on the Great Lakes*, Marie McPhedran wrote, "We are on Lake Ontario, the lake of many firsts in the history of Great Lakes shipping – the first recorded ship's voyage; the first steamboats launched on the lake; the real movement of settlers by boat to its shores; the first lighthouse ever to be built on the Great Lakes."

Now, Lake Ontario is home to another first: the first of the Great Lakes to have a Waterfront Trail along most of its shoreline. From Hamilton to Trenton, people are reclaiming and regenerating areas of the Ontario shoreline and its watersheds.

In Port Hope, two of the most active participants are two residents, retired labour relations executive Keith Richan and Peter Hussman, a welding contractor. Both spent countless hours chairing committees and knocking on doors, seeking funding and other support to clean up neglected areas and blaze what is now the Port Hope Waterfront Trail.

In 1994 boy scouts planted trees in an open area just north of the Waterfront Trail east of Hope Street, another example of community involvement in waterfront regeneration.

Without Hussman and Richan, and thousands of individuals, service clubs, community groups, and volunteer organizations along Lake Ontario's shore, the Waterfront Trail would still be a dream waiting to be transformed into reality.

The first pioneers arrived in June, 1793, and four years later Smith and Walton received a Crown grant of 294 hectares (726 acres) of land. In 1798, Smith built the area's first flour mill, on the east bank of the Ganaraska River and, within ten years, distilleries, foundries, breweries, more flour mills, and shipyards had been established. This prosperous community was said to rival Toronto. In fact, Port Hope was called Toronto from 1817 to 1819. Meanwhile, the other Toronto was called York until 1834.

On March 6, 1834, Port Hope, population 1,517, was incorporated.

Each day, ships travelled from Port Hope to Rochester, a major trading partner. Today, boats still ply the lake, but most are private sailboats or racing yachts. Trade with Toronto is still brisk: visitors come to see what remains one of the handsomest 19th-century main streets in the province.

As you enter Port Hope from the west, the Ferguson farm and Wildwood, circa 1858, both on your left, create a strong sense of history. Wildwood is a reminder of Port Hope's affluence and the building boom of the mid-1800s. Originally the home of John Shuter Smith, its story comes complete with an evil count, a kidnapping, and a happy ending. After Smith's death, his widow, Josephine, was said to have moved to a castle in Europe, where she married a member of the German nobility. But her former in-laws became suspicious as Smith's once-prosperous estate shrank steadily. Their suspicions turned out to be valid: Josephine had been duped and was being held captive by her wicked husband. Shortly thereafter, she was freed and returned to Port Hope.

To the west, on the same side, stands the Brand farmhouse, one of the area's most graceful examples of rural 1860 architecture.

South of the Brand home is Dunain, built in 1857 by Port Hope's first elected mayor, William Fraser and his bride, Augusta Williams. It stands on acreage received as a wedding gift from her father, a naval commander named John Tucker Williams. Remarkably, this private home is still owned by descendants of the original family.

Further east, south off Lakeshore Road on Victoria Street South, you will find, at number 82, a golfer's paradise - the Port Hope Golf and Country Club. Set on the lake, this semi-private club has a driving range and 18 holes with a 66 par. It is open from April to October. For further information or to book a tee time, call 905-885-6487.

There is also a public course, Hamilton Heights, which can be reached by heading east on Highway 2. Turn north on Highway 28 until you are a little more than 1.5 kilometres (1 mile) north of Highway 401. Turn east on Dale Road and drive for 2 kilometres (1.2 miles). The course has 18 holes, a 72 par, and a driving range.

At the foot of Victoria Street, the Waterfront Trail turns left onto Trafalgar Street where more-modern homes obscure Idalia, an Italianate villa on a beautiful ravine overlooking Lake Ontario. Just before making the turn east onto Trafalgar, a look west will reveal the Penryn homestead. Built in 1829, the Penryn home has an oval upstairs drawing room with its floors cambered slightly to replicate a ship's deck. The entire house, with the exception of the drawing room, was renovated in the 1890s.

At the point where Trafalgar and Bramley streets meet, there stands another turn-of-the-century house - Homewood. Reminiscent of a Virginia plantation home, it is something of an anomaly in Port Hope, especially because of its location at the head of one of the town's most architecturally significant streets. The Trail turns south for a short distance along Bramley before it bends east again. At this point, Bramley becomes Dorset Street.

Next to Homewood stand two cottages, constructed between 1860 and 1865. Although modest, they are popular examples of Ontario cottage architecture at its best.

Across the street, on the south side, at the top of the Dorset Street hill, sits Hillcrest, built in 1874, the only Port Hope mansion influenced by the French beaux-arts style. Hillcrest is now an elegant bed and breakfast; for more information, write Ruth Beaucage, 175 Dorset Street West, Port Hope, Ontario L1A 1G4 or phone 905-885-7367.

As the Trail curves down the hill, a mix of homes, large and small, impressive or merely charming, creates an eclectic streetscape. For example, Terralta Cottage, another Gothic treasure, contrasts with nearby Muidar, a decidedly Victorian home built in 1868.

Muidar is important to Port Hope's more recent history. Beginning in the mid-1930s, it was the home of Dr. Marcel Pochon, a protégé of the legendary Nobel-Prize winning Marie Curie. Pochon was recruited to supervise the process of refining uranium, which reshaped the town's economy. Pochon's home ("radium" spelled backward) recalls the years when Port Hope was a centre of uranium production. The element is no longer produced here, but the original company (once known as Eldorado and now called Cameco) still refines it in Port Hope.

Farther down the hill, on the ravine side, is The Cone, one of Port Hope's best-preserved homes. It was built in 1858 for Thomas Clarke, engineer and secretary of the Port Hope, Beaverton and Lindsay Railway.

At the corner of Dorset and Catherine streets, on a richly landscaped hillside, sits Wimbourne, built about 1851 for William Sisson, a wealthy Port Hope businessman. A typical Ontario cottage, Wimbourne stands out because of its unusual truncated gables and whimsical gingerbread.

To the south, Lakeview Terrace is a mix of row housing (now usually called town houses) and quaint cottages lining the street to where it meets John Street.

A northern excursion takes you into the business district, where you can find the post office and the Carlyle Bed and Breakfast, offering fine food and lodging. For information on rates or reservations, contact David or Jeanne Henderson, 86 John Street, Port Hope, Ontario L1A 2Z2 or phone 905-885-8686.

In addition to the Hillcrest and the Carlyle, there are two other bed and breakfasts near the centre of town. Just a five-minute walk from the business district is The Brimar, where your hosts are Brian and Marjorie Sorrell, 22 Ward Street, Port Hope, Ontario L1A 1L5 or phone 905-885-9396. For reservations at the Uppertowne Inn, contact Diane McCormick or David Priest

PORT HOPE VIADUCT AND STATION

Port Hope is home to a pair of railway landmarks, both near the Waterfront Trail. The largest and most spectacular is the long stone railway viaduct, which carries CN's Toronto-Montreal main passenger line across the broad valley of the Ganaraska River. Completed about 1856, this route was the longest section of continuous railway line at the time in Canada – more than 480 kilometres (300 miles). Then, as now, it was a vital link between Canada's two largest cities.

The bridge is very graceful, its stone arches painstakingly fitted together by masons. For more than a century, the Port Hope railway viaduct has been safely carrying trains weighing hundreds of tonnes more than their 19th-century predecessors. Tiny woodburning steam locomotives, pulling short trains of wooden cars, have given way to massive diesel engines, often in teams of three or four, hauling freight trains more than a hundred cars in length.

But the viaduct's designers did their work so conscientiously, creating a structure to last for centuries, that the bridge has never had to be replaced, even as trains grew heavier and bigger. Clearly, such a structure, like so many of our historical churches, libraries, municipal buildings, and post offices, is evidence of the Victorian zeal for building for the ages.

The bridge just north of the viaduct carries freight trains for CP. By the time the span was built in the early 1900s, concrete was being used for construction and so it, rather than massive stone blocks forms the piers.

Another Victorian relic in Port Hope is the railway station, about 300 metres (1,000 feet) west of the viaduct, off Hayward Street on the south side of the tracks.

The Port Hope station, originally constructed for the Grand Trunk Railway in 1856, may be the oldest one in continuous operation in Canada. A little limestone gem, it serves passenger trains, just as it did in pre-Confederation Canada.

Structurally, the Port Hope station has changed very little over the years. Note the beautifully curved arched windows, and the chimneys, which have been rebuilt in their original form. You can almost visualise top-hatted and hoop-skirted passengers of 1856 waiting for their trains or looking forward to hearing Sir John A. Macdonald on one of his campaign tours.

at 187 Walton Street, Port Hope, Ontario L1A 1N7 or phone 905-885-5694.

While you're on John Street, you can visit the Port Hope and District Chamber of Commerce, 35 John Street or phone 905-885-5519, it offers information and brochures about area amenities and can supply you with maps and details of walking tours.

The corner of Robertson and Queen streets offers you some options: north on Augusta Street, overlooking the Ganaraska River, is the old Town Hall, built when Port Hope was still flexing its muscles as a shipping port. In 1849, Commander Williams, the first mayor, along with the newly established town council, decided that a town hall was needed and it was constructed two years later.

In the 1840s, plans were made to enlarge the harbour, in order to keep pace with the fast-growing lumber and agricultural economy. In 1854, construction of the Port Hope and Lindsay Railway strengthened Port Hope's claim as an important trading centre. It was boosted further in 1856, when the Grand Trunk Railway passed through Port Hope on its route from Windsor to Montreal.

For a century, Port Hope remained unchanged, very much small-town Ontario. Thanks to that quiet period, the essentials of the town's architecture and way of life were left untouched, which is exactly what makes it one of today's best reminders of our early heritage.

If you do decide to leave the Trail by heading north on Queen Street, be sure to visit Memorial Park. Set among mature trees across from the public library, the park contains picnic tables, public restrooms, and a playground. There is also a refurbished bandshell, where there are free concerts twice a month throughout the summer.

At the north end of Queen Street, you will find Walton Street, which has been called the best-preserved commercial streetscape in Ontario. (Named for Captain Jonathan Walton who received the original land grant, like so many roads in Port Hope, Walton Street recalls the founding families and their offspring: Augusta, Julia, Caroline, Ellen, John, Peter, Shuter, Elias, William,

and Ward, among them.) Walton Street is an antique buffs'
delight, thanks to its intriguing mix of shops, bed and breakfasts,
and restaurants.

Side Trip
THE GANARASKA HIKING TRAIL

If you opt to head north on Queen Street, you can enter
a 3-kilometre (1.8-mile) section of the cross-country
Ganaraska Hiking Trail. It takes about 45 minutes to complete
the trip each way. Begun in 1968, the Ganaraska Trail now connects with the Bruce Trail to the west, ending near Collingwood
some 450 kilometres (280 miles) away. All sections are challenging and are for walking only. Sturdy shoes are advised at all times
when you follow the banks of the Ganaraska River to the Port
Hope Conservation Area. (However, the Trail should be avoided
in particularly wet springs, when river waters can be dangerously
high and especially hazardous for young children.)

There is a fish ladder at Corbett's Dam, beside the
Highway 401 underpass. A week or so before the opening of the
spring fishing season, it is filled with spawning trout and salmon
making their way upriver. At this dam, you can also see a well-
preserved reminder of Port Hope's early river industry - the
Molson Mill, built about 1850, and the Molson Millhouse which is
a decade older. The mill has historical links to one of Canada's
largest brewing empires, and once housed the Ontario College
of Art.

Beyond this section, the Ganaraska Trail passes through
various environments: from the sandy hills of the Ganaraska
Forest, through the Kawarthas to the rugged wilderness of the
Canadian Shield. For more information about the area, contact
Jack Goering of the Ganaraska Trail Association and the Pine
Ridge Ganaraska Trail Club, at 905-885-4430. ■

Alternatively, you may head south on Queen from the
corner of Queen and Robertson streets. South of the railway overpass, you will find yourself at the mouth of the Ganaraska River.
Here are small riverside parks, picnic areas, and year-round fishing.

Reputed to be the finest source of rainbow trout in
Ontario, the Ganaraksa River is the site of fishing derbies, both
spring and fall. The Ganaraska Spring Derby (rainbow trout) goes
from mid-February to late April; and the Northumberland Fishing
Quest (salmon chinook/cohoe, brown trout, rainbow trout,
walleye/pickerel, smallmouth bass, largemouth bass) continues
from early August to mid-October. For information on fishing or
charters out of Port Hope Harbour, contact the Port Hope
Chamber of Commerce at 905-885-5519.

From this point on the Ganaraska you can look across
the river to the Canadian Firefighter's Museum. If you decide to
visit, cross the river at the intersection of Queen and Robertson, go
under the viaduct past the Bi-Way store to the north and turn right.
This places you on Mill Street; the river is on your right and the
museum, less than half a kilometre (0.3 mile) away, is on the left.
There is a fascinating workshop, with a collection of restored
firefighting vehicles, both horse-drawn and hand-drawn, extinguish-
ers, rescue devices, and more.

The trucks are brought out a few times a year for local
parades and Fire Buffs events. The Canadian Firefighter's Museum
is open daily during July and August.

When you leave the museum, you can return to the
Trail by staying on Mill Street until you reach the lakefront, where
there is a tiny café, a marina (where charters are available) and a
beach picnic area. There is swimming, windsurfing, and wading in
Lake Ontario. Kids can expend their energy on the playground
equipment and cool off in the shallow water. At this point, Mill
Street ends as it curves east into Madison Street.

Directly across from the beach, to the north, is yet
another Port Hope gem: Canada House, circa 1822. According to
local lore, it was built by Captain Wallace and his brother-in-law,
Norman Brogdin, whose name is given to a lane in the downtown
business core. In the 1850s, the house was frequented by sailors and
travellers and was known as Seaman's Inn.

Following Madison around the bend brings you to
King Street, where, thanks to information and maps supplied by the
Chamber of Commerce, you can create a self-guided tour of historic

King Street. Houses here were apparently the homes of Port Hope's lake captains and crews. As you walk up the street, look left for a glimpse of the Ganaraska River and the Town Hall. Beyond them, you see the only uranium enrichment plant in Canada.

The Chamber's booklets are produced by the Port Hope branch of the Architectural Conservancy of Ontario. Founded in 1964, the group initially had only five members but has grown to become the second-largest branch in the province.

The Waterfront Trail heads north on Mill Street (you can also take King Street) to Peter Street (Highway 2), where it continues east to the town boundary. Along the way you will notice an impressive tapered tower. Built in 1877 by John Helm as a water tower, it is now empty and serves only as a reminder of the past. Next door, Helm built his home, which was known as Belgrave until 1920; now it is Greenwood Country Inn; phone 905-885-0000.

To continue along the water's edge, lace up your hiking boots and you're ready to enjoy the Port Hope Waterfront Trail.

Side Trip
PORT HOPE WATERFRONT TRAIL

This enjoyable route is 3 kilometres (1.8 miles) long – a 45-minute walk each way – with an unobstructed view of the lake. There is a parking lot east of Canada House.

Inexperienced hikers may find the shoreline section from the foot of King to Hope Street too challenging, in which case, a short car ride will get you to firmer ground. Take King north to Shuter Street and head east on Shuter to Hope. Make a right here and you will find parking facilities to your immediate right. From Hope Street east to Gage Creek is a hard-packed gravel trail, which makes for easy walking.

Here, you can take a leisurely stroll along the lake's edge to the wetland at Gage Creek, which is alive with wildlife. (See Gage Creek in Hamilton Township chapter.) But keep to the pathway: there are 4,000 tender seedlings alongside, planted by boy scouts. There are also great picnic areas close to the parking lots – perfect for a sunny day. ■

Port Hope is worth a visit any time of year. Each April there is a zany Float Your Fanny Down The Ganny Race, with canoes and kayaks as well as a small armada of homemade crazy crafts to commemorate the 1980 flood of the Ganaraska River.

Every Canada Day, Port Hope hosts a Calithumpian Parade and events throughout the day, culminating in a spectacular fireworks display. Later in the month comes the annual Sidewalk Sale while, in August, the Ganaraska Arts Festival presents "Art in the Park". In September, it's time for the Annual Agricultural Fall Fair, while October brings the very popular Historical House Tour: the Port Hope branch of the Architectural Conservancy of Ontario hosts visitors to different homes and buildings of interest. In December, there is an Olde Tyme Christmas with candlelight walks and carolling. For more information on these and other events, contact Port Hope at 905-885-4544 or the Chamber of Commerce at 905-885-5519.

As you cross the bridge over Gage Creek, you enter Hamilton Township and the town of Cobourg, where you will find one of the finest marinas and lakeside parks on the shore of Lake Ontario.

With *its more than one-hundred-year-old trees, its rose gardens, and white sandy beach...*

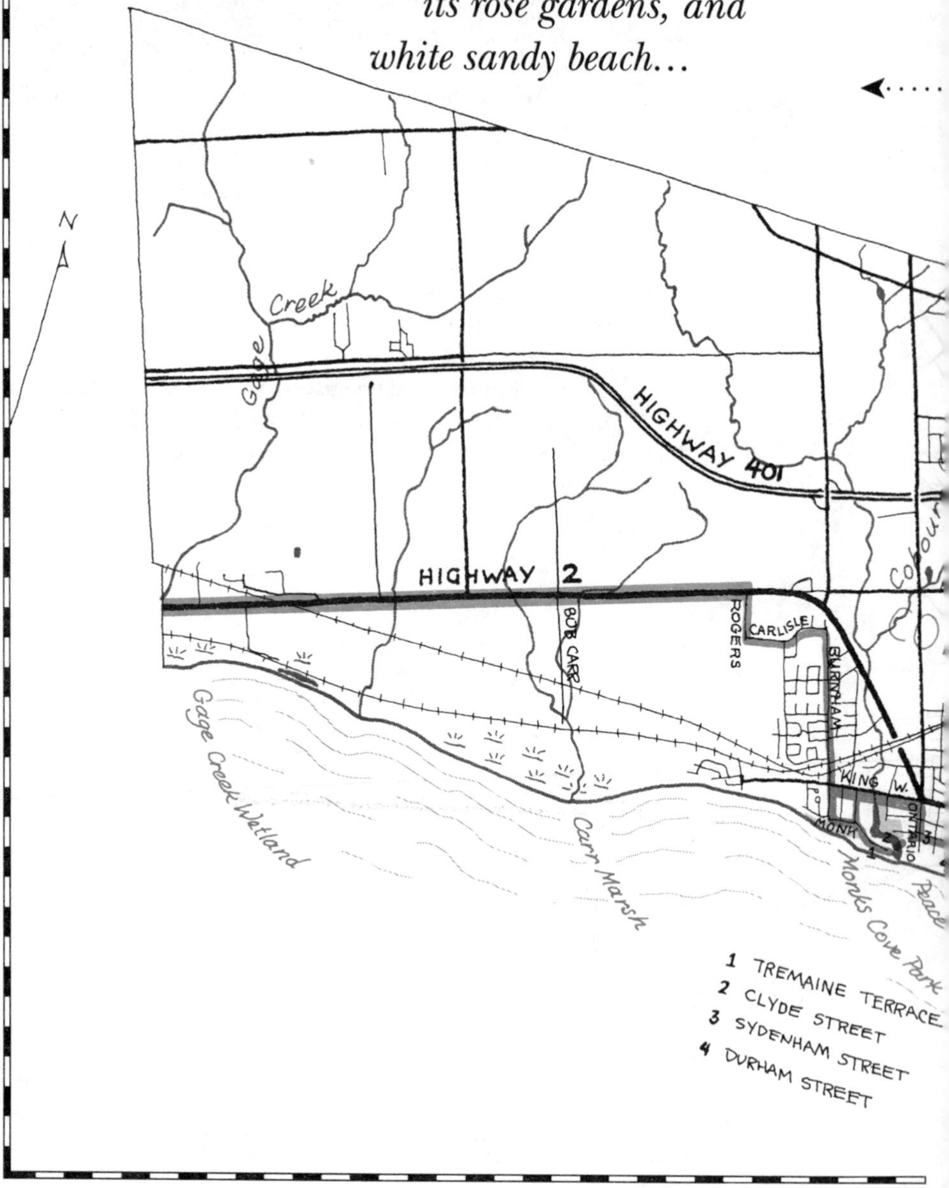

N

Creek

Gage

HIGHWAY 401

HIGHWAY 2

BOB CARR

ROGERS

CARLISLE

BURNHAM

Cobourg

KING W.

MONK

ONTARIO

Peace

Monks Cove Park

Gage Creek Wetland

Carr Marsh

1 TREMAINE TERRACE
2 CLYDE STREET
3 SYDENHAM STREET
4 DURHAM STREET

Hamilton
TOWNSHIP

TOWN OF
Cobourg &

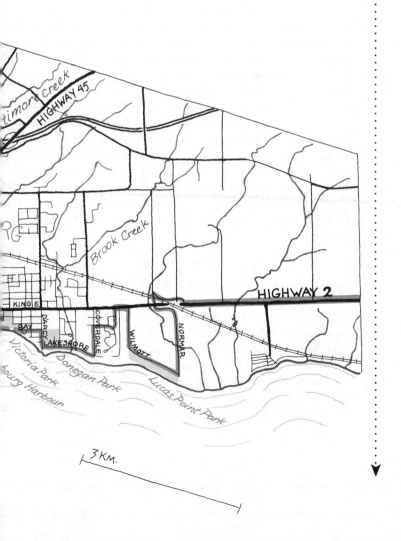

Baltimore Creek

HIGHWAY 45

Brook Creek

HIGHWAY 2

KINGE

BAY

DARCY

COVERDALE

LAKESHORE

WILMOTT

NORMAR

Victoria Park

Donegan Park

Cobourg Harbour

Lucas Point Park

3 KM.

AMED AFTER Henry Hamilton who succeeded Hector Cramahé as the Lieutenant Governor of Quebec, Hamilton Township rises from the lake at the Port of Cobourg, traverses the great moraine ridge to the north and descends into the beautiful island studded basin of Rice Lake. No strangers to the value of a good vista, the early native settlers who followed the retreating glaciers north, explored the hills and valleys above both lakes and wore pathways which later became routes such as Highway 45 or the ill-fated Cobourg and Peterborough Railway (see page 249).

Cobourg sits at the centre of a wide valley which used to be an "untraversable" cedar swamp, remnants of which can still be seen to the west of town. Proving that perseverance pays off, the town has grown from its first humble log building in 1798. The prosperity and hope of the 1850s is illustrated dramatically by the austere solidity of Victoria College to the north and dramatic Victoria Hall on the main street, both of which anchor the town.

Long a recreational destination for wealthy visitors from the American south among other places, Cobourg also has a well established tradition of involvement with the film industry. The town's thriving cultural life in the areas of theatre and music draws on talent from throughout this rural township.

Hamilton Township's section of the Waterfront Trail goes along paved shoulders on Highway 2 between Port Hope and Cobourg.

CARR MARSH

About midway between the two towns look for Bob Carr Road (unpaved) and follow it to the railway tracks that mark the marsh's northern border. You can get to the lake, but only on foot. In doing so you have to walk past a gun club, an archery range, and cross two sets railway tracks.

Past the southern-most tracks is a rough path that must be used cautiously. It is not easily accessible and can be a difficult hike. The 52-hectare (128.5-acre) marsh and woodlot are classed as Provincially Significant (see page 5 for wetland classification); their diverse ecology nurtures waterfowl, gulls, and numerous small mammals, including rabbit, muskrat, and fox. It is a nesting ground for the least bittern and black tern.

Although most of the marsh is privately owned, the remainder belongs to Hamilton Township and the Ganaraska Region Conservation Authority. Efforts are underway to create a public path into municipally owned sections.

In order to find places of particular interest to them, walking enthusiasts should contact the Ganaraska Region Conservation Authority for appropriate maps and handbooks; its office is on Highway 28, immediately north of Highway 401, across from Easton's gas station and the Comfort Inn in Port Hope.

Side Trip
HISTORIC HAMILTON TOWNSHIP

But there is another aspect to Hamilton Township – its historic environment, which is best seen by taking a loop of about 50 kilometres (30 miles).

A side trip north of Highway 2 offers opportunities for drivers (and only the hardiest and most expert cyclists) to enjoy the township's history. At the intersection of the highway and Burnham Street, turn north on the four-lane road for about 3 kilometres (1.8 miles) until you cross the bridge over Highway 401. At this point, the road narrows to two lanes of asphalt and, as part of Hamilton Township, becomes County Road 18.

Continue north until you reach Dale Road (County Road 74), which leads to one of the area's original hamlets, Precious Corners. Here, in 1811, a settler named Callaghan McCarty built his home. However, the hamlet was named for Joseph Precious and his family, who arrived in 1829. On your left is an abandoned cemetery with eight gravestones, the only historical remnant of the early settlement.

Back on the road and continuing north, you will find that sections of County Road 18 follow an ancient native trail from Lake Ontario to Rice Lake. Members of the First Nations lived in the area 11,000 years ago, drawn by waterways and by forests lush with deer and, possibly, caribou.

Succeeding generations of natives, drawn to the hunting grounds, found soil rich enough for planting corn and wetlands ideal for harvesting wild rice (hence the name of the lake). In the agricultural period, the predominant tribe was the Mississaugas, who had come from the region north of Lake Superior some 500 years earlier.

Further north, County Road 18 passes through other prominent early settlements in Hamilton Township, including Camborne, Lower Cold Springs, Upper Cold Springs, Gores Landing, and Harwood. This is the route Catherine Parr Traill wrote about in 1836, in *The Backwoods of Canada,* her classic description of pioneer life in the area.

If you would like more information, a pamphlet, or a friendly welcome, stop at the Hamilton Township office (between Precious Corners and Cold Springs) on the east side of the Country Road; or call 905-342-2810. Along the route you will see what is now Camborne United Church, originally built for a Methodist congregation in 1898.

A section of the original road breaks away from the main two-lane highway to a small paved spur where the McIntosh family still operates an old-fashioned general store. There have been McIntoshes in Cold Springs since the early 1830s.

Nearer Rice Lake, the topography changes rapidly because of the Oak Ridges Moraine. As the land rises, it offers a magnificent view of Rice Lake.

At Gores Landing, County Road 18 takes a sharp turn east and narrows. Those looking for casual dining and accommodation may want to stop at the Victoria Inn. Built in 1902 as a summer home for American artist Gerald Hayward (who came here annually from Larchmont, New York) it features a three-storey octagonal tower with finial and a large two-storey verandah with a bell-curved roof. The Hayward family crest is still visible in one of the original windows that light the staircase.

A general store stands at the northeast corner of the turn; north of it lies a short stretch of paved sideroad that leads to a public dock and boat launch on Rice Lake. There, you will find a replica of the historic Gores Landing gazebo, where ferries picked up settlers headed for Peterborough in the 1820s. As the area became more populated, the ferries took mail as well as passengers who wanted to tour the lake.

Along the south shore of Rice Lake are many resorts and campgrounds with variously priced accommodations. They give visitors a choice of places from which to explore the fine scenery and recreational activities, including camping, fishing, boating, and swimming.

Having made the turn, County Road 18 goes to Harwood; here the route of the old Cobourg to Peterborough Railway, owned by wealthy businessmen from Cobourg, cut across Rice Lake to Peterborough. The idea seemed sensible: build the railway as far as Harwood, construct a railway bridge across the narrowest point on Rice Lake, and continue the line all the way to Peterborough. Unhappily, however, within six years, nature had defeated entrepreneurship: the owners had not taken into account the wear and tear Ontario's winters would inflict on the bridge.

Leave County Road 18 at County Road 15 and go about 24 kilometres (15 miles) south to the junction of Country Road 15 and Highway 45. There, you will find Baltimore, the township's oldest village, and the final stop on this side trip.

Baltimore was settled in 1805 by John McCarty, six years before his brother Callaghan arrived at Precious Corners. Thanks to a large creek that runs through the village, it was an industrial centre, with several saw, grist, and carding mills. The last of these was built in 1842 and eventually sold, in 1884, to the Ball family. From then until 1971, three generations of Balls operated the mill. Ball's Mills, as it is called, is no longer in use, although it has been lovingly restored by owner Paul Rapati. Tours are available by calling 905-372-9815.

To learn more about the history of the mill and other significant sites, contact Clay Publishing in Bewdley, telephone number 905-797-2281, and order a copy of *Village Settlements of Hamilton Township*, by local historian Catherine Milne. ■

COBOURG

To get back to the Trail, continue south on Highway 45 to Highway 2; west to Rogers Road; then south into a residential area, just inside the town's border.

Cobourg's main section includes retail stores, restaurants, and fast food outlets tailored to all budgets. There are other amenities as well: a coin laundry, a liquor and a hardware store, a cycling shop, and major banks with ATMs. If you want to stay overnight, there are hotels, motels, and bed-and-breakfasts. For more information, phone the Cobourg and District Chamber of Commerce at 905-372-5831.

At the end of Rogers Road, the Trail turns east on Carlisle Street and continues through another residential subdivision before turning south on Burnham Street. Continuing south along Burnham will take you to Monk's Cove.

MONK'S COVE

Monk's Cove is a small park overlooking the lake at the bottom of Burnham Street. The park itself is lovely, with many kinds of birds passing through on their way to nesting and feeding grounds at nearby Cobourg Creek. The shoreline to the west is privately owned and, as in other places along Lake Ontario, property lines extend into the water; many owners do not welcome people on their grounds. Therefore, start walking east toward Cobourg Harbour.

From Burnham continue east along Monk Street to Tremaine Street. There is a historic building to the south: Villa St. Joseph, a retreat (originally an orphanage) that has been operated by an order of Roman Catholic sisters since the turn of the century.

Further east, Monk Street turns into Tremaine Terrace, which ends in a cul-de-sac. But if you look carefully, you will find a small paved pathway, open to the public, between the houses on the cul-de-sac. Follow it and you will reach the shore of Lake Ontario at the mouth of Cobourg Creek.

COBOURG CREEK

The creek is a significant fishery where trout and salmon come to spawn in the spring and fall, when the shores are lined with eager anglers.

A footbridge has recently been built, allowing those travelling on foot to cross the creek and continue following the Trail along the pebble beach to Cobourg Harbour. Some may prefer to go back to Tremaine Terrace, look for Tremaine Street, and go north on Tremaine Street to King Steet West, which is Highway 2.

Take Highway 2 east to Forth Street, and south on Forth. This will bring you to the main entrance of the Peace Park, one of a series of green spaces created by the federal Parks Service in 1992 (you have now returned to the Waterfront Trail). This park has places to rest and a small play area with swings for children. At its northeast corner, where the park joins Clyde Street, the Trail goes east along Clyde. At Ontario Street, Clyde becomes Sydenham Street and continues further east to Durham Street. Turn south on Durham Street and head to the beach, which is the beginning of the Cobourg Harbour area and waterfront promenade.

Alternatively you can head east on Tweed Street from Forth and continue to Hibernia Street; south on Hibernia leads to a large parking area at the western end of Cobourg Harbour. (Note that most of the roads you have been travelling on in this area are named for Scottish rivers.)

Side Trip
HISTORIC KING STREET

History buffs will want to take Durham Street north to King Street into the town's older areas, where striking architecture is a matter of great municipal pride; a walking tour has been designed by local conservationists. For information, visit the Chamber of Commerce, located in the Marie Dressler House Museum, 212 King Street West (a short distance west from Durham Street); or phone 905-372-5831. ■

MARIE DRESSLER HOUSE MUSEUM

 Born Leila Marie Koerber in Cobourg in 1869, she was a star of light opera, stage, and vaudeville by the time she made her first movie, *Tillie's Punctured Romance*, in 1914. The credits read like a Who's Who of early film: Charlie Chaplin was Dressler's co-star and the cast included Mabel Normand and the Keystone Kops. Mack Sennett (another Canadian-born movie pioneer) was the director. Dressler's pro-labour activities were a serious setback to her stage career and she began to concentrate on movies, winning an Academy Award in 1930 for *Min and Bill* (co-starring Wallace Beery). Described by one movie encyclopedia as a "homely woman of enormous girth", she was wildly popular and, for four years, was the industry's number one box office attraction. Her biography was unflinchingly (and poignantly) titled *The Life Story of an Ugly Duckling*. She might have been surprised to know that her home town still loves (and promotes) her: in recent years, the Cobourg Film Festival has featured some of the more than 30 films she made between 1914 and 1933.

A visit to the museum includes a tour of the Dressler house, which is filled with memorabilia of her career and of motion picture history. During July and August the Marie Dressler House Museum is open 9 a.m. to 5 p.m. seven days a week. There is no admission charge. Once you've seen it, you can return to the Waterfront Trail by taking a two-minute walk north from the inter-section of Clyde and Ontario streets.

As you walk north on Ontario Street you pass Cobourg's new public library, at the corner of King Street.

VICTORIA HALL

A short distance east of the Marie Dressler House Museum, on Highway 2, is Victoria Hall, the town's centrepiece, recognized by the Historic Sites and Monuments Board of Heritage Canada as a

structure of significant architectural merit. Completed in 1860
under the keen eye of internationally renowned architect Kivas
Tully, it was intended to be the centre of government for Canada
West, before the colony became Ontario and Toronto was chosen
for that honour.

Tully's other work includes the Welland County
Courthouse, asylums in London, Hamilton, and Brockville, and the
Bank of Montreal building in Toronto at Yonge and Front Street,
now home to the Hockey Hall of Fame.

In the mid-1800s, Cobourg's excellent harbour and
railway routes to Peterborough seemed to promise a busy commercial and industrial future. It was a place that deserved an architect of
Tully's stature and a public building with the grandeur of Victoria
Hall. Four years in construction, it housed council chambers, 26
offices, a concert hall, and a courtroom fashioned after England's
famous Old Bailey.

A century later, Victoria Hall had fallen into disrepair
and, by 1971, was beginning to collapse. The building was so
derelict that it was no longer safe for meetings of any kind.
Fortunately, that state of affairs was an affront to public-minded citizens in Cobourg and elsewhere: in nine years, they raised millions
of dollars for restoration and the hall was saved. Today, it is, once
again, a municipal building, with a concert hall, a meeting place,
and the town's art gallery. Furthermore, the courtroom is fully
restored and is used regularly for trials. One room upstairs is dedicated to James Cockburn, Northumberland County's Father of
Confederation; it is decorated with period furniture and artifacts.
Inquire at the municipality's offices for information about tours of
Victoria Hall. To return to the Waterfront Trail take Third Street
south to Cobourg Harbour.

COBOURG HARBOUR

In time, this part of the waterfront will undergo changes, as the
town proceeds with harbour revitalisation. Fishing charters are available. Further east, the beach leads to an unpaved parking area.
Cross the parking lot, where you will see an interlocking brick walkway beginning in front of the Cobourg Yacht Club.

This 1.6-kilometre (1-mile) promenade, popular year-round, goes through the marina, and along its north wall to Victoria Park, where it continues east to Bay Street. From here, you have a picture postcard view of the harbour with its sailboats and lighthouse. (The marina building includes washroom facilities and is accessible to people in wheelchairs.)

VICTORIA PARK AND BEACH

With its more than one-hundred-year-old trees, its rose gardens, and white sandy beach, Victoria Park offers 9 hectares (22 acres) of beautiful parkland on the shores of Lake Ontario. You will find a children's play area complete with spray pad, picnic tables, mini-golf, supervised swimming, and bandshell with weekly band concerts during summer months. For people intimidated by the colder lake water, there is an outdoor pool.

For those who want to spend a night or two, trailer and tent camping are available; however space is limited to only 75 sites for trailers and ten for tents.

EAST TRAIL

The walkway ends at Bay Street. Travelling east along Bay, the Waterfront Trail goes to D'Arcy Street. Directly in front is Donnegan Park, which has a children's play area and a number of baseball diamonds.

The Trail goes south to Lakeshore Road and then east, passing over Brook Creek and a small parkette that offers spectacular views of Lake Ontario. At Coverdale Avenue, the Trail goes north before turning east on to Hamilton Avenue. Turn north at Hawthorpe Avenue, this leads you back to Highway 2. Follow the highway east to Willmott Road and turn right, this will take you to Lucas Point Park. From there the Trail travels north along Normar Road to bring you back to Highway 2.

Travelling east on Highway 2 brings you to the eastern boundary of Hamilton township where the Trail enters the township of Haldimand.

The *terrain of Haldimand Township is gentle and its traditions sturdily rural, in touch with the land and the seasons* ◄······

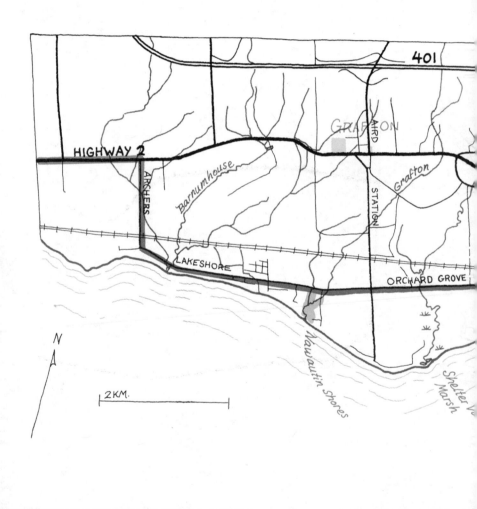

401

GRAFTON

HIGHWAY 2

AIRD

Grafton

STATION

ARCHERS

Barnumhouse

LAKESHORE

ORCHARD GROVE

Nawautin Shores

Shelter v
Marsh

N

2 KM.

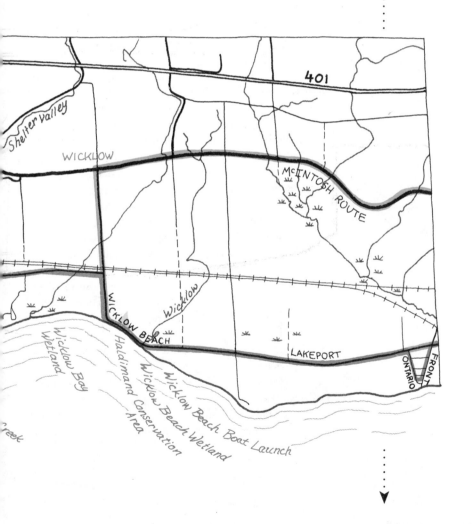

HE TERRAIN OF Haldimand Township is gentle and its traditions sturdily rural, in touch with the land and the seasons. It is bounded by Lake Ontario to the south, and three townships; Alnwick to the north, Hamilton and Cramahe townships to the west and east respectively. Settled by British immigrants on land sold by the Mississauga Indians in the late 18th and early 19th centuries, it was named for the Swiss-born governor of Quebec, Sir Fredrick Haldimand, who helped refugees from the American Revolutionary War settle in Upper Canada.

All this lends a strong sense of history to Haldimand Township, which enriches the way you experience the landscape as you journey through it.

In 1798, Asa Danforth was commissioned to construct the road that bears his name. The project, for which he was paid ninety dollars per mile, was completed over the following three years. It originated in Toronto and cut through Haldimand Township on its way to Kingston, the route of a stagecoach that began in 1817. Soon, at dizzying speeds, the journey from Toronto to Montreal could be completed in four and-a-half days with inns and taverns to serve hungry and tired passengers and horses. The old Danforth Road was eventually superseded by Kingston Road, but the local forms of transportation – horse-drawn buggies, cutters, and wagons – kept it a busy thoroughfare. In 1919, Kingston Road became a provincial road, Highway 2. Today, for about half its length, it follows the old Danforth Road.

The patterns of development in the township, the small communities and clusters of houses at intersections, are a legacy of styles popular more than a hundred years ago, when Haldimand comprised only seven hamlets: Burnley, Fenella, Wicklow, Vernonville, Centreton, Grafton, and Lakeport.

Each had its own general store, housing the local post office. These were the hamlets – a hamlet being defined as smaller than a village – that served as magnets for people and trade in rural areas. Each grew naturally at the crossroads of two early transportation routes and each provided locally needed goods and services:

the smithy, the cheese factory, the grist and flour mills, the carding and plaster mills, the cooper shops and barrel sheds; in the larger areas, there were furniture factories, breweries, and brick yards.

A good way to explore Haldimand Township is to follow the Trail route along the lakefront to the township's eastern boundary and then head north to Highway 2 and turn west, this time passing through the hamlets of Wicklow and Grafton.

As it weaves its way across Haldimand Township, Highway 2, the Heritage Highway, emphasizes the area's rural agricultural tradition as well as the buildings and businesses that have typified its hamlets for more than one hundred and fifty years.

The Trail enters the Township of Haldimand from the Township of Hamilton, as it travels east along Highway 2. There are no sidewalks along the Trail route in Haldimand so this section of the Trail is best journeyed by those travelling by bicycle.

Turning right on Archer's Road, the route heads south toward Lake Ontario; along the way, you pass farmers' fields, ravines, and the bridge that straddles the Canadian National Railway tracks. Descending this hill offers you a panoramic view of the lakefront – a view that is beautiful in all seasons.

Turn left at Lakeshore Road where the Trail runs parallel to the waterfront. You will notice the Grafton Shores subdivision, which has managed to develop large lots for homes while leaving surrounding woodland and wetland intact. To the south is the mouth of Barnum House Creek, where generations of anglers have waited patiently under the shelter of the black locust trees that fan out overhead. Opposite is the Hortop Conservation Area.

Further east is the Plast Ukrainian Camp; established in the late 1950s, its tennis courts, swimming pool, and outbuildings have provided the background for many happy memories. One camper from the early days recalls being able to drink the water directly from the lake. While not recommended for drinking by today's standards, the water here is very clean and free of debris.

Just east of the camp is the Nawautin Estates residential community and the Nawautin Nature Sanctuary.

Crossing Station Road, Lakeshore Road becomes Orchard Grove Road, and a variety of meadows and trees come into

NAWAUTIN NATURE SANCTUARY

Surely a summer morning walk through loamy woods beside a stream is a pleasure for the moment and for the memory. Add a meadow full of wildflowers, a waterfall or two, goslings on a pond, and the peeping of marsh frogs, and you have a small Eden.

There are many such small epiphanies on the Lake Ontario waterfront, most of them in private hands, firmly closed to visitors. But Margaret and Bob Marshall are as generous with their Grafton property as nature has been.

In 1987, they bought 26 hectares (65 acres) of land as a retirement project, some for homes that would be integrated into the existing landscape, some to be dedicated as a nature sanctuary with walking trails for others to enjoy. The key: everything would be in keeping with Margaret's philosophy: "What is there, let it be."

Today, the Nawautin ("peace by the water") Nature Sanctuary offers visitors 6 hectares (15 acres) of undisturbed beauty on the lakefront just south of Grafton. There are streams and waterfalls. In spring, lilac bushes, planted by settlers long ago, come into bloom and the meadow is lush with wildflowers sprung from seeds Bob sowed.

As you look around, it all seems so easy, so natural. But Nawautin represents years of work on the Marshalls' part: getting planning permission for the adjacent subdivision was only the beginning. The really tough problem was the presence of purple loosestrife. Years ago, this tall, elegant wildflower was introduced into North America from Europe and has thrived in its wetlands ever since. Only recently have naturalists and conservationists recognized that, however beautiful, loosestrife is deadly, spreading voraciously, choking out marsh plants and other wildlife. The Marshalls soon realized that if they were to create the self-sustaining sanctuary of their dreams they would have to rid their land of loosestrife.

So they learned about wetland regeneration, reading books, talking to experts, thinking, and planning. Bob, a contractor and building inspector before he retired, cut trails through the bush and cast wildflower seeds into the meadow. A filtration system was built, to prevent harmful sediments and chemicals from leaching into the watertable. In time, the loosestrife was eliminated, the wetland began to recover, and marsh plants had room to grow.

Now two waterfalls and rapids generate the oxygen needed for healthy growth of pond life.

Today, a walk through the sanctuary shows how much has been accomplished: tracks attest to the presence of deer; there are grouse; red-winged blackbirds call to each other; and sunlight filters through the leaves of black cherry trees. Trout and schools of smelt glide silently in the summer waters. Canoeists are welcome. In winter, the iced waterways are a pleasant and safe place for skating.

Margaret Marshall believes that the sanctuary "is heaven and now other people are going to be able to enjoy it". The Marshalls act only as its stewards: they have magnanimously turned their sanctuary over to the Township, for the enjoyment of all.

Cedar posts have been erected as bicycle racks, and parking is available. Visitors are asked only to step lightly and to leave this oasis as they find it, tranquil and lovely.

view. Milkweed, Queen Anne's Lace, and clover proliferate; in the winter, the land is covered by untrammelled snow, its austere beauty relieved by poplar, spruce, pine, and crabapple trees.

At Wicklow Beach Road, turn right toward the lake; you will pass the Jubalee Beach Trailer Park, a longstanding tourist facility. This lakeside park, open from the first of May until towards the end of October, features a swimming pool, recreation hall, showers, washrooms, and hook-ups for electricity. Call 905-349-2670 for more information and rates. As you follow the curve of the road, you are now parallel to Wicklow Beach, which provides direct access to Lake Ontario for walking, skipping stones, and picnicking.

Across the street is the Haldimand Conservation Area, which is designed for day use; you will find two public washrooms here. Up ahead lies the Wicklow Beach Boat Launch, the only such facility between Cobourg and Brighton, and a popular meeting place for people in the area. The boat launch is a prime example of unobtrusive and environment-enhancing development, an integral part of the Trail. It was built as the result of co-operative efforts by various levels of government, by private companies and individuals and is an important link to the early days of the township's history. In the 1800s, there were two harbour facilities in the area: Colborne Harbour, located in Lakeport, just east of the Wicklow Beach Boat Launch and Grafton Harbour, which lies to the west.

At that time, Colborne Harbour was visited twice a week, to pick up passengers and freight, by such steamers as the *Magnet,* en route from Toronto to Kingston, and to Oswego, New York. The harbour was an active centre of lumber shipments, as well as the location of shipbuilding operations that included schooners, ranging in length from 25 to 30 metres (82 to 97 feet). According to records of the time, forty master sailors, and cooks packed their gear and left "old Cat Hollow" (Lakeport) for service on sailing vessels, leaving behind wives and children to tend the garden plots and feed the geese.

Grain, flour, and whiskey were frequently shipped from nearby Grafton Harbour; on a busy day, horse-drawn buggies would stand in a line extending from the harbour to what is now Highway 2. The last known boat docking to take place at Grafton Harbour occurred in 1890, after which railway trains displaced lake vessels as a favoured means of transporting goods and people.

According to an 1893 report in the *Cobourg World,* "The ghost of the departed Indians [sic], whose bones were widely scattered by some fifty years of shipping, are now at liberty to rejoice that white man's schemes have passed away."

More than a century later, long after the era of industrial shipping ended, the Wicklow Beach Boat Launch was built; it brings us full circle back to the time when the fur trader's bateau and the native canoe slipped silently through the water, in harmony with nature. Today, small craft are launched for quiet recreation and enjoyment of the natural environment. Exploration on foot or by bicycle is mirrored by the experience of boating on Lake Ontario, which runs alongside the landscape like a ribbon of memory.

The boat launch offers the opportunity to fully experience both the present and a sense of the past, recapturing some of the original paradise that must have been familiar to the native peoples and early settlers in this area.

Interestingly, use of the boat launch has been shaped by the people who stop here for a picnic, to read a book in peace, or simply to sit and soak up – and be soaked up by – the water, rocks, and sun. Whatever its designers, builders, and planners envisioned, the Wicklow Beach Boat Launch has become a resounding success because it has been defined by local needs and preferences.

East of the boat launch is a stretch of private homes and farms, some of which date back to the township's earliest days. If you would like to stop for lunch, Sophie's Restaurant is open on Friday, Saturday, and Sunday. Or go next door, to the Challenge Antique Shop, if you're in the mood to browse. Looking north through patches of trees, you can see the rolling hills so characteristic of Northumberland County.

Direct access to the lake is possible by going south on Ontario Street; the road bends to the east and connects with Front Street, which will bring you back up to Lakeport Road and to the Village of Lakeport, which is on the boundary of Haldimand and Cramahe townships; the village was founded in 1793 by Joseph Keeler (for more about the remarkable line of men named Joseph Keeler, see page 278).

If you are in the mood for a little shopping or antique hunting, you will want to take a side trip up one of the north-south roads to get back onto Highway 2. Dotted along this route are the shops, businesses, and historical side trips so beloved of teachers, antique mavens, genealogists, researchers, and adventurous wayfarers. In fact, all the roads leading north from Lake Ontario in this area are inviting; and if the land seems uncluttered, note that each township lot is 81 hectares (200 acres) in size.

You will find fruit and vegetable markets selling such seasonal produce as apples, potatoes, corn, pumpkins, and squash – all grown locally. The presence of apple orchards in Haldimand Township continues an unbroken chain begun in the late 1800s, when the fruit was first grown in the area, through the development of the export market in the early days of this century. (See page 272 for information on the Apple Route, which makes its way into the Township of Haldimand from its beginning in the Village of Colborne.)

In keeping with the tradition of small-scale operations, there are many "home occupancies" in Haldimand Township, home occupancy being defined as a business that does not occupy more than one-quarter of the floor space in a home; does not advertise aggressively; and has a staff of family members only. Among the most successful such operations are the township's many antique shops, small engine repair businesses, cabinetmaking, accountancy services, and artists'/artisans' studios, all of which give the area an unobtrusive and individualistic commercial base.

In Grafton, for example, there is Our Country Home, a family business that specializes in reproduction pine furniture such as armoires, harvest tables, jam cupboards, and dry sinks. It, like such establishments as Jake Robinson's Come by the Farm Bed and Breakfast nearby, has a character that comes from the personality and hospitality of its owners.

HAMLET OF GRAFTON

If you are looking for a little get-away or mini-vacation, you may want to look into St. Anne's Bed and Breakfast. Just north of Grafton you see signs to St. Anne's where, in sophisticated spa surroundings, trained staff help clients exercise and unwind in the beautiful surroundings of the old Massey property, known locally as the Castle. For more information contact St. Anne's at 905-349-2493. Here, too, is the home of St. Anne's Water, taken from the property's artesian well and bottled for consumption throughout Ontario.

In Grafton there is a pleasant historical walking tour covering 1.7 kilometres (1 mile) – short enough to be stimulating, but long enough to offer opportunities to discover pieces of history that are both authentic and alive. In all, the tour visits twenty heritage buildings, dating as far back as the early 1830s, including a library, post office, inn, and several churches, among others.

Perhaps the best way to enjoy the walk is to pick up a complimentary copy of the brochure "Historical Walking Tour of Grafton", available from the Haldimand Township Local

Architectural Conservation Advisory Committee (LACAC), most of the shops in Grafton, and the municipal office during regular business hours, Monday to Friday.

If you are in need of refreshment, you will find a variety store at the eastern end of Grafton and the Pine Ridge Restaurant to the west.

If the tour only increases your appetite for more beautiful and historic homes, continue further west on Highway 2, approximately 2 kilometres (1.2 miles), where you will find some of the finest homes in the County of Northumberland.

Spalding's Inn and Brimley House are outstanding examples of Georgian architecture; both were built by Thomas Major Spalding, who had previously run the first halfway house on the stage coach line between Kingston and Toronto. Spalding also owned and operated a plant that made the bricks from which the two buildings were constructed.

Brimley House is on the corner lot of Highway 2 and Brimley Road; sometimes referred to as the Steele House, it was built for Spalding's daughter and son-in-law, John Steele.

The house is now a fine antique shop specializing in Quebec and Ontario primitive furniture. Spalding's Inn stands next to it. It, too, has a fine antique shop offering a full range of furniture and furnishings, glass, silver, and china.

A half-kilometre (0.3 mile) to the west are two businesses located on the other side of the road; one is Canadian Country Crafts and the other is a well-known local antique shop, Back-Bench Antiques, which carries furniture, jewelry, curiosities, books, china, and glass.

The Barnum House Museum, west of Grafton, is one of the finest examples of colonial architecture remaining in Canada. It was built circa 1821 by Eliakim Barnum, a wealthy distiller.

With help from the Province of Ontario, Barnum House was recently restored and an addition completed; the house is now officially designated a museum and is open to the public during the spring and summer months. For more information, call the museum at 905-349-2656.

Next door to Barnum House is Quaker's Pond, a residence once used as a Quaker meeting house; it was moved from its original location, about 1.5 kilometres (0.9 mile) west, and restored on its present site in the 1980s.

Side Trip
PETER'S WOODS

Naturalists may enjoy an excursion up to Peter's Woods, situated about 17 kilometres (10.5 miles) north of Grafton. To get there follow Lyle Street north from Grafton for about 9 kilometres (5.5 miles) to Centreton. Peter's Woods is about another 8 kilometres (5 miles) to the north; watch for the signs.

Peter's Woods is the gift of massive glaciers that, eons ago, scraped and jostled bedrock and soils into what is now the Oak Ridges Moraine; the moraine stretches from Orangeville to Trenton and is composed largely of sand, gravel, and small boulders.

Peter's Woods remains a virtually untouched maple-beech forest; it was named after a member of the Willow Beach Field Naturalists, the organization that helps maintain the woods as a nature reserve.

There is a 1-kilometre (0.6-mile) walking trail that begins at the parking lot, passes through an open field, and circles the forest; it gives you a glimpse of the magnificent hardwood forests that once covered much of southern Ontario. Because of the care with which this trail was developed – recognizing that the wet soils, spring banks, and delicate small plants are easily damaged –nothing has been lost. A brochure for taking your own walking tour of the woods is available at the entrance; the terrain makes the trip unsuitable for those in wheelchairs. ■

After your visit to Haldimand, the Waterfront Trail continues east along Lakeshore Road into the Township of Cramahe.

ONTARIO VERNACULAR HOUSE

The rural areas of Durham and Northumberland are distinguished by their fine examples of an architectural style known as Ontario vernacular. The style is a rectangular house, usually a storey-and-a-half, with a peaked gable in the centre. The lines of such houses, most of them were constructed between 1830 and 1880, are repeated with many variations.

The homes may be constructed of wood (clapboard or board-and-batten), stone (dressed or uncut), or brick (patterned or coloured). Doorways are simple or ornate and may draw on 19th-century classical, Gothic revival, or picturesque styles. The gable windows may be square, round, pointed, or, as in certain Cobourg homes, bottle-shaped. Gables and eaves display an imaginative diversity of gingerbread.

While houses in the vernacular style can be found throughout southern Ontario, those east of Toronto have certain unique features. Many still retain their original verandas, complete with lacy woodwork patterns known as treillage. (Verandas were introduced here in the 1820s, making treillage one of Ontario's earliest forms of wood-carved folk art.)

In Durham and Northumberland, the gable windows were sometimes replaced with doors, though the doors lead nowhere. There are not — and there never were — porches or balconies to support them. The openings, commonly referred to as suicide doors, have about them a hint of mystery.

The *route used by settlers almost two hundred years ago gives your trip here a strong sense of history.*

TOWNSHIP OF
Cramahe &
VILLAGE OF
Colborne

SALEM

HIGHWAY 2

UNION

2 Km.

HE FACT THAT, in Cramahe Township, the Waterfront Trail follows the route used by settlers almost two hundred years ago gives your trip here a strong sense of history.

Travelling east on Lakeport Road (also known as County Road 30), a visit to the Township of Cramahe begins as you cross Pine Street. Most of the land along the Lake Ontario shoreline is privately owned, limiting public access to the shore in this section of the Trail. However, that need not make your trip less enjoyable: the painstakingly carved-out roads you travel are a guide back to an important link to our history and heritage.

Pronounced "Crammy", the township is named for the remarkable Hector Theophilus Cramahé, a much-loved soldier and administrator who took part in the siege of Louisbourg and then spent the rest of his time in North America in the Quebec colony, stoutly defending people's rights.

The township named after him is apple country: in the mosaic of farms that stitch it together, McIntosh, Granny, Cortland, Northern spy, Empire, and Delicious apples are grown. Some farms welcome members of the public and offer opportunities for them to go into the fields to pick their fruit, and, in season, to sample freshly made apple cider.

As you enter the township from the west, the Trail is aligned along Lakeport Road; there are no paved shoulders along this segment and, given that the speed limit is 80 kph (50 mph), it is best enjoyed by an experienced cyclist.

Notice the clapboard house with the central chimney on the north side of Lakeport Road; this was one of the first homes built in the area. Still in private hands and now being restored to its original state, it was the home of Joseph Keeler, a United Empire Loyalist who was among the first to settle when people came to the area in the late 1700s and early 1800s. The house, built circa 1810, has been officially designated as a Heritage Home by the Local Architectural Conservation Advisory Committee (LACAC).

Just before Lakeport Road bends north, look to your right, where you can see the lakefront operations of the

PUBLIC TRANSPORTATION: VIA Train stops in Colborne. For scheduling information, call 1-800-361-1235.

THEOPHILUS CRAMAHÉ

Born in Dublin, Ireland on October 1, 1720, Cramahé was the youngest of ten children in a family whose ancestors had left France for Ireland near the end of the 1600s. At age 20, he followed in his father's footsteps and entered the English military; for 41 years, he served in the 15th Regiment, attaining the rank of captain and serving in Columbia, Cuba, Belgium, and the American colonies.

Having arrived in Quebec in June 1759, Cramahé began winding down his military career before completely giving up his command in 1761. In the years that followed, Hector Cramahé served as secretary and civil secretary under Brigadier-General James Murray and, later, under Governor Guy Carleton. Highly regarded as a wise and honest man, he was appointed lieutenant-governor of the Province of Canada on June 6, 1771, ten months after Carleton's departure.

In Cramahé, the people of Lower Canada found a just and able defender, one who urged London to address their complaints about a legal system functioning in English, a language most of them did not understand. On June 27, 1778, Cramahé was replaced by Frederick Haldimand and, in 1781, he returned home. He died in Devonshire, England in the spring of 1788, so intensely private a person that, to this day, no one knows whether he and his wife had children.

St. Lawrence Cement Company, which sits on what is known as Ogden Point. (Like most of the local areas, it was probably named after a family that lived nearby.)

ST. LAWRENCE CEMENT COMPANY

Since 1957, the St. Lawrence Cement Company has been mining limestone from this 300-hectare (750-acre) open pit. Because the company uses the province's oldest highway – Lake Ontario – to transport the stone to its Mississauga facility, there are no large trucks rumbling in and out of the property. Each year, between 1.4 and 2.3 million tonnes (1.4 and 2.3 million tons) of limestone are taken from the pit, which is 15 metres (50 feet) deep and estimated to contain a limestone layer that is approximately 150 metres (500 feet) thick.

Once the material is delivered to the Mississauga plant, it is ground into a powder and burned in a special rotary kiln, which, at 1,400 degrees Celsius (2,552 degrees Fahrenheit), transforms it from a solid into a fiery, lava-like substance. Rapidly cooled, it becomes "clinker", an abrasive material that is once again ground into a powder; in this form, it becomes more than 90 percent of the recipe for making cement.

As you travel north, you cross two separate sets of railway tracks, one belonging to Canadian National Railways (CN) and the other to Canadian Pacific Railways (CP). These are well-travelled routes, with VIA Rail and CP trains roaring by several times an hour. Not all crossings have barriers, so you should approach the area's railway tracks cautiously.

At Earl Street, the Trail turns right and heads east for a half-kilometre (0.3 mile), where it meets Division Street; turn left at the Colborne Pentecostal Church on the northeast corner and you will find yourself heading north through Colborne's fine residential area into its business section.

At King Street (the name given to Highway 2 within the Village of Colborne) you have several options of routes to consider. One is to take a side trip from the Waterfront Trail to follow a "spur" of the Apple Route.

APPLE ROUTE

Officially opened in a joint effort by the townships of Cramahe, Haldimand, Brighton, Murray, the Village of Colborne, Town of Brighton, and the City of Trenton in May 1994, the Apple Route highlights the importance of the apple industry to many of the municipalities on Lake Ontario's north shore.

The "core" of the Apple Route begins at Big Apple Drive in the Village of Colborne, near Highway 401, at what is known as "The Big Apple" (for more information about it, see page 275). It is only for a half-kilometre (0.3 mile) south of Highway 401 that the road bears the name Big Apple Drive; the original name of Percy Street is used from that point on, as the road leads to the Village of Colborne. This short section was renamed Big Apple Drive, after residents agreed that a Highway 401 sign using that name would draw attention to the Big Apple and the ramp leading into the area.

Travelling south on Percy Street into the downtown section of Colborne, the route heads east on Highway 2 and continues into the City of Trenton.

There are two spurs or side trip loops that can be taken from the core route. The first one (called the McIntosh) is in the Cramahe/Colborne area, while the second (the Empire), starting in the Town of Brighton, winds its way to Presqu'ile Provincial Park, then east along County Road 64 to Highway 33. From there it heads north to the City of Trenton.

Side Trip
McIntosh Route

To follow the McIntosh loop, head north on Toronto Street, which turns into Highway 2 as it curves and travels west; take Highway 2 west from the Village of Colborne toward Wicklow in Haldimand Township. Watch for signs announcing Deleeuw's and Knights, the two largest apple growers in the area. Both sell their apples directly to the public to complement their commercial operations.

Throughout the year, antique lovers and furniture seekers can be found at the auctions at Warner's Auction Hall, on the south side of Highway 2, at RR 3, just west of the village limits. There are sales every Thursday from 6 to 9 p.m., featuring new furniture and houseware items. There is also an auction every Saturday from 10 a.m. to 2 p.m., which includes antique furniture and collectibles; items can be viewed a few hours before bidding begins. The stock changes; to find out about a particular sale, call Warner's at 905-355-2106.

Deleeuw's Roadside Market, 5 kilometres (3 miles) west of Colborne, offers apples in varieties and grades not found in your local supermarket; its status as a small, family-owned operation enables Deleeuw's to specialize and cultivate fruit that appeals to people's delight in rare and particularly tasty food. As well as the McIntosh and Delicious favoured in most fruit markets (because they look handsome and have a long shelf life), older varieties of apples are available here; each has its own characteristics, its own distinctive flavour. Contact Dan Deleeuw at 905-355-1403 between 9 a.m. and 5 p.m. for more information.

Knights, about 1.5 kilometres (1 mile) west of Delweeuw's on Highway 2, has been in business for more than fifty years and is known for its Big A apples. Some two million bushels are grown yearly on this 162-hectare (400-acre) farm, where they are packaged and shipped to the United Kingdom, the United States, and the Caribbean. In order to keep the apples fresh, even in the off-season, Knights uses nine storage rooms that have been specially designed to strictly control air quality. The mix of carbon dioxide, oxygen, and nitrogen causes the apples to become dormant, preserving their freshness until they are ready for shipping. For more information, call 905-349-2521 between 7:30 a.m. and 5 p.m.

Given the local produce and the range of selection, it's a good idea to test different kinds before you choose; better to try several varieties than limit yourself needlessly in the midst of such apple bounty.

But the work being done on these apple farms has a value far beyond your taste buds: in the same way that some farmers use their small holdings to help preserve the breeding gene pool of cows, sheep, and goats, even for species that don't have a large market, apple producers are important in preserving apple types and in adding to the knowledge of their predecessors.

Continuing west along Highway 2, the McIntosh spur turns south on Wicklow Beach Road and passes through rolling farmland. At the intersection of Wicklow Beach and Orchard Grove roads, the Waterfront Trail begins its alignment along the Apple Route. Continuing south, it meets Lakeport Road and circles back into Cramahe Township, then into the Village of Colborne, completing a loop of about 24 kilometres (15 miles). ■

Another excursion that should not be missed, especially if you have children, is to the "Big Apple".

Side Trip
BIG APPLE

The people of Colborne have put the apple on a pedestal – literally. The town is famous for the "Big Apple" that can be seen from Highway 401. (Even New York City doesn't have one this big!) More than 10 metres (35 feet) high and 38 tonnes (37 tons) in mass, it is said to be the biggest apple in the world. Located just a few minutes north of the downtown section of Colborne, the Big Apple is a year-round park. The main building has a tourist centre, gift shop, bakery, and two restaurants (one a dining room and the other a cafeteria). Washrooms are wheelchair-accessible and there is a ramp to the second floor.

There are a miniature golf range, picnic and play areas, as well as a petting zoo featuring deer, llama, and pygmy goats. In addition to a display on the apple industry, the Big Apple is home to a working beehive. Viewed from behind the safety of plexiglass, the bees can be seen busily making honey. Without their work pollinating apple blossoms, the trees could not bear fruit.

In all but the winter months (when the golf range is also closed), you can climb the stairs to a lookout at the top of the Big Apple. Contact the Big Apple Tourist Centre at 905-355-2574 for further information.

As you head back toward Colborne on Percy Street, watch for the Hoselton Studios sign. Gord Hoselton's work – free-form sculptures of birds, and sea and land animals created in polished aluminum and mounted on Canadian marble – is widely collected and world-famous. Pieces are often given to visiting heads of state and other dignitaries. The Hoselton studio is located on Percy Street, about 2 kilometres (1.3 miles) south of the Big Apple. The showroom is open daily from 9 a.m. to 4 p.m. and can be reached by phone at 905-355-3933. ■

COLBORNE

WHETHER YOU HAVE just completed the trip along the Apple Route spur, are following the Waterfront Trail, or have just been to the Big Apple, you will enjoy a visit to the business section of the Village of Colborne.

On King Street West you will find the fire station that serves Colborne, and Cramahe and Haldimand townships. The structure beside it at One Toronto Street was built in 1922 and is a fine example of neo-classical architecture popular in the period between the wars. Originally designed as the town's high school, it now houses municipal offices and the public library.

Victoria Square Park, which is located directly across from the municipal offices, is a community park and occupies a full village block; the picnic tables, flowers, and trees provide an ideal setting for relaxation while the playground offers swings and a sandbox for kids.

You may want to start your visit to Colborne at Olde Seaton House Antiques, Collectables, and Gifts, at 57 King Street East (open Wednesday to Sunday, 9 a.m. to 5:30 p.m.). In addition to carrying antiques and collectibles, it serves as a visitors' centre where knowledgeable staff can provide information on places to eat, where to find accommodation, and points of interest from Colborne to Trenton; the telephone number for Olde Seaton House is 905-355-1804.

Turn east onto King Street (Highway 2) and you are at the point where the Waterfront Trail begins to follow the "core" of the Apple Route.

During the Victoria Day holiday the Village of Colborne celebrates the arrival of spring with the Apple Blossom Tyme Festival. It focuses on the community's heritage, and attracts visitors from surrounding municipalities. The festival features an array of craft, hobby, and antique exhibitions, held in the Colborne Cramahe Centennial Community Centre on Arena Drive; weaving and rug-hooking demonstrations take place in the Royal Canadian Legion Hall, 12 King Street East; and children's activities take place in the village square. For more information on festivals and events in the Village of Colborne, contact Jean Kernagham at the

Municipal Office at 905-355-2821 between the hours of 8:45 a.m. and 4:45 p.m., Monday to Friday.

In downtown Colborne, you will find the brown brick building that was once the County Registry Office; it's at 51 King Street East. Built in the mid-1800s, it housed all of Northumberland County's records until 1992, when they were transferred to their present location in Cobourg. An old regulator clock, one of the few surviving relics of the original registry office, is now in the municipal building and library on Toronto Street.

If you need to make a phone call, there is a booth directly across the street; however, it is not wheelchair-accessible.

Continuing east, the Trail follows the Apple Route along King Street (Highway 2). Sidewalks on both sides of the road make it possible to walk comfortably along the tree-lined residential street. There, you will find some beautiful century-old homes, one of which Roger and Margaret Lee operate as a bed and breakfast. Called the Maples, at 119 King Street, contact the Lees at 905-355-2059.

The white wooden building at 171 King Street East (at the corner of King and Parliament) near the eastern boundary of Colborne is the Keeler Inn, one of many houses that lined the stage coach routes of Lake Ontario's northern shore; there, in the early and middle 19th century, operators and passengers could stop to rest and eat, or to water and feed the horses.

Beginning at Coulton Street, which is the eastern boundary of Colborne, cyclists can enjoy a lane, 1.5 metres (5 feet) wide, that stretches along the north and south sides of Highway 2 for nearly 7 kilometres (4.5 miles), taking the traveller through the heart of Cramahe farmland. Highway 2 is a major road, with an 80-kph (50-mph) speed limit. The lane is popular with local children; therefore, drivers have to be on the lookout for them and for pedestrians in general. Notice the number of stands along the way where you can stop for a snack or load up with fresh fruits and vegetables.

No trip through the countryside is complete without a visit to a local flea market or antique and collectible shop. Watch for Colborne Country Accents at 206 King Street East; the barn behind the owners' home has been transformed into a cosy three-room

THREE KEELERS

Three men named Joseph Keeler – father, son, and grandson – were instrumental in establishing the industrial, commercial, and many of the social ventures that marked the progress of this area from untamed wilderness to thriving village and township.

The work of quarrying limestone began at Lakeport as early as 1830 and continues to this day: St. Lawrence Cement removes tonnes of stone daily from a 300-hectare (750-acre) site in Cramahe Township. The St. Lawrence pier is now the only commercial dock on this stretch of the lakeshore.

Limestone from this site was also used in the construction of Old St. Andrew's Presbyterian Church in Colborne, built between 1830 and 1833. Still standing, it is located on the north side of King Street East (45-49) at Victory Lane, and was the first of the village's seven churches.

Credited with being the first settler in Cramahe, Joseph Keeler, who lived in Vermont, visited the area in 1789, when he was in his late twenties, then returned in 1793, bringing with him some 40 families, and landing at what became known as Keeler's Creek, now Lakeport. In 1796 he was given a grant of land by Lieutenant-Governor John Graves Simcoe.

Joseph Keeler combined his skill in practical engineering with his entrepreneurial spirit and business acumen to build flour mills, saw mills, woollen mills, tanneries, and distilleries. The only remaining physical reminders of his presence are the majestic ruins of a mill (built from limestone quarried at Lakeport) located on the west side of Ontario Street just north of Earl Street in Colborne.

It is likely that the family lived for many years at Keeler's Creek, which later became known as Colborne Harbour, then Cat Hollow, now Lakeport. The most senior Joseph Keeler built a wharf there, the first of three that would eventually accommodate a thriving cross-border trade with Rochester and Oswego in upper New York State.

Joseph and Olive Keeler's son, Joseph Abbott Keeler, was an infant when the family came to Cramahe Township. In 1815, at age 27, he opened a small store in what would become the Village of Colborne; it included the community's first post office. He also served as justice of the peace for the entire Newcastle District, roughly the area covered by part of Durham Region and Northumberland County. In time, he founded the villages of Colborne and Castleton, and was a successful merchant and a postmaster; his was the planner's hand that laid out the wide main street and the park in the village square. He deeded the land for churches of various faiths, providing only that each keep a seat for his use. He named the village Colborne in honour of his good friend, Sir John Colborne, lieutenant-governor of Upper Canada between 1828 and 1836.

Joseph Abbott Keeler built Keeler House, which still stands at 9 Church Street East in Colborne. Constructed in the early 1820s in the same style as Barnum House (now a museum at Grafton), it was the birthplace of the third Joseph Keeler in 1822 and the place where the first Keeler died in 1839.

The youngest Keeler followed very closely in his father's and grandfather's footsteps: he was prominent in the family business as a merchant and he established the *Transcript*, Colborne's first newspaper. A Conservative, he was a strong supporter of Sir John A. Macdonald and of the prime minister's plan to build a trans-continental railway to British Columbia. This Joseph Keeler represented Northumberland in the Parliament of the Dominion of Canada at the time of Confederation and from 1879 until his death. He strongly supported the construction of the Murray Canal, which joins Weller's Bay to the Bay of Quinte, and which eliminated the need for travelling long distances by boat.

This Joseph Keeler, too, had a son named Joseph; however, the absence of further records may indicate that the fourth in the line died in infancy or very early childhood.

Some time after the third Keeler died in 1881, his wife Octavia and their family moved away. By then, the colony of the original Joseph Keeler's time was only a memory, and a fledgling country was taking its first steps to nationhood.

store featuring antique and collectibles, as well as a fine selection of homemade dried-flower arrangements. The wood-burning fireplace is an inviting place to warm up on a cool day.

Pieter's Appleyard, on the north side of Highway 2, about 1 kilometre (0.6 mile) east of Colborne Country Accents, is another orchard open to the public. Owned by Pieter and Anne Wyminga, it offers fun for the entire family: in September and October you can enjoy a cup of fresh apple cider or make your way out into the fields (on foot or by car) to pick apples; if your timing is right, you can watch how cider is made. In July, you can pick your own raspberries. The farm has three walking trails, ranging in length from 1 to 2 kilometres (0.6 to 1.3 miles); the shortest is flat and the other two are moderately hilly. Telephone 905-355-2863.

Just before you reach the Wyminga farm, you will see another fine heritage house, known as Cedar Wood, one of the few original homes that escaped the fire or other forms of destruction visited on so many structures over the years. It stands as a vital link to the heritage and history of the area and its people. The rear of Cedar Wood was built between 1840 and 1850, at a time when a section of land was given to those who wanted to settle in the area. The only stipulation was that settlers had to "prove" (cultivate) a portion of the land and build a liveable dwelling on the property.

For most people, that "liveable" home initially meant a small wooden structure, with brick additions being built as families grew more prosperous. The brick portion of this house was built sometime between 1869 and 1875. (Exact dating is impossible because the relevant files were destroyed by fire.) Cedar Wood remains a private residence and, thanks to a grant from LACAC, has been restored by its owners according to its original design.

East of Cedar Wood, you come upon an indelible image: on a hill, black wrought-iron gates and fence surround a cemetery. The names and dates on the well-worn headstones bear the names of some of the United Empire Loyalists who were among the area's original settlers.

Beside the graveyard stands Salem United Church, a white wooden structure dating from 1861, with its sense of peace and piety emphasized by the tree branches that sway quietly in the lake breezes. Historically recognized and frequently photographed from the road, the church can best be experienced by those who stop to linger in its serene setting.

LOYALIST INN

Continue east along this winding, hilly section of Highway 2 for about 3 kilometres (1.8 miles) and you come to Union Road. On the north side of the highway, just west of Union Road, stands a white building now known as the Loyalist Inn. Originally called the Rose Lane Inn, when it served the stage coaches, it sits on property that was part of a 120-hectare (300-acre) land grant given to Oliver Campbell; Campbell, whose land was apparently smaller than he felt was his due as a United Empire Loyalist, petitioned King George III for the same grant of land other soldiers had received.

THE FIRST STAGE COACH LINE

The first stage coach line ran from the Town of York (later Toronto) to Kingston, beginning in 1817. Operated by Samuel Purdy, it took passengers on a three-day excursion at a cost of 18 dollars each way. Under optimum conditions and on the best of roads, the coach could cover 125 kilometres (75 miles) per day. However, conditions were rarely optimum and, with the need to allow time for the horses to rest, the 250-kilometre (155-mile) trip was more likely to take three days over poorly maintained roads.

By the summer of 1830, William Weller of Cobourg was operating two trips a week between York and Carrying Place (near Trenton). The venture was so successful that soon there were five trips weekly and the route was expanded as far west as Hamilton and to Montreal on the east.

Rosewell Comstock acquired the land from Oliver Campbell and, in about 1812, built the inn we see today; in 1815 he received his operating licence from King George III, serving stage coach travellers on the Toronto-to-Kingston route along Highway 2. After use as a private residence for many years, the inn was once again opened to the public in 1990, when it was faithfully restored to its original classic Georgian design and became a bed and breakfast (thus serving travellers along much the same route as that used more than a century and-a-half earlier). However, the business did not remain open for long and the house is once again a private residence.

At the intersection of Highway 2 and Union Road, the cycling lane ends and the Trail turns south for 1.5 kilometres (1 mile), leading to Lakeshore Drive. (Caution is urged when crossing the railway tracks.) East along Lakeshore Drive the Trail leads you out of the Township of Cramahe and into Brighton Township. There, you will find some of Ontario's finest beaches and wetlands in Presqu'ile Provincial Park.

When train whistles blow in Brighton, the velvet sound resonates through a tranquil and rural setting

TOWNSHIP OF
Brighton &
TOWN OF
Brighton

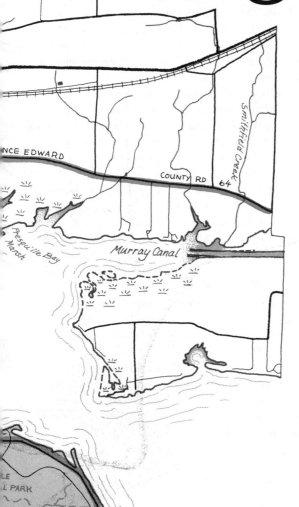

Smithfield Creek

NCE EDWARD

COUNTY RD 64

Presqu'ile Bay

Presqu'ile Marsh

Murray Canal

LE
L PARK

Presqu'ile Point

HEN TRAIN WHISTLES blow in Brighton, the velvet sound resonates through a tranquil and rural setting. Just two hours east of Toronto, set among the hills of Northumberland's apple country, along the shores of Lake Ontario, the town and township of Brighton are gentle links to Ontario's storied past.

The land was included in the vast tract of land ceded to Canada by the Mississaugas in the Gunshot Treaty of 1787. In 1792, when Lieutenant-Governor John Graves Simcoe divided Upper Canada's districts into 19 counties, Brighton became part of Northumberland County. (Because of a lack of precise descriptions in the treaty, it was amended in 1805 and the final document is known as the Toronto Purchase.)

As in many townships along the northern shores of Lake Ontario, the early settlers were United Empire Loyalists, refugees who fled the United States because they wished to remain loyal to the British Crown. Obadiah and Mary Simpson of North Carolina, who arrived in the spring of 1796, were the first Loyalists to make Brighton their home.

Since that time, Brighton's population has grown: there are slightly more than 4,000 people in the town and another 4,000 in the rest of the township. Overall, the pace of life is relaxed and the people are friendly. The area is home to one of southern Ontario's most diverse provincial parks, Presqu'ile Provincial Park.

The best way to visit the Brighton section of the Waterfront Trail is by following Highway 2 east to Union Road in Cramahe Township; turn south until you reach Lakeshore Road. (The Cramahe-Brighton line is just a short distance east.)

Lakeshore Road has a gravel surface with no shoulders; although it is a fairly quiet rural route, cars sometimes travel at considerable speeds, so vigilance is required. This is primarily a residential area with a variety of clapboard and brick houses situated on large lots that back onto Lake Ontario. Trail users should note there is no public access to the lakeshore between Union Road and Presqu'ile Provincial Park.

As you journey east along Lakeshore Road, you can see several radio and telecommunications towers on the hilltops just north of Highway 401. They mark what was once the shoreline of the lakes created some 10,000 years ago, when glaciers covering the area receded. The result was enormous quantities of water, the runoff filling the basin to a depth of 184 metres (603 feet) to create Lake Iroquois.

This portion of the Trail traverses the plain that formed just offshore as the glacier deposited sand and silt; the finer clay particles that washed into Lake Iroquois would have been carried further out.

The sandy, well-drained soil of Brighton Township is ideal for orchards; when the apple trees bloom in late spring, their beauty draws many visitors.

The land to the north has second growth forest. The predominant tree species are those that do best in full sunlight, including poplar and some white birch. Here and there are scraggly medium-sized Manitoba maples that have spread from plantings started in Toronto's Don Valley more than a century ago. Wetter sites have more evergreens, particularly white spruce and eastern white cedar.

Not far west, you will find Huff Road; a kilometre (0.6 mile) east of Huff, the Trail turns sharply south to offer an excellent view of marshland.

Lakeshore Road ends at Harbour Street, where you will find the Parkside Variety Store and Restaurant. Both are open year-round: the store is the only one in the area; the restaurant offers daily specials and is a popular attraction for visitors heading to the entrance of Presqu'ile Provincial Park, which is immediately south.

Just in front of the store you will find a stone cairn erected by the descendants of Obadiah and Mary Simpson. The plaque reads in part:

In yonder sand dune
lie the remains of
the first settlers of
Brighton District.

Toward the end of the 18th century, Lieutenant-Governor Simcoe conducted a survey of the property and, because of the fine harbour, decided it was an ideal site for a town and district capital. Ambitious plans were drawn up for the construction of the town of Newcastle, and in the spring of 1804 the first building was begun. All the ambitious plans, however, came to nought when the schooner Speedy was lost at sea (see vignette *The Speedy*).

PRESQU'ILE PROVINCIAL PARK

Presqu'ile, Ontario's fourth oldest provincial park was created in 1922 to protect distinctive habitats and to offer city-dwellers an opportunity to experience and enjoy the natural heritage that is so much a part of the province's history.

In 1920, most of Presqu'ile was transferred from federal to provincial ownership; some of the original cottages remain on the peninsula, but only one, Stonehedge, lies within the provincial park's boundaries. Built in 1945 and named for its walls of stone, this 1,525-square-metre (5,000-square-foot) cottage was originally owned by a member of the Board of Toronto Harbour Commissioners.

Although it's not part of the Waterfront Trail route, a visit to Presqu'ile Provincial Park is a must, whether for an afternoon or for several days of camping. The 400-campsite park features a variety of recreational facilities including, wide sandy beaches, 17 kilometres (10.5 miles) of walking trails, a cycling path, picnic areas with barbecues, a public boat launch, and, in winter, cross-country ski trails.

The asphalt road, which winds throughout the park, is an excellent (but busy) place for a stroll, a cycle, and in-line skating; although it is bumpy in places. There is a convenience store where bikes can be rented during the summer.

Unlike the western shoreline's beach, most of the eastern shoreline comprises natural marshland. More than 161 hectares (398 acres) of wetland stretch along Presqu'ile Bay, making it the largest protected wetland on the north shore of Lake Ontario. Unless you're canoeing, the best way to experience the wetland is

THE SPEEDY

Except for a terrible accident off the shores of the Presqu'ile peninsula nearly two centuries ago, there might easily be no Presqu'ile Provincial Park. What is now parkland would have been a town, with market square, shops, hospital, school, and a graveyard.

Construction on the courthouse was already under way in the spring of 1804 and a celebrated murder case was being transferred from the town of York. But something went horribly awry: the schooner Speedy, carrying the accused, court officials, and witnesses, was blown out to sea and vanished with all on board. It was never found.

The loss of the Speedy rocked York: 20 people had vanished, five per cent of the colonial capital's population. But it was not merely a matter of numbers. Except for the accused, these were leading citizens of York: Thomas Cochran, a judge; Robert Isaac Dey Gray, the Solicitor-General of Upper Canada; and a member of the House of Assembly, to list a few.

The prisoner, an Ojibwa native named Ogetonicut was accused of killing John Sharp, an agent for the fur-trading Farewell brothers of Oshawa. The transfer was the result of a survey which showed that Washburn Island in Lake Scugog, where the killing took place, was in Newcastle District.

With the loss of the Speedy, the Presqu'ile site was judged inconvenient as a town centre. (Instead, Cobourg was chosen as the district seat.) But the incident resonated in other ways as well. First, it was evidence that the system had different standards for dealing with aboriginal people.

A year earlier, Ogetonicut's brother had been killed by a settler, but no charges were ever laid – although there was a suspect. On the other hand, the alleged killing of a settler by a native pushed the system into high gear.

There was another issue as well: The Speedy's captain, Thomas Paxton, had reported that his vessel was unfit and in desperate need of repair. But Paxton was overruled and the ship sailed. To this day, no one knows where the Speedy sank, or whether the tragedy was caused by the storm raging on the lake or unseaworthiness of the vessel itself.

on the one-kilometre (0.6-mile) boardwalk that has been constructed over the water, out into the marsh.

The Presqu'ile Layer Cake Recipe

If you would like a Presqu'ile of your own, consider the recipe for this layered delight: To make the base, grind a mixture of 450-million year-old marine fossils. On top of the base, combine 937 hectares (2,315 acres) of limestone and sand peninsula to produce a middle tier. In order to get the perfect topping, you will have to blend pristine marsh, richly mixed forest, a wide sandy beach, and offshore islands. Ice generously with plants and animals, sprinkled with just a few nationally rare species. To finish, marinate in Lake Ontario for about 10,000 years and wait for the waters to recede. Voilà, Presqu'ile.

Birding

For many, Presqu'ile's main attraction is not on the land but in the air and on the water surrounding Gull and High Bluff islands, a short distance from the southwestern corner of the peninsula.

Waterbird colonies there are audible long before they are visible, in the individual sounds of more than 70,000 pairs of nesting gulls, cormorants, terns, and night herons. In order to protect breeding birds, the site is closed from March 10 to September 10; however, you can easily view the islands, without intervening foliage, from the south end of the beach. You may even see members of two of Ontario's "species of special concern", the great black-backed gull and the caspian tern.

Spring is an especially impressive time for bird-watching, especially if you're interested in watching ducks. As many as 10,000 of them fill the bay and at least 25 different species have been spotted during the spring migration.

If you would like to be part of the annual Waterfowl Viewing Festival, plan to be in the park the last weekend of March or the first weekend of April. Well-informed volunteers, armed with telescopes, point out the various species and their habits.

There is a special joy each spring in the sights and sounds of returning songbirds. From mid-April, the morning chorus

GULL ISLAND

It is so noisy on Gull Island, which lies just off Presqu'ile's beach, that you can suffer permanent hearing damage. Even on a calm day, the tumult can be heard for several kilometres. The odour is a wall that repels all but the most determined visitors and those braving that defence could find themselves showered by regurgitated fish from a startled cormorant perched overhead.

Everywhere, there is evidence of nature at its most basic. In fact, the ground is littered with thousands of dead birds, part of the natural order of life on the island. The landscape more closely resembles a deserted plain on another continent than an island in Lake Ontario. That may be why Gull Island has been described as hell on earth.

Nonetheless, it is one of North America's great wildlife factories. At the height of the breeding season, from mid-March to mid-September, Gull Island is off-limits to people, because even a single visitor can cause mass desertion of nests and the death of thousands of birds. More than a quarter of a million seabirds make their homes on this and nearby High Bluff islands.

Although gulls, especially ring-billed ones, are in the vast majority, several other species of colonial waterbirds, including double-crested cormorants, common terns, and black-crowned herons, and Caspian terns, use the islands as breeding grounds.

The concentration of wildlife gives researchers a rare opportunity to study behaviour, migration, and dietary habits, as well as the survival rates of the many species. Some of the earliest warnings of the dangers of DDT and other toxic chemicals came from studies here.

It may not be inviting, but Gull Island is a valuable sanctuary for birds and a vital source of environmental knowledge for humans.

grows stronger daily, reaching a glorious zenith by mid- to late-May. At the migration's peak, the trees fill with the gem-like colours of scarlet tanagers, yellow warblers, indigo buntings, purple finches, and hosts of others. To help birders recognize the many different species, park naturalists offer guided walks, beginning in May and continuing until about Thanksgiving weekend.

In all, the peninsula that comprises the park is inhabited by several hundred species of birds (313 have been reported). Although the best time for birding is during spring and fall migrations, there are interesting birds in the park year-round.

Wildflowers for All Seasons

The wide range of park vegetation reflects the diversity of its natural areas. Visit Jobes' Woods Nature Trail for May wildflowers; scout Calf Pasture for July blooms; and check the natural beach for the flowers of August. From mid-August to September, the harsh growing conditions in the pannes (the areas between the fore-dunes and back-dunes) produce rare flowers. Botanists have found regionally, provincially, and nationally rare species in this habitat. Among the most interesting are false dragonhead, three species of ladies'-tresses orchids, and many kinds of sedges.

Creatures of the Night

A cool spring twilight in the pannes, a warm summer evening at Calf Pasture, or a moonlit night at the edge of the marsh – these offer the pleasures of discovering Presqu'ile's abundant night wildlife. In spring, thousands of tiny frogs sing their mysterious chorus in the panne's shallow pools. In summer, the dusk offers glimpses of shy and easily startled deer, while an evening stroll on the marsh boardwalk may reveal muskrat, beaver, or the occasional otter.

Lighthouse and Museum

Built in 1840, Presqu'ile lighthouse, located on the southern tip of the peninsula, is the second oldest still operating on the Canadian side of the Great Lakes. Until 1872, William J. Swetman, the first lighthouse keeper, alerted passing ships to the presence of land. Converted to electrical operation in 1935, the lighthouse no longer

MONARCHS ARE MIGRANTS TOO

An autumn walk along Presqu'ile beach yields the sight of many butterflies: yellow sulphurs and delicate whites, among other species. But the most spectacular in size and numbers – and the one that usually excites the most comment – is the monarch.

Monarchs are at once familiar and mysterious: The metamorphosis from striped and furry caterpillar to gold-trimmed cocoon and, finally, into orange and black butterfly fragility, fascinates children and adults alike.

In late summer and early fall, thousands of monarchs flutter along the Lake Ontario shoreline, particularly at such vantage points as Presqu'ile Park. In favourable weather, the butterflies head out over the open lake, moving south or west. While it was long understood that they were migrating somewhere, their precise destination remained a mystery until recently .

The solution came from the work of Dr. Frederick Urquhart, professor emeritus of zoology at Scarborough Campus of the University of Toronto. A leading world expert in the field, he sought a substitute for the metal tags that biologists use to study bird migration. Dr. Urquhart devised an adhesive tag so small it could be fastened to the leading edge of a butterfly's wing. The tag, which is about a one-fortieth the weight of the monarch itself, bears a number and address; in 1975, after he and associates had tagged almost half a million monarchs, Urquhart's team was able to track them to their winter home: Mexico.

We now know that, in the early spring, the butterflies head north. What is uncertain – and what will remain unknown until and if a tagged butterfly is found back at Presqu'ile – is whether they are actually returning to their place of birth. Significantly, one tagged butterfly is known to have flown south, wintered in Mexico, then completed about 1,000 kilometres of the northern journey before being found. This suggests that some monarchs may, indeed, return to the place where they were hatched. The ones that reach the Great Lakes area are females – very weary and tattered by the time they get to Presqu'ile in early June. They immediately lay their eggs on the abundant milkweed plants in the area and then die.

Depending on weather conditions, about four generations of monarchs are born on the Presqu'ile peninsula each summer, emerging as

insects, feeding as caterpillars for two to three weeks, then pupating into butterflies. Most die within 30 to 40 days, with members of only the last
generation living long enough to migrate south. Those that do migrate survive
from 10 to 11 months.

Like an orange and black tide, the fall flight begins, almost
imperceptibly, in mid-July, although the timing varies considerably from year to
year. The exceptionally mild autumn in 1994 allowed significant numbers to
remain at Presqu'ile until early November.

If you would like to see how these handsome insects are
tagged, there is a demonstration annually at Presqu'ile Provincial Park on Labour
Day weekend. For more information, call the park's office.

needed a keeper by 1952. Swetman's house and the foundation
of the fog station are being incorporated into a new marine
heritage site.

Presqu'ile is a 90 minute drive east of Toronto. From
Highway 401, take exit 509 south on Highway 30 for about 8 kilometres (5 miles) to Highway 2. Turn right and drive half a kilometre
(0.3 mile) to Ontario Street, turn left (south), and proceed to the
main gate. There are signs all along the route. For further information, contact Presqu'ile Provincial Park, RR 4, Brighton, Ontario,
K0K 1H0 or call 613-475-2204.

THE TRAIL TO BRIGHTON

If you've chosen to remain at Harbour Street, continue along the
Waterfront Trail by going east; a walking path runs along the south
side of the causeway for part of its length. Elsewhere, if you are on
foot, keep to the limestone shoulder. The high causeway is a good
vantage point for scanning the marsh to the south, where you will
see many varieties of songbirds and waterfowl.

Just before you reach the intersection of Harbour
and Ontario streets, the Trail veers off to the right and heads
toward the foot of Ontario Street. There you will find a public boat
launch with some parking, as well as picnic facilities, fishing, and

views of the marsh. Some of the high sand dunes of the Presqu'ile peninsula are visible to the west.

The Trail heads north along Ontario Street (a bicycle path parallels the road on the east side) for about a kilometre (0.6 mile), passing through a small, quiet residential community. Then it turns east along a right-of-way that is an extension of Raglan Street. From this point, however, you may want to pay a visit to the centre of town by continuing on Ontario Street to Main Street, which is 4 kilometres (2.5 miles) north.

TOWN OF BRIGHTON

A right turn takes you into the downtown section of Brighton where you can find the conveniences you may need. On Main Street, between the bank and the beer store, is a tourist information booth, open seven days a week from July 1 to Labour Day. Knowledgeable staff have information about the excellent antique shops in the Brighton area as well as the bed-and-breakfast establishments known for their hospitality.

On Saturdays from May through November, Brighton's Farmers' Market goes into full swing behind the bank building. You can purchase everything from fresh fruit and locally grown vegetables to fresh or smoked fish, baked goods, and plants. Rain or shine, more than 20 vendors set up their wares each week to serve local residents and visitors.

There are a number of fresh produce markets on the edge of town. Rundle Farms, on the south side of Highway 2, about 1 kilometre (0.6 mile) west of Ontario Street, provides a wide variety of fruits and vegetables and is open seven days a week year-round. To the north of town on Highway 30 is Spring Valley Farms, open seven days a week from spring to Thanksgiving weekend.

PROCTOR HOUSE MUSEUM

North of the centre of town is Proctor House, the restored mansion of Lake Ontario shipping magnate Josiah Proctor and his family, who came to Brighton from Vermont in the mid-1800s. The family prospered and soon owned mills, a general store, a hotel, various other properties, and a small fleet of ships. The house was built in the late 1860s, on a plot of land with commanding views of Lake Ontario and surrounding landscape.

In time, the estate was donated by the Proctor heirs to the Lower Trent Region Conservation Authority (LTRCA). In turn, LTRCA leased the property to Save Our Heritage, an organization that refurbished and renovated the house, and opened it to the public.

The conservation area of 40 hectares (100 acres) of forest and park that surrounds the house is well worth a visit. Its blend of manicured parkland and rugged forest makes it ideal for picnicking in the summer or cross-country skiing in winter.

To reach Proctor House, take Main Street east to Prince Edward Street and go north for about 1 kilometre (0.6 mile) to the top of the hill; it's at 96 Young Street. The museum is open daily during July and August, weekends in June and September. For hours and other information phone 613-475-2144.

APPLEFEST

Brighton is on the "apple route", which follows Highway 2 from Colborne through Brighton to Trenton. Each September the town holds its Applefest: a gala event featuring a parade down Main Street, country fair, carnival rides, concerts, tractor pulls, beef barbecues, bazaars, and pancake breakfasts. The weekend is popular among local people as well as tourists, so if you want to join in, you might call ahead to arrange accommodations. For more information, call the Applefest Committee at 613-475-APPL (2775).

If you choose to follow the Trail instead of taking the trip downtown, head east on the Raglan Street extension from Ontario Street, on the path for little more than half a kilometre (0.3 miles) through a forest of poplars and cedars. At the end of the path, turn right on Cedar Street and follow it to the marina at Harbour Street.

You will note the marina's white metal tower with the red beacon to the left. Along with the four small lighthouses (range lights) and various buoys found in the bay, it is a navigation aid. Once upon a time, Freeman House stood nearby. Long gone it was built in 1807 and may have been used as a jail or barracks during the War of 1812 or the rebellion of 1837.

Leaving the marina, the Trail continues east along Harbour Street. At Cedar Street look to your right, where you will find an observation point providing a view of the bay.

GOSPORT

Continue east on Harbour Street until you reach Baldwin Street. A side trip of 1 kilometre (0.6 mile) south on Baldwin leads to historic Gosport, originally called Freeman's Point. In earlier days, after the original plans for Presqu'ile were abandoned, Gosport became important as a shipping centre. There were three wharves in the town, the oldest dating from 1841.

Gosport also depended on commercial fishing: In 1875, only five places on Lake Ontario had larger fisheries. Gosport's commercial fishing was at its peak in the 1920s, but there has been a steady decline since then, locally and on Lake Ontario in general.

At the foot of Baldwin Street, just before you reach the water, you will find the Harbourview Motel Marina, with accommodations and fishing boat rentals by the day. Staff know the best places to fish on Presqu'ile Bay and local boat operators have made several award-winning catches. There is also a well-stocked bait and tackle supply. For more information, contact Bill Rudland at the Harbourview Motel Marina, 613-475-1515.

Farther along Harbour Street you pass Butler Creek and a pumping station. In 1860, a large mill pond was located a little upstream. Harbour Street ends at County Road 64 (known as Prince Edward Street in Brighton); the Trail continues east from this intersection along County Road 64. The exact age of the white wooden home at the corner is uncertain, but it is believed to be about 140 years old and was reportedly built using white pine from the site.

The first house on the opposite side of the street (211 Prince Edward Street) was constructed in 1848 by the Butler family. Contemporary accounts indicate that some bricks were made from clay found on the Butler farm; the brick on the north side differs from that on the west side.

Leaving Brighton's built-up area, the Trail turns east and follows County Road 64. This is a paved road with a speed limit of 80 kph (50 mph). The road stretches for about 6.5 kilometres (4 miles) through a rural setting of farms and marsh. On the left are farms and, on the right, private homes with long grassy front yards reaching up to the road, and back yards rolling down to Presqu'ile Bay. You will pass many roads leading south to the water but most are private.

The main sewage lagoon, which can be seen from the roadside, is home to a surprising array of wildlife. Flocks of ducks come here during migration, and at times it has a greater diversity of waterfowl than any location on the bay. The lagoon is perhaps the most reliable place to see such species as green-backed herons. The birds most people hope to glimpse are, of course, the rarest ones, such as eared grebe and cattle egret, which have both been sighted here. There are also healthy populations of painted and snapping turtles. Unfortunately, some of them often attempt to cross the busy roadway, with deadly consequences.

Just east of the red barn at the pig farm is a final view of Presqu'ile Bay, including the large lighthouse at the tip of the peninsula. Two of the smaller range lights are also visible, one on the near shore at the right (west) and one on the far shore, just to the right of the main light. The spit of land on the far shore extending from the left side is Stony Point. Just beyond the near shore, the small green buoy at the far left marks the entrance to the Murray Canal. Completed in 1889, the canal links to the Bay of Quinte and the Trent-Severn Waterway.

BRIGHTON SPEEDWAY

About 6.5 kilometres (4 miles) east of Harbour Street is the Brighton Speedway. Stock car races are held every Saturday night beginning in April and continuing until September's Applefest Weekend, when the finals of a nine-part Ontario and Quebec racing series are held. For more information, contact Brighton Speedway Park at 613-475-3250.

Just past the race track, the road crosses Smithfield Creek, whose headwaters are near Highway 401. Like so much other landscape in the area, the topography was created by melting glaciers. As they receded, they deposited tremendous amounts of soil and rock in a long line of hills called a moraine.

Some geologists believe that the Trenton Moraine is a detached eastern extension of the Oak Ridges Moraine that starts north of Toronto, while others believe the two are separate. Whichever, the topographical feature is referred to as a kame moraine, which means the sediments were partially sorted by meltwater streams before being deposited. After they were formed, the area's hills were flattened when the moraine was submerged beneath the waters of Lake Iroquois.

At Stoney Point Road, the Trail leaves Brighton Township and enters Murray Township, where a trip alongside the Murray Canal awaits.

As *the sun rises to the east, sailboats glide silently through the morning mist, looking not unlike tall Victorian ladies out for a morning stroll.*
The quiet is bliss

◄·····

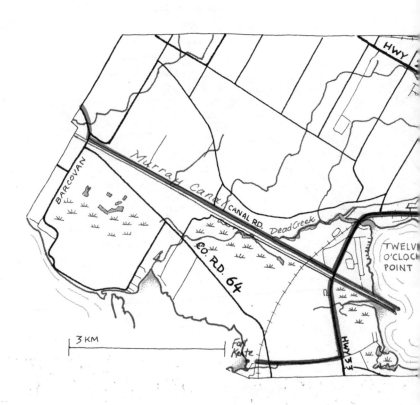

Murray &

TOWNSHIP

CITY OF
Trenton

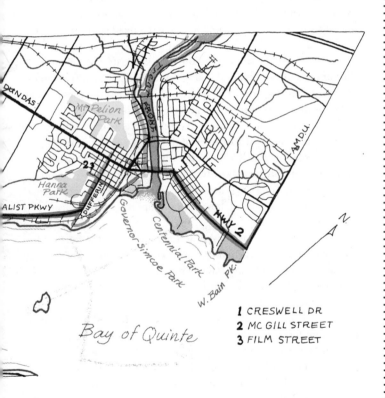

DUNDAS

Mt Pelion Park

Hanna Park

ALIST PKWY

2

FRONT

Governor Simcoe Park

Centennial Park

A.M.D.U.

HWY 2

W. Bain Pk.

N.

Bay of Quinte

1 CRESWELL DR
2 MC GILL STREET
3 FILM STREET

URRAY TOWNSHIP, with the Murray Hills at its back and Lake Ontario in front of it, marks the entrance to the Bay of Quinte at the Murray Canal. This is Loyalist country, first surveyed in 1791 and again in 1796, and settled by refugees created by the American revolution.

MURRAY CANAL

It's early morning and you pause at the County Road 64 bridge over the canal, watching the attendant lower the gates and prepare to swing the bridge. A cluster of boats has gathered overnight, nervously treading water, impatient to get a head start on another perfect day.

As the sun rises to the east, sailboats glide silently through the morning mist, looking not unlike tall Victorian ladies out for a morning stroll. The quiet is bliss, though the canal will get busier as the day progresses. Begun in 1884, the canal provides access from Lake Ontario to the Bay of Quinte; (for a profile of one of the most influential advocates of the canal, see the story of Joseph Keeler on page 278). In its early years, the canal was busy with freighter and steamboat traffic going to and from Trenton's very busy port. Today, it is most often used for pleasure craft: on a summer holiday weekend, it becomes a superhighway for fishers and boaters.

As you turn east onto Canal Road on the north side of the canal, you have reached the approximate mid-point of the eight-kilometre (five-mile) long canal. Three road swing bridges and one railway swing bridge (continuously open from May to October) cross it at various points.

This section of the road alongside the Murray Canal is level but loose gravel can make it quite dusty in dry periods. The delicate pinks and whites of the spring wildflowers, by autumn, give way to richer purples and golds. (But if you're walking or cycling, don't let the palette of colours distract you: the road is amply potholed.)

The Canal Road is a shortcut from County Road 64 to Highway 33 and into Trenton; it, too, can be very dusty when there

Murray Township has many roadside stands loaded, throughout warm weather, with produce: they begin in June with ruby-red berries, followed by a cornucopia of fresh fruits and vegetables, and marking summer's end with silky golden ears of corn. For more information on the many amenities in Murray Township, including its two golf courses, contact the County of Northumberland Tourism Bureau at 1-800-354-7049.

has been little rainfall. On late summer afternoons, scores of bicycles are parked along the bank, while kids take advantage of the intervals between boats to leap into the canal's cool waters.

If fishing is your passion, you are about to enter paradise: The Murray Canal, Lake Ontario, the Bay of Quinte, and the Trent River provide many favourite fishing holes and the best fish stories. Local sports stores have everything from a Blue Fox to a Daredevil, even a Hulapopper or two. And don't forget: around here, dew-worms still work.

As you reach the swing bridge at Twelve O'Clock Point Road, turn left onto Highway 33, which is a section of the Loyalist Parkway, a route that covers much of that followed by early settlers from the United States.

TWELVE O'CLOCK POINT ROAD

Located where the Murray Canal enters the Bay of Quinte, Twelve O'Clock Point has been a favourite fishing place for years: At one time, fish were so plentiful there were commercial fishing operations. (Even now, commercial fishing nets can be spotted along the point, in the early spring.)

The eastern pier of Murray Canal is a popular spot for casting a line, but be there early, especially on holiday weekends. The road on the north side of the canal (access is from Highway 33) leads to one of the busiest fishing sites along the bay.

A small greenbelt area borders both sides of the eastern section of the canal, beginning at the entrance to Twelve O'Clock Point Road; there are picnic tables, barbecues, and cool green grass. Outhouses are available on the north side of the canal; however, they are not accessible to people in wheelchairs.

At the intersection of the canal service road and Highway 33, the Waterfront Trail turns left and follows a segment of the Apple Route (see page 272 for more details on the Apple Route). You may, however, decide to turn right and follow Highway 33 south through Carrying Place for a side trip to historic Fort Kente.

Side Trip
CARRYING PLACE AND FORT KENTE

Carrying Place was the name native people gave to the narrow isthmus at the head of the Bay of Quinte; it was also the place where they signed the Gunshot Treaty, by which they gave up most of what is now Eastern Ontario.

Today, Carrying Place is a thriving community and a popular weekend destination for craft and flea market aficionados, as well as for fishers. Parents should note the excellent playground at the corner of Highway 33 and County Road 64; there is also a public boat launch east of Carrying Place on the Bay of Quinte.

Upon reaching County Road 64, turn right; you are now heading west on the oldest travelled road in this province. A thousand years ago it was a native trail used as a portage between Weller's Bay and the Bay of Quinte. (You will notice a few heritage buildings as you pass by.)

Enthusiasts will enjoy the antiques and art gallery at Asa Weller's Tap House, built after the War of 1812, and still standing. Nearby Weller's Bay is named for Asa. ∎

FORT KENTE

Continuing west 1.4 kilometres (0.9 mile) along County Road 64, you will reach an intersection. Continue straight on Fort Kente ("ken-tay") Road for half a kilometre (0.3 mile) to Weller's Bay, where you will find Fort Kente. The name comes from a native word for meadow, which was the way native people described the land between Lake Ontario and the Bay of Quinte.

The fort dates from 1813, when it was built by the Provincial Dragoons to protect the portage route, then an important link in the military route during the War of 1812.

The Kente Portage Heritage Conservation Society has rebuilt the fort on its original site and you see it today much as it was in 1813. Face Lake Ontario from the fort and you appreciate what a strategic stronghold it was: the bay and lake are visible for some distance, ensuring that the enemy would be unable to gain access to this important route.

Fort Kente is open during the summer months and admission is free. The best time to visit is mid-July, during the three days of the Kente Portage Festival, when there are re-enactments of military battles, canoe races, games, and concerts, as well as historical displays and demonstrations. For more information, call 613-394-2313. ■

To continue along the Trail, follow the same route back to Twelve O'Clock Point Road and wind your way north along Highway 33. Stop for an ice cream cone and, if it's Sunday, while away a few hours at the antique and flea market that is not quite a kilometre (0.6 mile) north of the bridge on the right side – paradise of another sort, for the collector.

Dead Creek is the name given to the marshy area on the right, where the bay opens alongside the highway. It is home to many different species of wildlife, including mallards, blue herons, and, occasionally, a family of loons. (And, if you think you've seen a loon, take another look: it may actually be a cormorant, a bird that dives and fishes continuously and is entertaining to watch. It obviously knows the good spots: this is the place to pick up a large-mouth or smallmouth bass, catfish, or pike, among other kinds.)

As you continue toward Trenton along Highway 33 (known locally as the Carrying Place Road), the Bay of Quinte shoreline offers spectacular views.

CITY OF TRENTON

The early River Trent settlement, later named Trent Port, began on both sides of the Trent River, much the way Trenton is now. The Trent became one of the main routes for French fur traders travelling from the St. Lawrence to the Upper Lakes. Once a part of Murray Township, Trenton separated from it and was incorporated as a village in 1853, a town in 1880, and a city in 1980.

By the 1960s, Trenton had grown from a booming lumber town to a thriving manufacturing-based economy; in more recent recessionary times, the people of the city have worked tirelessly to broaden their economic foundations.

A mix of old and new, Trenton's skyline includes such heritage buildings as the City Hall, built in 1888 as the Post Office and Customs House. There are also many examples of Regency cottage and early 19th-century architecture. To see beautifully gabled Gothic homes and Victorian gingerbread, get the Trenton Walking Tour guide from City Hall or the Trenton Memorial Public Library (across from Fraser Park).

As you enter Trenton along Carrying Place Road and curve left on to Dufferin Avenue, you will notice an unusual business building on the right side: the round house, which was used to store and switch railway cars during the first half of this century. Today, only a few of these railway turntables remain in Canada. Railway buffs will want to check out the Trent Port Historical Society's displays at the Dufferin Centre, which is at the top of Dufferin Avenue.

At the point where Carrying Place Road curves to join Dufferin Avenue, boaters may want to turn right onto Dufferin and continue south, where they will find the public boat launch at the Bay of Quinte. (In future, the Waterfront Trail will follow this route and then pass through the waterfront abandoned railway lands to Bayshore Park.)

BAY OF QUINTE

With or without a camera, you will not soon forget a sunset or sunrise along the Bay of Quinte. A naturalist's dream, the craggy shoreline of the Bay of Quinte is rich with wildlife, including many varieties of geese, ducks, and other birds. From this part of the Trail, you get a panoramic view of the bay, including Indian Island. After an unoccupied island home burned to the ground, the island became a popular weekend docking spot for local boaters.

The Waterfront Trail continues north on Dufferin Avenue. You are now entering an area of Trenton that was once home to a thriving movie industry.

In 1919, when a production studio was established here, Trenton became the site where numerous films were made, including such hits as *The Great Shadow,* starring Tyrone Power Sr. and parts of the classic *All's Quiet on The Western Front* (1930). Unfortunately, Trenton's film-making industry peaked in the late 1920s, just as talkies were being introduced. Today, all that remains of the city's brief time in celluloid sunshine is a walk down Film Street, which is parallel to and two blocks west of Dufferin Avenue.

When in the area, you may want to consider a short detour to Hanna Park.

HANNA PARK

At McGill Street, turn left off Dufferin Avenue to reach Hanna Park, which includes a playground for children. Although it is tucked away in the southwest corner of the city, Hanna Park offers year-round access to walkers, joggers, cyclists, people in wheelchairs, and cross-country skiers. Its paths and trails are a refreshing breather from city life. Parking is available.

The 17-hectare (42-acre) park is home to a wide variety of plants and wildlife. Birders will be delighted at the rest spots thoughtfully provided on the park's trails.

Off Highway 33, at the western entrance to the city, the paths in Hanna Park will soon be connected to the Waterfront Trail.

Leaving Hanna Park, the Trail heads east on Cresswell Drive, which bends to the north a short distance along and leads into Bayshore Park.

Instead of heading east on Cresswell Drive, you may wish to continue north eight blocks on Dufferin Avenue to reach the base of Mount Pelion, known in the area as "the mountain", which is one of Trenton's most significant landmarks.

MOUNT PELION

While not exactly Olympian in height, over time it has carried the names of two mountains in Greek mythology. According to the myth, two young children attempted to climb Mount Ossa to reach Mount Pelion, so they could get to Mount Olympus, the home of the gods. The children were killed before they could complete the task; hence "piling Ossa on Pelion" has come to mean battling an obstacle that cannot be overcome. Although Trenton's mountain was initially given the more modest name of Ossa (the shorter peak) it later became called Pelion.

Samuel de Champlain may have been the first European to set foot on the mountain, in 1615. At the time, he was travelling through the area with 500 Hurons to present-day northern New York State to attack Iroquois enemies. A native story also tells of a giant who rose from the mountaintop to chase away the Iroquois, who were bent on capturing a nearby French garrison in the 1600s.

At the top of Mount Pelion is a old canon that may have been used to guard the settlement from American attackers during the War of 1812. After the war, it was dragged to the top of the mountain by six teams of horses. By the late 1800s, its main job was to boom out on Victoria Day, but the gun was retired after an incident in which all Trenton's downtown store windows were shattered.

While they are not marked or groomed, well-worn paths have been beaten over time, and steps will take visitors to a lookout tower at the top of Pelion. It offers breathtaking views of Prince Edward County to the south, the Murray Hills to the north, and Belleville and Canadian Forces Base Trenton to the east. The tower was completed by the city as a centennial project in 1980.

BAYSHORE PARK

We are now entering Trenton's busy downtown area, with its many specialty shops. Nearby Bayshore Park is popular all year long, but especially in summer, when it is the official base for the Trenton Summer Festival, which includes the TUBS Society Bathtub Races: the vessels are modified bathtubs that are raced from Trenton to Belleville and back. The cosy cottage at the entrance serves as a seniors drop-in centre, and is also home to the Downtown Business Improvement Area (DBIA) association.

The DBIA is busy year round, planning festivals and events for Trentonians and visitors. In September, kilts are the order of the day and haggis is on the menu during the Scottish-Irish Festival, which features a parade, mass bands, band competitions, and highland dancing. For further information on these festivals and other community events, call Festivals Trenton at 613-392-3243.

FRASER MEMORIAL PARK

Nestled between Trenton Cold Storage and the entrance to the Trent River is Fraser Park. Originally dedicated as a memorial to soldiers from the Trenton area who died in the two World Wars, it is a favourite spot for a lunchtime break, to soak up the sun or enjoy a good book from the library across the street.

Trenton's Waterfront Development Committee plans to build a scale model lighthouse at the head of the Waterfront Trail, where the committee's Trenton Renaissance Project will begin to take shape.

If all phases of the development are completed, there will be, among other things, a path around the lighthouse; a connection between Fraser Park Marina and Front Street; a riverside walk behind Front Street (to include landscaping, restaurants, parking, and complete upgrading of the backs of the Front Street buildings); a multi-use building, with an open-air section, in the centre of the Front Street parking lot; a visitors' centre; an ecological pond; and a river pier and fishing park. This will connect the Waterfront Trail from Fraser Memorial Park to Lock One on the Trent-Severn Waterway.

FRASER PARK MARINA

Some years ago, the City hoped to expand its marina space – at one point to 500 slips; however, the project turned out to be very costly and did not go ahead. Determined to revitalize the Fraser Park Marina, a small group of people decided, nonetheless, to create a people place in the heart of the city, an attractive marina with up-to-date facilities to draw boaters from the Bay of Quinte to Trenton.

That goal is now realized: tall masts welcome visitors to the entrance of the Trent-Severn Waterway. A modern marina with shower and washroom facilities, power hookups, three new docks, and pumpout services attracts boaters. An outdoor patio and green space complete the amenity.

Beside the marina, the new Skyway Bridge, opened in 1990, spans the Trent River. Built adjacent to its permanent site and then eased into place on a thin sheet of Teflon 10 metres (33 feet), it was the first bridge in North America and the longest in the world to be constructed in this way.

TRENTON GREENBELT WATERFRONT TRAIL

Beginning at Fraser Park and travelling north on Front Street, the Trenton Greenbelt Waterfront Trail runs along the Trent River to the Jack Lange Memorial Walkway. Its downtown section has many shops and restaurants; between May and October check out the Trenton Farmers Market on Tuesday, Thursday, and Saturday mornings for the best local produce and crafts. Relax on one of the park benches along the river and enjoy a leisurely lunch, while you watch the fishing boats and pleasure craft cruise by.

This portion of the Trail can be enjoyed whether you're travelling on foot or by bike; however you should avoid heavy traffic times, because Front street feeds both bridges, which are the only crossing points over the Trent River. Along the street's east side is a wide grassy boulevard with weeping willows and only portions of the street's west side have sidewalks. Parking is available at either Fraser Park or at the Jack Lange Memorial Walkway.

Stop in at the Chamber of Commerce (613-392-7635) located at the north end of the Front Street parking lot, for a friendly hello and information. If you would like to see Trenton and area from the water, they can tell you about the city's many boat charter companies.

As you continue along the Trail, you approach McDonald Bridge (named for former Mayor J. D. McDonald), passing Trenton's fire hall on your right. Along the river's edge, you will find picnic tables that provide a place to stop and rest. This section of the river has large numbers of the pickerel and pike that love the cold water for which the Trent is known.

JACK LANGE MEMORIAL WALKWAY

Continuing north on the Trenton Greenbelt Waterfront Trail, past the fire hall, you will find a public boat launch immediately south of the Lower Trent Region Conservation Authority office. The Jack Lange Memorial Walkway begins at this point; park at the launch area or just north of the Conservation Authority building. Perfect for a lazy stroll or for vigorous jogging, the walkway is accessible to cyclists and people in wheelchairs, and has strategically placed benches so that you can watch the mallards and gulls on its marshy shoreline. The walkway is named for Dr. Jack Lange, a local veterinarian dedicated to conservation and the environment. Sheltered picnic tables and portable washrooms (not accessible to people in wheelchairs) are also available.

LOCK ONE INTERPRETATION CENTRE

Approximately 2 kilometres (1.2 miles) further along the Jack Lange Memorial Walkway, north of the Lower Trent Region Conservation Authority office, is the Lock One Interpretation Centre of Environment Canada's Parks Service. The Interpretation Centre can also be reached from Highway 33 just below Highway 401. Parking is available.

It took almost a century to complete the Trent-Severn Waterway, begun with a small wooden lock in Bobcaygeon in 1833. Now it is one of central Ontario's major tourist attractions.

Canal lock systems – chambers for transferring vessels from one water level to another – have been in use for more than 2,000 years. Once a boat enters the lock, the gates at each end are closed and water is let in until the vessel reaches the level of the second body of water. Lock One of the Trent-Severn system takes only about eight minutes to fill.

The Centre, which contains a gift shop and canal-related exhibits, was built on the site of the former lockmaster's house. Display boards placed around the park offer interesting information about the Trent-Severn and the lock operations.

Side Trip
ROYAL CANADIAN AIR FORCE MEMORIAL MUSEUM

East on Dundas Street (Highway 2) approximately 2.2 kilometres (1.3 miles) from the Skyway Bridge, you will find Amdu Road. Turn left on Amdu (an acronym for Aerospace Maintenance and Development Unit) and continue north for 1 kilometre (0.6 mile) to the Royal Canadian Air Force Memorial Museum.

Since 1931, the men and women of Canadian Forces Base Trenton have served Canada, in war and peace. In their honour, and in commemoration of those who died carrying out their duties, the Royal Canadian Air Force Memorial Museum was opened in 1984 – the only one in Canada dedicated to the RCAF.

The museum includes an impressive collection of aircraft, from the Second World War's DC3 Dakota to the MIG 21, donated by the German government after reunification. This gift was an expression of gratitude for the years of service by Canadian forces in Germany and to commemorate the end of the Cold War. It is open weekends only from June 1 to September 1. For more information, call 613-965-2208. ■

In Murray Township and the City of Trenton, you have had the chance to travel the route of natives and French fur traders, stand guard at an important military fort, catch the biggest fish ever, climb a Greek mountain, walk in Tyrone Power Sr.'s footsteps, watch a bathtub race, sit in a MIG 21, and raise a boat several metres.

Not bad for a walk along a Trail.

LIST OF PLACES, ATTRACTIONS, PUBLIC MARINAS, AND TOURIST OFFICES	WASHROOMS	WATER FOUNTAIN	FOOD	PHONES	WHEELCHAIR ACCESSIBLE	ADMISSION CHARGE	PARKING	PICNIC TABLES	BBQ	RECREATIONAL ACTIVITIES	TRAIL SURFACE
CONFEDERATION PARK • Wild Waterworks • Adventure Village	■	■	■	■	■	■	■	T/B	■	Playground Wild Waterworks Mini-golf Batting cages Arcade Campground for recreational vehicles and tents	Asphalt
LAKELAND COMMUNITY CENTRE	■	■	■	■	■	■	■	■		Swimming pool Volleyball Basketball Playground Go-carts	Asphalt
WINDERMERE BASIN										Birding	Natural
KINSMEN PARK	■	■			■			■		Wading pool Playground Basketball	Natural
HARBOURFRONT AND PIER 4	■	■	S	■	■		■	■		Playground Boat launch Fishing	Natural

P – Partial
S – Seasonal
L – Limited
B – Benches
T – Tables
W – Wheelchair Accessible

List of places, attractions, public marinas, and tourist offices	Washrooms	Water Fountain	Food	Phones	Wheelchair Accessible	Admission Charge	Parking	Picnic Tables	BBQ	Recreational Activities	Trail Surface
Burlington Canal/ Beachway Park	■		S	■	P		■	B		Swimming Boating Beach volleyball Playgrounds	Granular Asphalt
Joseph Brant Museum	■	■		■	■		■	B		Museum	Sidewalk
Royal Botanical Gardens	■	■	■	■	P	■	■	■		Floral exhibits Birding Nature interpretation programs Restaurant Photography	Sidewalk Woodchip
Cootes Paradise										Hiking trails Birding	Natural
LaSalle Park • LaSalle Park Marina	■	■	at scheduled events only	■	■		■	■	■	Wading pool Baseball Birding Marina – 211 slips Boat launch Playground	Granular Grass
Spencer Smith Park	■	■	S	■	■		■	■		Playground Gazebo – concerts Floral displays	Granular Asphalt Concrete Grass
Sioux Lookout Park					■		■	■		Birding	Asphalt Granular
McNichol Park					P		L	■		Birding	Granular Natural
Burloak Waterfront Park					P		■	■		Playground Birding Canoeing	Asphalt Granular Sidewalk

P – Partial
S – Seasonal
L – Limited
B – Benches
T – Tables
W – Wheelchair Accessible

OAKVILLE AT A GLANCE

LIST OF PLACES, ATTRACTIONS, PUBLIC MARINAS, AND TOURIST OFFICES	WASHROOMS	WATER FOUNTAIN	FOOD	PHONES	WHEELCHAIR ACCESSIBLE	ADMISSION CHARGE	PARKING	PICNIC TABLES	BBQ	RECREATIONAL ACTIVITIES	TRAIL SURFACE
BRONTE CREEK PROVINCIAL PARK	■						■	T		Swimming Fishing Hiking Tennis Basketball/volleyball courts Shuffleboard Winter skating Tobogganing Children's playloft	Various
SOUTH SHELL PARK							■	T/B		Children's climber	
SHELL PARK	W	W			■		■	T/B		Playground Four soccer fields Softball Rose gardens	
BRONTE BLUFFS PARK							■			Sovereign House/ Mazo de la Roche Heritage display Centre	Gravel
BRONTE BEACH PARK • Bronte Harbour Marina • Metro Marine Ltd.	■						■	T/B	■	Sandy beach Public marina – 274 slips Fishing Marina – 20 slips	
C. VOLKES MEMORIAL PARK								B		Memorial	Asphalt
FISHERMAN'S WHARF	W		■	■	■		■	B		Fishing	Lockstone walkway Boardwalk
VISTA PROMENADE					■			B			
WATER'S EDGE PARK					■			B		Trail	Gravel
CORONATION PARK	W	■	S				■	T/B	■	Trails Large children's play area Water spray pad Volleyball courts Skating	Gravel Lockstone walkway

List of places, attractions, public marinas, and tourist offices	Washrooms	Water Fountain	Food	Phones	Wheelchair Accessible	Admission Charge	Parking	Picnic Tables	BBQ	Recreational Activities	Trail Surface
Oakville Harbour Development										Marina – 316 slips	
Tannery Park	■	■					■	T/B		Trail	Lockstone walkway
Shipyard Park								T/B			Granular
Navy Flats							■	T/B		Canoe club	
Busby Park								T/B		Public docks	Granular Lockstone
Civic Park								T/B		Lawn bowling	
Erchless Estate • Oakville Museum	W	■		■	■	■	■	B		Formal gardens Museum	Granular
Lakeside Park	■	■				■		T/B		Playground Bandstand	Granular
Gairloch Gardens • Oakville Galleries Studio	■						■	B		Formal garden Gallery	Granular
Arkendo Park								B		Trail	Gravel
Joshua's Creek Trail							■			Hiking Cross country skiing	Gravel Woodchip

P – Partial
S – Seasonal
L – Limited
B – Benches
T – Tables
W – Wheelchair Accessible

MISSISSAUGA AT A GLANCE

List of places, attractions, public marinas, and tourist offices	Washrooms	Water Fountain	Food	Phones	Wheelchair Accessible	Admission Charge	Parking	Picnic Tables	BBQ	Recreational Activities	Trail Surface
Lakeside Park							■	T		Playground	
Lewis Bradley Pool	■	■		■			■			Playground Pool	Asphalt
Bradley Museum	■		■	■	■	■	■	T		Museum Gift shop Tea room	
Meadowwood Park	■										
Watersedge							■	T		Playground Tennis courts Outdoor ice rink	
Rattray Marsh										Birding Wildlife NO BIKING	Boardwalk Natural
Jack Darling Park	■		■	■			■	T	■	Viewing decks Playground Water spray pad	Asphalt
Richard's Memorial	■	■		■			■	T	■	Playground	
Rhododendron Park	■						■	T/B	■	Manicured gardens NO BIKING	Asphalt
J.C. Saddington Park	■		■	■			■	T	■	Playground Fishing Remote-control power boats	Asphalt
Port Credit Harbour • Port Credit Harbour Marina • Tourist office								T		Fishing Marina – 966 slips Boat launch	Asphalt
Adamson Estate						■	■	T/B			Asphalt

P – Partial
S – Seasonal
L – Limited
B – Benches
T – Tables
W – Wheelchair Accessible

LIST OF PLACES, ATTRACTIONS, PUBLIC MARINAS, AND TOURIST OFFICES	WASHROOMS	WATER FOUNTAIN	FOOD	PHONES	WHEELCHAIR ACCESSIBLE	ADMISSION CHARGE	PARKING	PICNIC TABLES	BBQ	RECREATIONAL ACTIVITIES	TRAIL SURFACE
LAKEFRONT PROMENADE • Lakefront Promenade Marina	■	■	■	■	■		■	T/B	■	Fishing Marina – 167 slips Bike and in-line skate rentals Playground Splash pad	Asphalt Boardwalk

P – Partial
S – Seasonal
L – Limited
B – Benches
T – Tables
W – Wheelchair Accessible

ETOBICOKE AT A GLANCE

LIST OF PLACES, ATTRACTIONS, PUBLIC MARINAS, AND TOURIST OFFICES	WASHROOMS	WATER FOUNTAIN	FOOD	PHONES	WHEELCHAIR ACCESSIBLE	ADMISSION CHARGE	PARKING	PICNIC TABLES	BBQ	RECREATIONAL ACTIVITIES	TRAIL SURFACE
MARIE CURTIS PARK	W	■	S	■	■		■	T/B	■	Boat launch Playground Wading pool Baseball diamond	Asphalt
LONG BRANCH PARK										Gazebo with seasonal concerts	
COLONEL SAMUEL SMITH PARK					■		■	T/B		Marina Birding	Asphalt
PRINCE OF WALES PARK	■						■			Tennis courts Playground Wading pool Artificial skating rink in winter	
HUMBER BAY PARK	W	■		■	■		■	T/B		Boat launch Fishing pier Model boating	Asphalt

P – Partial
S – Seasonal
L – Limited
B – Benches
T – Tables
W – Wheelchair Accessible

TORONTO AT A GLANCE

List of places, attractions, public marinas, and tourist offices	Washrooms	Water Fountain	Food	Phones	Wheelchair Accessible	Admission Charge	Parking	Picnic Tables	BBQ	Recreational Activities	Trail Surface
Sir Casimir Gzowski Park	WS	■		■	■		■			Playground Wading pool	Asphalt
High Park	■	■	■	■			■	T/B		Tennis courts Swimming pool Zoo Outdoor theatre	Asphalt
Sunnyside	W	■	S	■	■		■			Swimming pool Playground Wading pool	Asphalt
Budapest Park	■	■					■			Playground	Asphalt
Marilyn Bell Park		■			■		■	B		Tennis courts Rugby	Asphalt
Exhibition Place	S	S	S	■	■	S	■	T/B		Various events year round	Asphalt
Ontario Place • Ontario Place Marina	■	■	■	■	■	■	■	B		Waterpark Childrens amusement area Mini-golf Summer concerts Imax theatre 350 slips	Asphalt
Coronation Park								B		Baseball diamond	
Fort York						■	■			Tours	
Little Norway Park	S	■								Playground Wading pool	

P – Partial
S – Seasonal
L – Limited
B – Benches
T – Tables
W – Wheelchair Accessible

continued on next page

TORONTO AT A GLANCE

List of Places, Attractions, Public Marinas, and Tourist Offices	Washrooms	Water Fountain	Food	Phones	Wheelchair Accessible	Admission Charge	Parking	Picnic Tables	BBQ	Recreational Activities	Trail Surface
Harbourfront & Queen's Quay Terminal • Marina Quay West • Harbourfront Centre • Marina 4	■		■	■	■					Antique Market Outdoor ice rink in winter Theatres Shopping In-line skate rentals Marina – 160 slips Marina – 20 slips Marina – 100 slips	Asphalt
SkyDome	■		■	■	■	■	■			Sports and entertainment stadium Site tours	
CN Tower	■		■	■		■	■			EcoDek Lazer tag game Glass floor Observation deck Revolving restaurant Virtual reality centre Motion simulator ride Mini-golf & games Arcade & games	
Toronto Islands • Hanlan's Point Public Dock • Toronto Island Marina	■	■	■	■	■	■	■	■	■	Centreville children's amusement area Tennis Baseball Bike rentals Boat rentals Marina – 100 slips Marina – 450 slips	Asphalt Boardwalk
Outer Harbour Marina										Marina – 654 slips	

P – Partial
S – Seasonal
L – Limited
B – Benches
T – Tables
W – Wheelchair Accessible

TORONTO AT A GLANCE

LIST OF PLACES, ATTRACTIONS, PUBLIC MARINAS, AND TOURIST OFFICES	WASHROOMS	WATER FOUNTAIN	FOOD	PHONES	WHEELCHAIR ACCESSIBLE	ADMISSION CHARGE	PARKING	PICNIC TABLES	BBQ	RECREATIONAL ACTIVITIES	TRAIL SURFACE
CHERRY BEACH	S			■			■		■	Swimming	
LESLIE STREET SPIT TOMMY THOMPSON PARK					■		■			Open only on weekends Birding	Asphalt
ASHBRIDGE'S BAY PARK		■	S	■	■		■	T/B	■	Swimming pool Boat launch Baseball Beach volleyball	Asphalt Boardwalk
BEACHES	■		■	■				B		Shopping Restaurants Tennis courts Baseball diamond Fitness course	Asphalt Boardwalk

P – Partial
S – Seasonal
L – Limited
B – Benches
T – Tables
W – Wheelchair Accessible

List of places, attractions, public marinas, and tourist offices	Washrooms	Water Fountain	Food	Phones	Wheelchair Accessible	Admission Charge	Parking	Picnic Tables	BBQ	Recreational Activities	Trail Surface
Rosetta McClain Gardens	W	■			■		■			Formal gardens NO BIKING	
Scarborough Heights Park					■		■			Hiking	
Bluffer's Park • Bluffer's Park Marina	W	■	■	■	■		■	T	■	Hiking Boating Swimming Marina – 500 slips	
Cathedral Bluffs Park							■			Playground	
Cudia Park							■				
Sylvan Park							■			View of Shipwrecked "Alexandria"	
Guildwood Park/ Guild Inn	■		■				■			Formal gardens Guest room Tennis courts Swimming pool Fitness and games room Shopping Museum and Art gallery Hiking	
East Point Park							■			Sports field	
Colonel Danforth Park (Side Trip)	■				■		■	T	■	In-line skating Birding Hiking	
The Rouge Park	■			■	■		■			Birding Hiking Boating, canoeing Boat launch Fishing	

P – Partial
S – Seasonal
L – Limited
B – Benches
T – Tables
W – Wheelchair Accessible

PICKERING AT A GLANCE

List of places, attractions, public marinas, and tourist offices	Washrooms	Water Fountain	Food	Phones	Wheelchair Accessible	Admission Charge	Parking	Picnic Tables	BBQ	Recreational Activities	Trail Surface
PETTICOAT CREEK CONSERVATION AREA	W		■	■	■	■	■	T/B		Pool Trails	Asphalt Natural
BRUCE HANDSCOMB MEMORIAL PARK					■			B		Playground	Asphalt
FRENCHMAN'S BAY	W		■	■	■		■	B	■	Birding Fishing Sailing Canoeing Windsurfing Rentals	
• Port Pickering Marina										212 slips	
• Moore Haven Marina										90 slips	
• East Shore Marina										625 slips	
• Swan's Marina										80 slips	
WEST SHORE COMMUNITY CENTRE	■	■	■	■	■		■				
DOUGLAS PARK								T/B		Playground	
BEACHFRONT PARK						■	■	T		Playground Swimming	
HYDRO MARSH										Playground	
ALEX ROBERSTON COMMUNITY PARK					■		■	T/B		Playground	Natural
BAY RIDGES KINSMAN PARK	■	■		■	■		■	T/B		Tennis Baseball Playground Soccer Canada Day celebrations	
PICKERING NUCLEAR GENERATING STATION										Information centre	
SIMCOE POINT PIONEER CEMETERY										Heritage plaque	

P – Partial
S – Seasonal
L – Limited
B – Benches
T – Tables
W – Wheelchair Accessible

AJAX AT A GLANCE

LIST OF PLACES, ATTRACTIONS, PUBLIC MARINAS, AND TOURIST OFFICES	WASHROOMS	WATER FOUNTAIN	FOOD	PHONES	WHEELCHAIR ACCESSIBLE	ADMISSION CHARGE	PARKING	PICNIC TABLES	BBQ	RECREATIONAL ACTIVITIES	TRAIL SURFACE
DUFFINS CREEK AND WETLAND							■			Birding Fishing Canoeing	Asphalt Boardwalk
ROTARY PARK	W		S		■		■	B		Playground Cross country skiing, snowshoeing Boat launch	Asphalt
AJAX WATERFRONT PARK					■		■				Asphalt
PICKERING BEACH										Tennis courts Baseball diamond Playground	

P – Partial
S – Seasonal
L – Limited
B – Benches
T – Tables
W – Wheelchair Accessible

List of places, attractions, public marinas, and tourist offices	Washrooms	Water Fountain	Food	Phones	Wheelchair Accessible	Admission Charge	Parking	Picnic Tables	BBQ	Recreational Activities	Trail Surface
Lynde Shores Conservation Area							■			Birding Fishing Canoeing Ice skating in winter	Boardwalk Natural
Cranberry Marsh							■	T		Birding	
Iroquois Park and Arena	■			■			■			Swimming pool Soccer Baseball diamond Ice rinks	
Whitby Station Gallery										Exhibits Classes Workshops	
Whitby Harbour • Port Whitby Marina										Fishing Marina – 410 slips	Asphalt
Heydenshore Kiwanis Park							■	T	■	Public beach	Asphalt
Intrepid Park											
Cullen Gardens and Miniature Village	■		■	■		■	■	.		Shopping	
Family Kartway	■					■	■			Go-carts	
Heber Down Conservation Authority	■									Camping Nature trails Cross country skiing Sleigh rides in winter	

P – Partial
S – Seasonal
L – Limited
B – Benches
T – Tables
W – Wheelchair Accessible

OSHAWA AT A GLANCE

List of Places, Attractions, Public Marinas, and Tourist Offices	Washrooms	Water Fountain	Food	Phones	Wheelchair Accessible	Admission Charge	Parking	Picnic Tables	BBQ	Recreational Activities	Trail Surface
Lakefront West Park	■	■	S	■	■		■			Baseball diamond Playground	Concrete
General Motors Oshawa Complex										Tours	
Pumphouse Marsh Wildlife Reserve					■					Nature interpretation Birding	Asphalt
Lakeview Park	■	■	S	■	■		■	■		Swimming Volleyball Baseball Softball Rugby	Asphalt

Oshawa-Sydenham Museum										Splash pad
										Playground
										Historical museum
										Rentals
										   Wind surfers, kayaks,
										   peddleboats	

Second Marsh					■					Nature interpretation Birding Observation tower	Asphalt
McLaughlin Bay Wildlife Reserve							■			Nature interpretation Birding	Woodchip

P – Partial
S – Seasonal
L – Limited
B – Benches
T – Tables
W – Wheelchair Accessible

List of places, attractions, public marinas, and tourist offices	Washrooms	Water Fountain	Food	Phones	Wheelchair Accessible	Admission Charge	Parking	Picnic Tables	BBQ	Recreational Activities	Trail Surface
Darlington Provincial Park	W	■	■	■		■	■	T	■	Camping Canoe rental	Woodchip
Darlington Nuclear Generating Plant–Hydro Information Centre	W	■					■	T		Baseball diamond Track	Gravel
Bowmanville Harbour Conservation Area	■	■		■	■		■	T	■	Public boat launch: fee Playing field Picnicking Rental of BBQ, corn pots	Asphalt Gravel
Clarington Tourist and General Information	W			■	■		■				
Bowmanville Zoo	W	■	■	■	■	■	■	T		Camel and mechanical rides	Asphalt
Clarington Museum	W				1 Floor		■	T			
Port Darlington Marina	W		■	■	■		■	T		Charter boats 200 slips	
Jungle Cat World	W	■	■			■	■	T		Night safaris Zoo	Packed Gravel
Bond Head Parkette	■			■	■		■	T		Fishing Boat launch	Gravel Boardwalk
Wiggers Marina										15 slips	

P – Partial
S – Seasonal
L – Limited
B – Benches
T – Tables
W – Wheelchair Accessible

HOPE TOWNSHIP AT A GLANCE

List of places, attractions, public marinas, and tourist offices	Washrooms	Water Fountain	Food	Phones	Wheelchair Accessible	Admission Charge	Parking	Picnic Tables	BBQ	Recreational Activities	Trail Surface
Richardson's Lookout	■						■			Lookout tower	Natural
Dorothy's House Museum	■			■			■			Museum (call for hours)	
Garden Hill Conservation Area	W	■			■		■	T		Fishing Birding	Natural
Ganaraska Hiking Trail							■			Hiking	Natural

P – Partial
S – Seasonal
L – Limited
B – Benches
T – Tables
W – Wheelchair Accessible

List of places, attractions, public marinas, and tourist offices	Washrooms	Water Fountain	Food	Phones	Wheelchair Accessible	Admission Charge	Parking	Picnic Tables	BBQ	Recreational Activities	Trail Surface
Port Hope	■		■	■			■			Shopping Heritage buildings	Sidewalks
Canadian Fire Fighters' Museum	■		■							Museum	
Port Hope Marina	■		■	■	■		■	T		Fishing Public boat launch	Natural Sidewalks
Memorial Park	■			At Events Only			■	T		Playground Bandstand	Natural
Port Hope Golf and Country Club	■		■	■	■	■	■			Golfing	

P – Partial
S – Seasonal
L – Limited
B – Benches
T – Tables
W – Wheelchair Accessible

Cobourg at a Glance

List of Places, Attractions, Public Marinas, and Tourist Offices	Washrooms	Water Fountain	Food	Phones	Wheelchair Accessible	Admission Charge	Parking	Picnic Tables	BBQ	Recreational Activities	Trail Surface
Gage Creek Wetland							■			Birding	Packed earth
Carr Marsh										Birding	Natural
Monk's Cove											
Cobourg Creek										Fishing – Trout, Salmon	Pebble beach
Peace Park										Playground	
Chamber of Commerce 212 King Street West	■			■	■		■			Tourist information	
Marie Dressler	■			■	■		■			Museum	
Victoria Hall • Municipal Building • Concert Hall • Court House • Art Gallery	■	■		■	■		■			Tours available, through Chamber of Commerce	
Cobourg Harbour (Marina)	■		S	■	■		■	T S		Marina – 197 slips Yacht Club Salmon charters available Boating	1.6 km (1 mile) promenade, interlocking brick
Victoria Park	■	■	■	■	■		■	T S		Playground Mini-golf Bandstand (weekly concerts in summer) Pool (supervised swimming)	Sandy beach
Donnegan Park										Playground Sports field	

P – Partial
S – Seasonal
L – Limited
B – Benches
T – Tables
W – Wheelchair Accessible

HALDIMAND TOWNSHIP AT A GLANCE

List of places, attractions, public marinas, and tourist offices	Washrooms	Water Fountain	Food	Phones	Wheelchair Accessible	Admission Charge	Parking	Picnic Tables	BBQ	Recreational Activities	Trail Surface
Nawautin Nature Sanctuary					■					Birding Wildlife	
Hamlet of Grafton • Barnum House Museum	■		■	■			■			Antique shopping Heritage buildings	
Wicklow Beach										Boat launch	
Peter's Woods										Hiking	

P – Partial
S – Seasonal
L – Limited
B – Benches
T – Tables
W – Wheelchair Accessible

CRAMAHE AT A GLANCE

LIST OF PLACES, ATTRACTIONS, PUBLIC MARINAS, AND TOURIST OFFICES	WASHROOMS	WATER FOUNTAIN	FOOD	PHONES	WHEELCHAIR ACCESSIBLE	ADMISSION CHARGE	PARKING	PICNIC TABLES	BBQ	RECREATIONAL ACTIVITIES	TRAIL SURFACE
PIETER'S APPLEYARD							■	B			
THE BIG APPLE • Tourist information	W	■	■	■	restaurant		■	T/B		Mini-golf Playground Petting zoo Trail	

P – Partial
S – Seasonal
L – Limited
B – Benches
T – Tables
W – Wheelchair Accessible

List of places, attractions, public marinas, and tourist offices	Washrooms	Water Fountain	Food	Phones	Wheelchair Accessible	Admission Charge	Parking	Picnic Tables	BBQ	Recreational Activities	Trail Surface
Victoria Square Park	■	■	■	■			■	T/B		Heritage park Playground	Asphalt
Seaton House • Tourist information										Tourist information centre Shopping	

P – Partial
S – Seasonal
L – Limited
B – Benches
T – Tables
W – Wheelchair Accessible

List of places, attractions, public marinas, and tourist offices	Washrooms	Water Fountain	Food	Phones	Wheelchair Accessible	Admission Charge	Parking	Picnic Tables	BBQ	Recreational Activities	Trail Surface
Presqu'ile Provincial Park	W	■	S	■	■	■	■	T	■	Camping Canoeing Hiking and biking trails Birding Boat launch	Asphalt Natural Boardwalk
Harbour Street Boat Launch	■				■		■	T		Public boat launch	Gravel
Harbour Street Park					■		■	T			Asphalt
Cedar Street Lookout										Birding	Asphalt
Gosport Park	■			■			■			Playground Baseball diamond	Asphalt
Harbourview Motel Marina	■		■	■	■		■	T		Room rental Boat rental Fishing	
Proctor House	W				■					Public tours Cross country skiing	
Brighton Speedway Park	■		S	■	■	■	■	T	■	Stock car races	Asphalt
Brighton Speedway Fun Centre	■		S	■	■	■	■	T	■	Go carts Mini-golf Batting cages	Asphalt

P – Partial
S – Seasonal
L – Limited
B – Benches
T – Tables
W – Wheelchair Accessible

Murray Township at a Glance

List of places, attractions, and public marinas, and tourist offices	Washrooms	Water Fountain	Food	Phones	Wheelchair Accessible	Admission Charge	Parking	Picnic Tables	BBQ	Recreational Activities	Trail Surface
Murray Canal							■	T		Boating Fishing Swimming	
Twelve O'Clock Point Road	■		S				■	T/B	■	Fishing Interpretive display	Grass
Carrying Place										Crafts Flea markets Playground Boat launch	
Fort Kente							■			Historical re-enactments, mock naval and land battles, canoe races, and storytelling during July festival	

P – Partial
S – Seasonal
L – Limited
B – Benches
T – Tables
W – Wheelchair Accessible

List of places, attractions, public marinas, and tourist offices	Washrooms	Water Fountain	Food	Phones	Wheelchair Accessible	Admission Charge	Parking	Picnic Tables	BBQ	Recreational Activities	Trail Surface
Hanna Park					■		■	T/B	■	Playground Birding Tennis courts Cross-country skiing	
Bayshore Park								T/B		Fishing Birding Base for Trenton Summer Festival	Natural
Fraser Park and Marina	W		■	■	■		■	T/B		Outdoor patio Flower gardens Fishing Public marina	Asphalt
Jack Lange Memorial Walkway	■				■			T/B		Hiking	Gravel
Lock One Interpretation Centre	W				■		■	T/B	■	Canal related displays Gift shop	Asphalt
RCAF Memorial Museum	W		■		■		■	T/B		Indoor and outdoor displys Aircraft park	
Chamber of Commerce	■	■					■			Information centre	

P – Partial
S – Seasonal
L – Limited
B – Benches
T – Tables
W – Wheelchair Accessible

References

Abbott, W. 1980 *Images of the past.* N.p.:

Ajax (Ont.). Business Development Dept. *The 1994 community profile for the town of Ajax.* Ajax: Ajax (Ont.). Business Development Dept.

Argyris, Eileen. "Three men named Joseph Keeler, shapers of history." *Colborne Chronicle, Cramahe Heritage Edition:* 1992 June 23.

"The Augusta." *SOS Newsletter.* (Fall 1991).

Bacher, John. "Quirky circumstances and political zigzags are carving out the world's largest city forest." *Now Magazine* 1994 September 22-28: 14-15.

Bailey, T. M. 1983. *Hamilton chronicle of a city.* Hamilton: Windsor Publications Inc.

Bergeron, S. 1992 "Van Sicklen Cemetery, in cemeteries, Northumberland Co." Brighton: (Brighton Public Library).

Brown, R. 1994. *Ghost railways of Ontario.* Peterborough: Broadview Press.

Brueckner, J. N.d. *Four gardens of the world.* Dr. Brueckner's personal video documentary.

Cadman, M. D., et al. 1987. *Atlas of breeding birds of Ontario.* Waterloo: University of Waterloo.

Calnan, M. ed. 1987. *Gunshot and gleanings of the historic Carrying Place, Bay of Quinte.* Ameliasburgh: 7th Town Historical Society.

Canniff, W. 1894. *A history of the early settlement of Upper Canada.* Toronto: Dudley & Burns.

Carney, M. "Victory at Second Marsh." *Seasons* 33, (1993) no. 2 :16-19.

Cecile, C. P. 1983. *Oshawa Second Marsh baseline study - final report: documentation, integration and interpretation of ecological data.* N.p. Canada. Environment Canada.

Chapman, L. J., and D. F. Putnam. 1966. *The physiography of Southern Ontario.* 2d ed. Toronto: University of Toronto Press, Ontario Research Foundation.

Clarkson, B. 1967. *Credit Valley gateway; the story of Port Credit.* Port Credit: Port Credit Public Library Board.

Coleman, J. T. 1875. *History of early settlement of Bowmanville and vicinity.* Bowmanville: West Durham Steam Printing and Publishing House.

Collins, J. "Second Marsh: flowers gratefully declined." *Ontario Naturalist* (Summer 1979) 25-26.

"Cramahe was Lieutenant-Governor of Quebec and Detroit." *Colborne Chronicle, Cramahe Heritage Edition:* 1992 June 23.

Creighton, S. 1993. *The Oakville book: Oakville then and now.* Oakville: Rubicon Publishing.

Cruickshank, T. 1987. *Port Hope: a treasury of early homes.* Port Hope: Bluestone House Inc.

Dictionary of Canadian biography. N.d. Toronto: University of Toronto Press.

Duncan, B. "Project paradise." *Bruce Trail News* (Fall 1994).

Dutton, D. N.d. "Divers now allowed to see Toronto's shipwrecks." *Toronto Star* .

Etobicoke Historical Board, and Local Architectural Conservation Advisory Committee. 1995. *Villages of Etobicoke.* Weston: Argyle Printing Co.

Fairbairn, J. B. 1906. *History and reminiscences of Bowmanville.* Bowmanville: New Print.

Farewell, J. E. 1907. *County of Ontario.* Whitby: Whitby Gazette-Chronicle Press.

Filey, M. 1982. *I remember Sunnyside: the rise and fall of a magical era.* Toronto McClelland and Stewart.

_____. 1987. *A walker's, jogger's, cyclist's, boater's guide to Toronto's waterfront* Toronto: Toronto of Old.

Goddard, M., and S. Johnston. 1986. *Haldimand historical background.* N.p.

Goodwin, C. E. 1988. *A birdfinding guide to the Toronto region.* Westin: Clive and Joy Goodwin Enterprises Ltd.

Goulin, J. M., and R. Hussey. 1990. *Rattray Marsh: then and now: articles on the human settlement and natural history of the Rattray Marsh Conservation Area.* Ajax: Rattray Marsh Protection Association.

Greenwald, M. 1973. *The historical complexities of Pickering, Markham, Scarborough, and Uxbridge.* N.p.: North Pickering Community Development Project, Ontario. Ministry of Treasury, Economics and Intergovernmental Affairs.

Griffiths, M. 1988. *Aquatic environment of Humber Bay.* Toronto: Ontario. Ministry of the Environment. Water Resources Branch.

Griffiths, R. W., et al. "Distribution and dispersal of the zebra mussel (Dreissena polymorpha) in the Great Lakes region." *Canadian Journal of Fisheries and Aquatic Sciences* (1985) 48.

Grimm, W. C. 1970. *Home guide to trees, shrubs and wildflowers.* New York: Bonanza Books.

Guillet, E. C. 1939. *Pioneer travel.* Toronto: Ontario Publishing Co.Ltd.

_____. 1948. *Cobourg, 1798-1948.* Oshawa: Goodfellow Printing.

_____. 1957. *The valley of the Trent.* Toronto: Champlain Society.

_____. 1963. *Early life in Upper Canada.* Toronto: University of Toronto Press.

H. Belden & Co. 1972. *Illustrated historical atlas of Northumberland and Durham counties, Ontario.* Belleville: Mika Silk Screening.

Hamilton Naturalists' Club. 1994. *Naturally, Hamilton!: a guide to the green spaces of Hamilton-Wentworth.* Hamilton: Hamilton Naturalists' Club.

Hamlyn, R. G. [1958]. *Bowmanville: a retrospect.* [Bowmanville: Centennial Committee].

Henley, B. 1993. *Hamilton: our lives and times.* Hamilton: The Spectator.

Heyes, E. 1974. *Etobicoke: from furrow to borough.* Etobicoke: Etobicoke (Ont.). Borough of Etobicoke Civic Centre.

Hitsman, J. M. [1965]. *The incredible war of 1812: a military history.* Toronto: University of Toronto Press.

Hope and its port: two centuries of change. 1992. [Lindsay]: [East Durham Historical Society].

Innis, M. Q. 1965. *Mrs. Simcoe's diary.* Toronto: MacMillan of Canada.

Johnson, L. 1973. *A History of the county of Ontario, 1615-1875.* Whitby: The Corporation of the County of Ontario.

Kohl, C. 1990. *Dive Ontario.* Chatham. Cris Kohl.

LaForest, S. M. N.d. 1987-1995 unpublished field notes of natural history observations in Brighton.

_____. N.d. *A guide to the common spring waterfowl of Presqu'ile Park.* Brighton: The Friends of Presqu'ile Park.

_____. 1989. Presqu'ile Provincial Park wildlife update. Ontario. Ministry of Natural Resources.

_____. 1993. *Birds of Presqu'ile Provincial Park.* Brighton: Friends of Presqu'ile Park, Ontario. Ministry of Natural Resources.

The Landplan Collaborative Ltd. December 1994. *Waterfront experiences: an analysis of waterfront experiences for the Lake Ontario greenway strategy* (draft). Toronto: Waterfront Regeneration Trust.

Loverseed, H. V. 1988. *Burlington: an illustrated history.* Burlington: Windsor Publications.

Luste, T. 1993. *Listing of attractions, festivals, amenities, and services in support of tourism, recreation and other economic opportunities.* Toronto: Waterfront Regeneration Trust.

Martin, N. C., C. Milne, and D. S. McGillis. 1986. *Gore's Landing and Rice Lake plains:* Gores Landing: Heritage Gore's Landing.

Mathews, H. C. 1953. *Oakville and the sixteen: the history of an Ontario Port.* Toronto: University of Toronto Press.

McBurney, M., and M. Byers. 1979. *Homesteads, early buildings and families from Kingston to Toronto.* Toronto: University of Toronto Press.

McCarthy, D. *Autobiographies: a fool in paradise and the good wine.* Toronto. MacFarlane, Walter & Ross.

McCowell, L. D., J. L. Pikor, and W. M. Cain. 1981. *Hamilton Beach in retrospect: report of the Hamilton Beach education, alternate, community and history project.* Hamilton: Hamilton-Wentworth (Ont.: Regional municipality).

McKay, W. A. 1961. *The Pickering story.* [Pickering]: Township of Pickering Historical Society.

McPhedran, M. 1952. *Cargoes on the Great Lakes.* Toronto: McMillan Co. of Canada.

Mead, E. "The view from Mt. Pelion." *Trenton Trentonian* . 8 March 1978.

Metropolitan Toronto and Region Conservation Authority. 1989. *The greenspace strategy for the Greater Toronto Region.* Downsview: Metropolitan Toronto and Region Conservation Authority.

Middleton, G. V. 1971. *Notes on the geology of the Hamilton area, technical report 71-1.* Hamilton: McMaster University. Dept.of Geology.

Mika, N., and H. Mika. 1979. *Trenton, town of promise.* Belleville: Mika Publishing Company.

Mikel, W. C. 1943. *City of Belleville history.* Picton: Picton Gazette Publishing Company, Limited.

Milne, C. 1991. *Village settlements of Hamilton Township.* Bewdley: Clay Publishing.

Moffatt, P. C. 1972. *Time was: the story of St. Mark's Anglican Church, Port Hope.* Cobourg: Haynes Printing Co. Ltd.

Morley, B. D. 1970. *Wild flowers of the world.* London: New York: G. P. Putnam's Sons.

"Mt. Pelion cannon to boom twice monthly." *The Trentonian* 4 September 1970.

Oakville (Ont. : Town). Parks and Recreation Dept. N.d. *Joshua's Creek trail guide.* Oakville: Oakville (Ont. : Town). Parks and Recreation Dept.

O'Brien, B. 1992. *Speedy justice: the tragic last voyage of his Majesty's vessel Speedy.* Toronto: The Osgoode Society.

Ontario Historical Society. 1967. *Profiles of a province; studies in the history of Ontario; a collection of essays commissioned by the Ontario Historical Society to commemorate the Centennial of Ontario.* Toronto: [Ontario Historical Society].

Ontario. Conservation Branch. 1956. *Rouge-Duffin-Highland-Petticoat valleys: conservation report.* Toronto: [Toronto. (Ont.). Dept. of Planning and Development].

Ontario. Ministry of Natural Resources. 1992. *Zebra mussels cottager's guide.* N.p.: Ontario. Ministry of Natural Resources.

Oshawa Second Marsh Steering Committee. 1992. *Oshawa Second Marsh: management plan.* Oshawa: Oshawa (Ont.). Community Services Dept.

Persaud, D., et al. 1985. *Historical development and quality of the Toronto waterfront sediments – Part 1.* Toronto: Ontario. Ministry of the Environment. Water Resources Branch. Great Lakes Section.

Peterson, R. T. N.d. *Field guides to the birds.* N.p.

_____. 1968. *A Field guide to wildflowers of Northeastern and North-Central North America, a visual approach arranged by colour, form, and detail.* Boston: Houghton Mifflin.

Petrides, G. A. 1988. *Eastern trees.* New York: Houghton Mifflin.

Pictorial Brighton, 1859-1984. 1984. Brighton: Anniversary Book Committee.

Port Hope (Ont.). Dept. of Parks, Recreation and Culture. *Walk it: walking trails of Port Hope, Cobourg and district areas.* Port Hope: Port Hope (Ont.). Dept. of Parks, Recreation and Culture.

Pullen, L. 1985. *The Bowmanville West Beach wreck "Juno", archaeological report.* Oshawa: Save Ontario Shipwrecks.

Reeve, H. 1967. *The history of the township of Hope.* Cobourg: Cobourg Sentinel Star.

Reeves, W. 1992. *Metropolitan Toronto Waterfront: regional heritage features on the Metropolitan Waterfront.* Metropolitan Toronto (Ont. : Regional municipality). Planning Dept.

Richards, I, S. M. LaForest, and D. McRae. 1991. *Bird checklist, Presqu'ile Provincial Park.* The Friends of Presqu'ile Park.

Richards, J. 1964. *Birds of the Oshawa-Lake Scugog region, Ontario.* Np.

Riddell, W. R. 1920. *Old province tales: Upper Canada.* Toronto: Glasgow, Brook & Co.

Rossiter, W. H. N. 1983. *Canadian Pacific in southern Ontario, Volume II.* Calgary: The Calgary Group of the British Railway Modellers of North America.

Rukavina, N. A. 1969. *Nearshore sedimentary survey of western Lake Ontario, methods & preliminary results.* N.p.: International Association of Great Lakes Research.

Sauriol, C. 1981. *Remembering the Don.* Scarborough: Consolidated Amethyst Communications Inc.

_____. 1984. *Tales of the Don.* Toronto: Natural Heritage/Natural History Inc.

_____. 1991. *Green footsteps.* Toronto: Hemlock Press.

_____. 1992. *Trails of the Don.* Orilla: Hemlock Press.

Scadding, H. 1966. *Toronto of old.* Toronto: Oxford University Press.

Skeoch, A. N.d. *Stonehooking*. N.p.: South Peel Historical Society.

Squair, J. 1927. *The township of Darlington and Clarke, including Bowmanville and Newcastle*. Toronto: University of Toronto Press.

Stevenson. W. 1976. *A man called intrepid: the secret war*. New York: Harcourt Brace Jovanovich.

_____. 1983. *Intrepid's last case*. New York: Villard Books.

Stinson, J. 1990. *The heritage of the Port Industrial District, Vol 1*. Toronto: Toronto Harbour Commissioners.

Stinson, J., and Moir, M. 1991. *Built heritage of the East Bayfront. Environmental audit of the East Bayfront/Port Industrial Area phase II, technical paper no. 7*. Toronto: Royal Commission on the Future of the Toronto Waterfront.

Traill, C. P. 1971. *The backwoods of Canada; selections*. [Toronto]: McClelland & Stewart.

Turcotte, D. 1989. *Burlington: memories of pioneer days*. Erin: The Boston Mills Press.

_____. 1987. *The sand strip: Burlington/Hamilton beaches*. St. Catharines: Stonehouse Publications.

"Tweed man reveals cannon came to Trenton in 1877" *Courier-Advocate* 1 July 1950.

Urquhart, F. A. 1987. *The monarch butterfly: international traveller*. Chicago: Nelson-Hall.

Verman, H. B. 1979. *Geology and fossils: Craigleith Area, Ontario*. Toronto: Ontario. Ministry of Natural Resources.

Vincent, J. 1994. *Toronto waterfront habitat rehabilitation pilot projects: technical report, 1993*. Downsview: Metropolitan Toronto and Region Conservation Authority.

Weeks-Mifflin, M. 1989. *Harbour lights: Burlington Bay*. Erin: Boston Mills Press.

Westerman, S., and M. A. Bachellor, ed. 1978. *The CBS news almanac*. Maplewood, New Jersey: Hammond Almanac, Inc.

Wilson, B. G. 1981. *As she began: an illustrated introduction to Loyalist Ontario*. Toronto: Dundurn Press.

Winter, B. 1967. *A town called Whitby*. Whitby: R. Huff Productions.

Wood, W. 1911. *Past years in Pickering; sketches of the history of the community.* Toronto: William Briggs.

"The wreck of the S.S. Alexandria" *Birchcliffe Beacon* January.

Index